COLUMBIA UNIVERSITY STUDIES IN LIBRARY SERVICE

Number Six

WHAT'S IN A NOVEL

What's in a Novel

By HELEN E. HAINES

IN LITTERIS
LIBERTAS
1754·1893

COLUMBIA UNIVERSITY PRESS   NEW YORK

COPYRIGHT 1942 BY COLUMBIA UNIVERSITY PRESS, NEW YORK

LONDON: GEOFFREY CUMBERLEGE, OXFORD UNIVERSITY PRESS

First printing 1942
Second printing 1943
Third printing 1946

MANUFACTURED IN THE UNITED STATES OF AMERICA

TO MY MOTHER

From the light of her mind the spark was kindled,
from the fire of her heart the flame was fed.

PREFACE

THE PURPOSE of this book is to set forth simply and clearly some of the values that in ever widening radiation exist in present-day fiction. Its chief incentive has been my conviction, established through many years of book-selection teaching in library schools, of public book lectures, and of book reviewing, that contemporary fiction, as a great pervasive medium of public education and enlightenment, deserves fuller recognition and much more constructive utilization than it receives.

In professional library service the rigid dividing lines of "fiction" and "nonfiction," that separate "serious" from "recreational" reading, and a traditional attitude of mixed condescension and repression toward the body of literature that holds the greatest influence over the largest public are barriers to the fullest productive use of books and to the most rounded cultural development of the individual reader. In the field of education the novel is primarily considered as a literary composition to be analyzed in terms of aesthetic criticism; comparatively little attention is directed to the enlarging range and power of current fiction as record and interpretation of every aspect of life or to the values of fact, of utilitarian information, that infiltrate its substance and relate it to the materials of knowledge in history, science, social study, and many other fields. Even the reading public, in spite of the magnetic appeal of the novel as a source of pleasure and as illumination of human character and experience, accepts in a measure the stigma of triviality that rests upon current fiction. Reading for entertainment is apt to be a conscious self-indulgence, passively enjoyed, or trial-and-error experimentation carried on hopefully, but in confusion. Many intelligent readers pride themselves on their indifference to fiction, shutting out from their minds the spark of imagination that kindles the powers of the human race. It may be that a compact, practical, and objective consideration of the novel in a few of its significant manifestations today will help to strengthen confidence in its potentialities and bring them to wider effectiveness.

No complete presentation of contemporary fiction has been here attempted. It has been sought only to show "what's in a novel," as its forms change and multiply and its materials absorb new elements in the catalysis of time; and to do this, not by critical analysis from the standpoint of literary art, but by specific factual indication of substance and purpose and effect.

For the whole field there is brief preliminary generalization and synthesis, designed to bring out specific points of denotation, definition, and characterization, to consider variant reading tastes, and to offer a few suggestions to readers. Practical counsel for nonprofessional reviewing of novels, in women's clubs or similar groups and for radio audiences, given in the final chapter, involves somewhat similar treatment. Otherwise the general gives place to the particular in a survey and characterization of the present-day novel in certain familiar categories. The range of this survey is varied, but necessarily limited, and the selection that it represents is illustrative and, also necessarily, more or less arbitrary. The novel of character and family life; the biographic study shaped and colored by the novelist's art; the chronicle of social change, unfolding from past to present; the fiction that rehearses and challenges our economic and industrial problems; the great fields of regional and historical fiction; novels that mirror world horizons and reflect portents of world destiny; the iridescence of imaginative romance and the provocative play of fantasy; the fictional web of crime and mystery, with its lure for a multitude of readers—these are the kinds and type-groups of fiction that are here considered in the terms of the novels themselves: their essential substance, their obvious values, their pervasive influences.

Much, of course, has been left untouched, in broad subject groups, in novels of specialized topical relationship, and in the application of fictional method to unusual material. There are the novels of the sea, which in a hundred years have built a great literature of their own, solid in values, curiously immune to the withering touch of time, carrying man's universal experience of adventure, danger, and endurance through the changing patterns of navigation by sail and steam to modern mechanics of destroyer, seaplane, and aircraft carrier. There are the novels of multiple relationships to the professions, to all fields of art, science, and industry. Novels concerned with the medical profession have during a decade gained enormously in range and popularity, have brought solid substance of factual knowledge to the portrayal of different aspects of medical practice, and have undoubtedly built up strong popular support for the principles of socialized medical service. There are many significant novels of specific industries, of crafts and skills; and an ever-enlarging body of fiction has become essentially a factual medium for popularization of science, valid in authority, provocative in method, as in George Stewart's effective transmission of modern meteorological research and service in his novel *Storm*. To include these and other notable specialized groups would have meant an expansion far beyond the scope of what must remain a "token" demonstration of what's in a novel.

It may be objected that the more controversial aspects of contemporary fiction have been passed over. Thus, no consideration has been given to novels of recognized mass appeal that are in fact stereotypes for indiscriminate quantity production: the trivial, moralistic, or sentimental "light fiction"; the mechanized and garish "Westerns"; the crude melodramatized compositions that find their destined place on the "asbestos shelf" of the commercialized rental library. Nor has there been any exploration of the Debatable Land of forays and reprisals on moral issues, the embattled, fog-enveloped ramparts of censorship. These aspects have not come within my purpose, for my concern has been with the values, the materials of information, the influences for enlightenment and intelligence, that are common to so large a proportion of present-day novels. And it has seemed that the presentation of values should be in itself an indication of standards for the discriminating application of individual judgment.

Informality of treatment has prevailed throughout. In the few special illustrative lists the usual bibliographical record (place of

publication, publisher, and date) is given; but most of the novels
mentioned in the text are familiar components of the body of contemporary fiction, and the briefer indication given should be adequate. My basic source has been the novels themselves; I have read
and made my own notes for most of them, although reviews have
been freely culled, and standard selection aids constantly drawn
upon. Among aids of greatest usefulness special acknowledgment
should go to Elbert Lenrow's *Reader's Guide to Prose Fiction,* published by Appleton-Century in 1940. From this classified bibliography of 1,500 novels shines a bright light of promise for broader
appreciation and greater constructive use of fiction in the whole
educational field. Prepared for the Commission on Secondary
School Curriculum of the Progressive Education Association, it is
modern in outlook, mature in selective range, and perceptive
throughout of the varieties and realities of experience, the intricacies of personal problems, on which the novel today casts illumination. Agnes Camilla Hansen's little manual, *Twentieth Century
Forces in European Fiction* (Chicago, American Library Association, 1934) has been of immediate help in furnishing exact bibli-
ographic detail within its special field; and I should like to express
my admiration for this unpretentious contribution to fuller realization of the significance and function of the novel in world literature.
For the consideration of Latin American fiction Alfred Coester's
compact, sympathetic study, *The Literary History of Spanish
America* (2d ed., New York, Macmillan, 1928) has been especially
drawn upon, and other correlative material has been used, in addition to that cited in the text; but here, also, the novels themselves
have yielded their substance directly through personal reading.

Help from friends in the library and the book world must be
gratefully noted. The admirably developed fiction collection of the
Los Angeles Public Library has been indispensable; its staff always responsive and co-operative. Especially from Rhoda Marshall
(head of the Fiction Department of that library), from Margaret
Hickman (head of the Foreign Department), and Leslie I. Hood
(manager of the Library Department of A. C. Vroman, Inc., Pasa-

dena) practical help and cordial interest have been forthcoming in
generous measure. To Dr. Charles C. Williamson, Dean of the School
of Library Service of Columbia University, this volume owes its
existence, as did its predecessor, *Living with Books;* his unfailing en-
couragement and forbearance under unforeseen delays have been a
lifeline in heavy weather; and sincerest appreciation for many
kindnesses goes also to Donald Geddes, Charles G. Proffitt, and
other friends in Columbia University Press.

HELEN E. HAINES

Pasadena, California
May 20, 1942

CONTENTS

WHAT'S IN A NOVEL

1. THE PROVINCE OF THE NOVEL

*. . . in my judgment, the province of the novel is
the entire range of human experience and the vast
area of mortal destiny.*—ELLEN GLASGOW: *Saturday
Review of Literature, January 23, 1937*

IN THE most ephemeral and transitory fiction of the past the
social historian traces emerging patterns of social change. But
it is only within the last half century that the province of the
novel has so widened that Ellen Glasgow's affirmation justifies itself in any comprehensive consideration of contemporary fiction.
Today readers have in the novel a life-extension agency: a means,
not to the prolongation of physical existence, but to an expanded
mental participation in the whole range of human experience. As
Bernard de Voto has said: "The mass and tension of modern fiction
have opened up areas of experience, states of consciousness, and a
variety of themes if not of emotions that the novel did not deal
with before." Modern fiction has overpassed former boundaries—
strengthened, varied, developed its processes and scope. It reflects
the activities, the complexities, the human, social, and moral problems, the satisfactions and inquietudes of the modern world with
a more pervasive radiation than any other form of writing. In
the full extent of its manifestation it represents the strongest and
most continuous appeal that literature has for the commonalty of
readers. It has long held the dominating place in book production
and book use.

Through the decade of the thirties American book production
ranged from 8,000 to 11,000 publications a year, decreasing in the
middle years (with a low of 8,092 in 1933) and rising to its peak of
11,067 in 1938 Fiction consistently held first place as the largest
individual class, though with a continuous lessening in volume (ex-

cept for a sudden rise in 1935), from a peak of 2,103 in 1930 to a low of 1,547 in 1939. There are many minor variations in the record of these successive years that should be taken into account in drawing conclusions. Thus, the highest fiction output for the period was that of 1930, with its 2,103 volumes, or 556 more than are recorded for 1939; but the number of new novels (not new editions) was only 215 fewer in 1939 than in 1930. So far as decrease in current fiction can be traced throughout the period, it is apparent that it was greater in reprints than in original publications. More fiction is published than any other single kind of literature, and more people read fiction than read books in any other specific class. Nearly a hundred years ago Thackeray spoke of the appetite for novels that exists in the vast army of readers extending over the earth; and neither the appetite nor the army have diminished since then. Fiction represents virtually one-half the home circulation of books in American public libraries; it furnishes a much larger proportion of the circulation from the myriad rental libraries that exist in almost every community, large and small, throughout the country; it constitutes probably a third of the individual book buying done through bookstores and other trade outlets.

How much novel reading is done in a year by the American public cannot be fairly approximated. Best-seller records and book-trade records in general are based on the number of books sold, not on the number of persons who have read those books; records of library circulation apply only to public libraries; a very wide margin of reading remains unrecorded. Novels that top the best-seller lists are likely to sell from 275,000 to 300,000 copies in the year— Margaret Mitchell's *Gone with the Wind*, with a sale of two million copies in three years, is the phenomenon of the decade; those lower in the list may run from 50,000 to 200,000 copies in a year's sales. But neither these nor any other statistics can register the degree to which the novel has become a factor in the self-education of daily living. It could hardly be otherwise. The range of fiction today is as wide as the range of human interests; its standards of quality, its trends of influence, are as varied as are the gradations of individual taste, the diversities of group mores. There is more effective work-manship than ever before; there is unflagging inventiveness, an emergence of new patterns, and a linking of fiction more and more closely to every problem and phase of the immediate present. Novel-ists now approach their raw material—the material of human ex-perience—realistically, as ordinary human beings rather than as con-scious artists apart from the common herd, and thus come nearer to the plain truth than ever before. Somerset Maugham points this out in *The Summing Up* and adds:

When I compare my early novels with those that are written by young men now, I cannot but see that theirs are vastly more accomplished. . . . Girls still in their teens, youths at the university, produce books that seem to me well written, well composed, and ripe with experience. I do not know whether the young mature sooner than they did forty years ago or whether it is that the art of fiction has in that time so much advanced that it is now as easy to write a good novel as then it was difficult to write even a mediocre one.

In the mass, of course, fiction is a composite. Much of its sub-stance is immediately perishable; much is inferior, mediocre, trivial. From Thomas Mann to Jerome Weidman, from John Steinbeck to Ethel Dell, it rises to heights of spiritual vision, of insight into hu-man experience; it sinks to depths of tawdry vulgarity, of inane flatulence. This mixed substance makes fiction the body of litera-ture most exposed to attack and most vulnerable. As art, save for a few supreme exceptions, it provokes unending strife, in which critics and experts theorize and analyze and baffle the reading public with the conundrum of the workshops: "It's pretty, but is it Art?" As entertainment its many values of mental enlightenment and social stimulus are too often disregarded; even now it wakens disapproval or distrust among those who cling to traditional moral rigidities. In a letter to his father, in 1820, young Thomas Babington Macaulay spoke with indignation of having been called "a novel-reader—a commodious name, invented by ignorance and applied by envy, in the same manner as men without learning call a scholar a pedant, and men without principle call a Christian a Methodist."

That was nearly a century and a quarter ago, but the implication that irked that ardent young novel reader of the past still lingers. The time-wasting consumption of trashy novels by idle women, the regrettable preoccupation of misguided youth with the profanities and indecencies of modern fiction, are favorite themes for reprobation from pulpit and platform, usually set forth by expositors who pride themselves on their ignorance of the subject. Few seem aware of the part current fiction plays in the continuous, advancing popularization of knowledge. In the organization and development of public education programs, as in the book service of public libraries, an invisible barrier separates "serious reading" from novel reading, disregarding the correlation, the mutual dependence, that exists between contemporary fiction and almost every other kind of literature and that offers the strongest stimulus to informal mass education, the most effective incentive to fruitful individual reading. For fiction is one of the formative influences in everyday life; it enlarges the mind's horizons; it instills or increases understanding of human nature. Novels and newspapers are still chief sources of our general information. "Novels, be they good or bad, useless or necessary," said Sir James Fitzjames Stephen, with grim resignation, "circulate over the land in every possible form, and enter more or less into the education of almost everyone who can read. They hold in solution a great deal of experience." If that was true in 1855, it is much more certainly true today, as the diversified alluvium of fiction sifts into every problem and phase of living.

The chief reason for reading novels is that the reader enjoys, or expects to enjoy, doing so. This fact, I think, explains the severity of mentors who believe that pleasure is not a component of edification; it also has established among educators and librarians the tendency to regard what they call "recreational reading" as a public self-indulgence that may be tolerated, but should not be approved. Yet the pleasure derived from reading has always been a lure leading the mind to wisdom and understanding; the classics became the classics because they gave more pleasure to more readers than did other books. Fiction is one of the great and continuing sources of pleasure;

and as current fiction succeeds in diffusing pleasure from authentic material of human experience—from biography, history, social study, individual and mass psychology—it draws into closer and more vital relationship to the whole literature of knowledge. There are, of course, many levels of reading. Although pleasure is the motive that underlies all others, readers' motives vary, intensify, or weaken on different levels. On the upper levels there is intellectual curiosity, response to aesthetic appeal, desire to accept or to test for oneself the approval of critics, willingness to overcome instinctive resistance to a repellent surface. On the lower levels there is passive satisfaction in the familiar, adherence to traditional standards, adolescent sentimentalism, a craving for crude stimulants. There is fiction for every reading level.

For a generation accusing prophets have foretold the doom of the book in our machine-made civilization. The automobile, the moving picture, and the radio are successively to be the instruments of its annihilation. Georges Duhamel, distinguished French novelist, essayist, and publisher, in his volume *In Defence of Letters*, says that "little by little people are finding ways of satisfying their thirst for knowledge without having recourse to books"; and he looks forward gloomily to the time when "the human race will keep its recipes for living, not in libraries, but on ebonite disks and gelatine films." In this country, at least, evidence is lacking to justify these forebodings. Book manufacture increases steadily; the use of books through libraries mounts by its own momentum and is constantly extended by the opening of new areas and the development of reading ability and reading interest among the less literate. The crucial, tragic world conflict of our immediate day intensifies public eagerness to clarify, through books, knowledge and judgment. Novels have become the mainstay of the movies, and they win new readers as they come to life on the screen. Through radio's reviewers commendation of popular books is spread abroad and their readers are multiplied; the books featured in the picture magazines or condensed in the digest periodicals rise promptly to increased sales and reading revival. The nationwide celebration of five hundred years of printing, in 1940, deepened public realization of books as the foundation, expression, and impetus for human aspirations and activities. Only for rhetorical reasons need we envisage extinction of the book in the world of the future.

In the mass, reading taste improves. There is little reason nowadays for the contemptuous reference to best sellers that has so long signalized intellectual superiority. More and more do we find work of sound literary quality and other assured values in the novels numbered among the year's best sellers. *Northwest Passage*, giving vigor and color to authentic materials of history; *The Yearling*, regional fiction instinct with simplicity and truth; *The Mortal Storm*, graphic but tempered portrayal of the rise of Nazi power in Germany; the panorama of life in India unrolled in *The Rains Came; Children of God*, revitalizing one of the strangest epical chapters of America's past; *The Grapes of Wrath*, transmuting an immediate economic problem into human terms of pity and passion—these are best sellers of the last few years that in range and significance reveal the province of the contemporary novel.

That the currents and forces which continuously shape our social history are registered in the fiction that offers their most spontaneous literary expression is a commonplace to students of literature and to intelligent general readers. But to realize the transformation and expansion in materials and in treatment that make modern fiction so powerful a medium of public enlightenment, we may cast a retrospective glance upon successive phases of a single enlarging current of influence. From the detritus of the minor English fiction of the past—artificial, trivial, preposterous, the dayfly of its own moment in time—there may be traced the changing pattern of woman's position and behavior during two centuries of economic and social change. In *Pamela's Daughters* [1] Dr. Utter's delightful study of the heroines of English fiction, this pattern is set before us with freshness and cogency. Pamela Andrews, "born in 1740 at the age of fifteen from the pen of Samuel Richardson," is seen as the

[1] Robert Palfrey Utter and Gwendolen Bridges Needham, *Pamela's Daughters*, New York, Macmillan, 1936.

mother of all the heroines of English fiction. Her experiences furnished plot patterns for their vicissitudes throughout two centuries; her traits and qualities were inherited by a multitude of type-form descendants, who may be classified according to those traits, as the prude, the weeper, the fainter, the "fallen" heroine, and the poor working girl. All these, with a few others who show relationship in collateral branches, Dr. Utter brings before us for identification and analysis: examples of feminine mores, from the tight little old world of economic repression and social Procrusteanism to the freedom of the twentieth-century "multiverse."

Virtue was the sole working capital of Pamela and her daughters, to be so invested as to yield a dividend of security in a world where economic opportunities were closed to women: "chastity was the only thing God had given to women that commanded a price." Here are the heroines confronted with Pamela's economic problem and enforced to assume the protective coloration of helplessness and "delicacy." As "delicacy" becomes a social requirement, prudery flourishes, as does the "sensibility" that for at least a century afflicted heroines (and heroes, too) with "liquid sorrow," in a continuous flow of tears, trickling singly by drops or flooding in torrents from page to page, from volume to volume. Here is analysis of the code for fainting, compulsory for all self-respecting heroines in the age of tight lacing; of the literary tradition that endowed blondes with angelic qualities, brunettes with sinister or aggressive dispositions; of the caricature figure of the old maid, established in English fiction by Smollett, and not extinguished until the nineties, when the "bachelor maid" entered the scene; of the application and effect of "Goldsmith's law" concerning female frailty, as proclaimed in his famous utterance, "When lovely woman stoops to folly"; and of the triumphal progress of the poor working girl through the centuries, as she eludes or vanquishes the villain who still pursues her. As the Victorian age closes, the daring new patterns of the nineties and the complex designs for living of the twenties take shape; and in the last analysis we see in confrontation Pamela, preordained to dependence on her parents, on authority, on the social order, on God, and her modern descendant, endowed with a self-sufficiency born of free intelligence and accumulated experience, conscious that salvation is in herself and to be attained only by exercise of the will. Between Ann Vickers and Pamela lie the human, moral, social, and intellectual perspectives of the novel as it records and interprets the modern world.

The changing status of woman is only one of the powerful currents of influence that have brought the modern novel into being. More fundamental, more deeply reconstructive, has been the transforming influence of science upon modern life. With the breakdown of age-old stabilities of belief there has come an ever-widening pursuit of meanings and values in living, expressed in questionings, insistencies, conflicting voices of doctrine, or prophecy, or doom, but also in a deepening realization that man must sustain alone a world that is his own creation. This pursuit, this realization, runs through contemporary fiction in those successive moods of illusion, disillusion, revulsion, reassurance that arise from the spirit and the issues of the time in a continuous process of generation, growth and dissolution; and enlarging territories of human experience are taken over as in this process fiction becomes both more universalized and more individualized.

The method of science, with its objective of tested truth and its requirement of exactitude in the observation and record of perceived fact, has established the accuracy of detail and the authenticity of accessory material that are now prerequisites of the novelist's craft. The solid factual specialization of novels that center on a single subject field is evidence of this influence, which affects fiction of all types and all degrees of literary art. There may be old-fashioned sentimentality or equally old-fashioned melodrama in the current novel of medical practice or hospital setting that has come into such wide popularity, but there will certainly be also an interfusion of precise technical detail. In the same way, the scientific spirit of detachment, of impersonal analysis, carries its emanation into objective yet sensitive studies of human behavior, such as Elizabeth Bowen's *The Death of the Heart*, and gives penetration and validity to many minor novels that outline character in simple strokes. The practical effect of applied science upon the material structure of life has produced a body of fiction concerned with man in his relation to the machine age, in industry and in business, as well as in broader, less tangible, aspects of personal experience.

Modern psychology is a manifestation of science; but it is an independent, pervasive, and dominating influence in the development of fiction. The whole art and substance of the novel have taken on new dimensions, have been charged with new energies, as the study of psychology, in theory and in practice, has penetrated more and more deeply into the mystery of the human mind. From the concepts and doctrines of William James, Freud, and Jung a generation of novelists has drawn inexhaustible materials and evolved varied, subtle, and bizarre methods of handling them. The continuous flowing current of consciousness, the experiential timelessness of immediate perception, the sex instinct as motor and motive of the unconscious, the complexes and inhibitions that are attributes of a multifold personality in conflict with itself, and the indeterminateness of the border line between normality and abnormality—these are tenets of psychology or psychoanalysis that have been objectified for the common reader by the work of Dorothy Richardson, Virginia Woolf, D. H. Lawrence, Dos Passos, Faulkner, and a multitude of others.

Vagaries and violences have been involved in this translation of psychological precept into the terms of fiction. Preoccupation with abnormal elements of personality, sex obsession, intense egocentricity have fostered neuroticism and cultism and reinforced the current of sadism released in the literature as in the life of our day. This, however, is but a single aspect of the extension of fiction into regions of psychopathology and psychiatry. In general the effect of experimental psychology upon the novel has been to break up traditional and artificial patterns of character portrayal, to eliminate black and white contrasts of vice and virtue, to elicit and elucidate impulse and motive rather than to center on action; to expose the individual personality, latent as well as overt, by presenting not only actualities of emotion and experience but also impressions and perceptions within the inner self. One obvious result is the mounting inflow of biographic and autobiographic novels concerned with influences that affect individual development. They offer evocations of the memories and experiences of childhood; or exploratory analyses of adolescence, sexual initiation and adventure; or introspective studies of the struggle for mental or emotional adjustment to life; sometimes singly, sometimes in evolutionary process. They may and often do represent a consecration of personal trivia, repetitive or monotonous; but in the mass they are eliciting new values from familiar areas of experience and deepening common understanding of why human beings (including ourselves) are as they are.

"Social awareness" is the strongest present influence in contemporary fiction. The term is vague, but useful; for it is elastic enough to stretch back through the hundred years in which the novel has been the champion of social reforms and humanitarian ideals and to spring forward into new regions of amplified social consciousness and intensified social conflict. In its full scope it takes us from Dickens and the mid-Victorians through the broadening stream of sociological fiction and the rising realism of the later nineteenth century and the early twentieth to the war novels and the postwar current of caustic social criticism in the 1920's; and through the "depression decade" of the 1930's, with the rise of proletarian fiction and the far-spreading inflow of novels reflecting social, economic, and political problems. It is not strange that social awareness should pervade the literature of a decade that opened in bewilderment, demolition, and experiment, that teemed with crucial issues of social and political reconstruction, that moved through clashing opinions, antagonistic principles, to converging conflict between opposed forces of democracy and dictatorship, and that closed as its portents were fulfilled in new world war.

In novels conditions were recorded, ideas transmitted, new areas of experience opened. Problems of labor, of industry, of agriculture, of unemployment and relief were projected into imaginative reality for a multitude of readers immune to sociological and economic texts. Communism, capitalism, social revolution, social reconstruction, democracy, regimentation, warring political doctrines, became realizable, not simply as political theories, but as factors in everyday living. Olive Dargan's *Call Home the Heart*, in 1932, gave impetus to the long succession of novels that visualized industrial and agricultural conditions in the South; labor's struggle for unionization was reflected in novels of lumber camps, factories, and mining regions. *It Can't Happen Here*, in the mid-channel of 1936, set a fantastic portent of things to come. In 1939 *The Grapes of Wrath*, translating a crucial national problem into unforgettable living human experience, brought the cycle to its culmination. Many of these novels are inept or crude as literary art; many are exaggerated, overweighted with homily or partisanship or violence. But in their exposition and challenge of social injustice and economic pressures nearly all possess specific values of authentic background, often of close personal knowledge. They contribute valuable related material to the factual literature of social study.

If the advance of woman, the dominance of science, experimental psychology, and an expanding social awareness have been the strongest influences in fiction's growth, many other factors are interlinked with these. The first World War, in impact and aftermath stamped its influence on the whole body of literature through a quarter century—in revulsions and negations, in passionate urgencies for ideals of peace, and in impulsions toward spiritual appeasement or assurance by way of emotional metaphysics. From portents and tensions of world conflict in the mid-thirties have emerged the realities of the world revolution that must still further shape the development of modern fiction.

Modernity, of course, is simply relationship to the present moment in time; modern fiction is the fiction of the fleeting present. In broader interpretation the term is fairly enough applied to the fiction that through half a century has conveyed the spirit of what we like to call the "modern age"—the spirit of a world in transition, turning from old traditions, building on new bases, keyed to a different pitch of expression. For present consideration the term is narrowed down more closely. Our concern is with the fiction of the last twenty years, especially with that of the last decade, and with specific, practical aspects of its range and values rather than with critical analysis of its qualities. There seems little reason to add another to the many studies devoted to the novel as literary art. Novelists, critics, essayists, and scholars have surveyed and charted modern fiction from every angle of structure, technique, theme, power, purpose, and artistic achievement. Our leading novelists are studied in school and college courses, in study groups, and in individual reading; the character of their work and in a measure their personalities as writers are familiar to all intelligent readers. Such contemporary literature of criticism as Carl Van Doren's inclusive study of the American novel, H. J. Muller's comprehensive exposition of modern fiction, E. M. Forster's penetrating analysis of aspects of fiction, Joseph W. Beach's provocative demonstration of significant influences in American fiction from 1920 to 1940, Dr. Canby's thoughtful critical commentaries—not to mention the overflowing stream of current reviewing—establishes the importance of the novel as a form of creative art and guides to its analysis, interpretation, and appraisal. But there is, perhaps, place for a broad, though selective, survey of present-day fiction from a general and factual, rather than a critical, standpoint. Such a survey is here attempted—necessarily inadequate and incomplete, for only the Genie of the Bottle could compress so vast a substance into a small container. It aims to present novels, predominantly American and English, of different kinds and types, in a few distinctive groupings; to consider their subject range, their substance and characteristics; to indicate their inherent, practical values of informational background and social significance, and to note some of the reading relationships that link modern fiction to the materials of knowledge in every field.

These values exist in fiction of all types and different degrees of literary art; they seem to me stronger and more pervasive today than ever before. Often, of course, they merge or overlap. Many of the finest novels hold them all. Consider Thomas Mann's "Joseph" sequence, not only as a masterpiece of creative genius, an evocation of the spirit of man seeking through eternity knowledge of good and evil; but in the magnificent factual detail of its background, its diffusion of specific historical knowledge, its distillation of philosophic thought, and its reading relationship that ranges from primitive religion and Egyptian archaeology to Biblical history and modern psychology. *The Grapes of Wrath* has similarly inclusive values: specific, basically authentic informational background; dynamic social significance; vital reading relationship to important sociological and economic studies in its particular field.

Many novels are stronger in one value than in another. Informational background is perhaps most common, providing carefully realized settings even for adventure tale or light romance, and evident in the specialized factual and technical detail found in much of the better crime-and-mystery fiction. The great body of historical and regional fiction offers rich informational background and valuable reading relationships; there is strong social significance also in the synthesis of human experience carried on the time-flow of the years or shaped by environment and social heritage that is built up by the "saga" chronicles, the cyclical family histories, which appear in endless succession. American novelists, especially, have turned to the past quite as much to trace the rise of social forces operating today as to express the deepening mood of nationalism or to cherish memories of days that are gone. Within the decade they have raised a structure of American history that covers the ground from the early colonial period through the Revolution and the formative years of government, the whole pioneer era of ever-advancing frontiers, the Civil War and its aftermath, and the era of rising industrial power, of increasing social and economic problems. Necessarily this structure is composed of many regional units and has many inequalities and variations in substance; but as a whole, in extent, in the careful research and personal knowledge of regional backgrounds that it represents, in illumination of the American past and the many-faceted irradiation cast upon contemporary experience, it seems to me the most impressive achievement of present-day American literature.

There are other less tangible values in the novels that flow ceaselessly into every channel of interest today. Values of emotional release, of emotional appeasement, of imaginative stimulus, of imaginative surrender, simple values of entertainment—these are all implicit in the art of the novel. Accepted by the ordinary reader instinctively, without conscious recognition, these values hold the secret of the novel's universal appeal; and as the province of the novel is enlarged and enriched by new channels of communication, by an increasingly insistent factual reality, they make it more and more the great medium of human understanding, the most satisfying means to vicarious participation in the common emotions, the moving aspirations, the tragic experiences, the obscure vicissitudes, and the simple pleasures of human life and human nature.

II. VALUES AND RELATIONSHIPS

But deeper study always, sharper senses, profounder living; never an end to curiosity.—THOMAS WOLFE: *Of Time and the River*

FICTION in many kinds rises from, moves upon and passes over the surface of contemporary life. Beneath its "muchness and manyness," to use Thomas Wolfe's phrase, may still be traced the two pristine sources, romance and realism—imagination and fact—which singly and together carry back to its origins. During some two hundred years these sources have drawn into themselves new elements of invention and realization, have filtered through new deposits of knowledge, penetrated into new channels of perception and experience. They have merged, separated, reunited, and have brought all the diverse kinds and types of modern fiction into different degrees of relationship to one another. If we no longer keep the formal distinctions between the romance and the novel, it is because "novel" is the term now commonly accepted to denote all prose fiction except the short story. But the novel in its individual nature, in its particular "kind," still reveals its romantic or realistic heritage.

The romance once wove elaborate tapestries of chivalry and love and heroic combat; in its familiar meaning a romance is still a tale of love. It drew upon the supernatural, turned to fantasy and allegory, invested adventure and peril with glamor, was seeded with horror by the "Gothic tale," and enshrined both passion and sentimentality. Its transmigrations bring us the modern fiction of fantasy and allegory, symbolism, satire, and make-believe—from *Brave New World* to *The Sword in the Stone* and *Road of Ages*—and of exotic adventure—from *Sard Harker* to *The Seven Who Fled*. Its element of make-believe and wish-fulfillment tinges our "light fiction," from the delicate simplicities of Elizabeth Goudge to the synthetic love thrills of Kathleen Norris. But its idealism, its exaltation of passion, are reflections of human nature quite as truthful as are those conveyed by a stark realism that records only the trivial, the mean, or the brutal.

Under the shadow of the romance the novel first appeared, as the short tale of real life, concerned chiefly with domestic intrigue, jealousy, and a ribald acceptance of life as it is. Reality was its field, not make-believe. The novelist was historian rather than romancer, his purpose to convey to the reader a sense of participation in actual experience. Fuller record, deeper exploration, of realities of human character and experience were part of a continuing process of enrichment and expansion, until imagination and fact, romance and realism, were blended in a powerful, flexible art that more than any other medium of communication reveals man's nature to himself and registers and molds opinions, manners, and morals. Romance and realism find separate expression in modern fiction, but in its substance they are indissolubly mingled. For the essence of the romantic spirit is idealism, and, as George Meredith says in his Letters, "Between realism and idealism there is no natural conflict. This completes that."

The structure of the modern novel stands upon the foundations laid by Defoe, by Richardson, Fielding, Scott, Austen, Dickens, Thackeray, Balzac; built upon by Hawthorne, Melville, Meredith, Henry James, Conrad, and Galsworthy. It is a structure that ranges over many different levels, is planned according to new specifications, incorporates much new material, and is equipped with numerous mechanical conveniences. But it still utilizes an assortment of its traditional furnishings and reconditions or adapts many of its older parts. Most novels find a place for themselves on some level and in some part of the general structure; a few make a compartment of their own, which will later attract other tenants. The so-called "forms," "kinds," and "types" of fiction furnish a rough guide-chart to the whole structure. These terms are often used interchangeably, but they convey different meanings.

"Form" is defined by the *Concise Oxford Dictionary* as "arrangement and style in literary composition"; "kind" is "class, sort, variety"; "type" is "person, thing, event, serving as illustration, symbol, or characteristic specimen of another thing or of a class." Thus, we may characterize a novel as realistic, or romantic, or expressionistic, or naturalistic, or stream-of-consciousness in form (which is its arrangement and style); we may recognize it as belonging in nature, though not necessarily in form, to a particular kind or class of fiction (historical, biographic, crime-and-mystery); we may consider that works composed in a given form or representing a specific kind of fiction are types. Proletarian fiction, for example, is not a specific form, for it may be composed in expressionistic style or it may be plain, direct, realistic narrative, but it is a distinctive kind of fiction and examples of it are accepted as types. Historical novels belong to an old, very familiar class; individually they may be romantic, realistic, epic, dramatic, or a combination of these and other forms (like *Anthony Adverse*); they merge into other kinds, such as saga, regional, and biographic fiction, and this merging produces various specific, though subsidiary, types. "Type" is the word commonly used to indicate examples of both form (or technique) and kind (or class) of fiction, and though its interchangeable application is sometimes confusing its use in this duplex or even triplex fashion seems legitimate enough. For Virginia Woolf's *Mrs. Dalloway* may be regarded as a type of two forms, the stream-of-consciousness form and the form of the so-called "time novel," and also as a type of the particular kind of fiction concerned with psychological character study of woman. Morley's *Kitty Foyle* is stream-of-consciousness in form and character-study of woman in kind. In *The Big Money*, by John Dos Passos, several different types are represented: a highly expressionistic form of "time novel"; a realistic and dramatic narrative form; and the kind of fiction concerned with immediate social problems of its day. His later novel, *Adventures of a Young Man*, is plain biographic narrative in form and belongs both to character-study and to social-problem fiction in kind.

Such differentiation of fiction into types and type-groups is an

arbitrary exercise, and a superficial one, so far as it is concerned with
the mold of form rather than with intrinsic substance. But it is a base
for some of the most penetrating and stimulating contemporary
criticism, and it possesses an index or guidance value that is useful to
the student and to the general reader. Anyone who reads novels at
all will find their reading more enjoyable, their field of interest
widened, as they make more extensive acquaintance with novels of
different kinds and especially as they come to recognize, even if not
to respond to, the particular way or ways in which a novelist has
chosen to shape his work. Even mere identification acquaintance
with the type names that emerge and succeed one another in current reviewing, in critics' summaries and literary commentary will
give the ordinary unliterary reader a certain realization of changing
concepts and new trends of development in contemporary life.

Realism in form and in mood dominates the modern novel. The
romantic element appears in it chiefly as idealism in theme, or as
compassion for human beings, or as a warm, sensitive response to
loyalties of the heart. The romantic glamor of the happy ending and
the assured reward of virtue has faded away under the light of
common day in which novelists in increasing numbers observe,
study and record realities of human experience. But glamor does
not lose its lure. Readers who have long expected to find in fiction
escape from realities into a happy never-never-land, or at least com-
forting assurance that the best is yet to be, resent the novel's acceptance of the tragic certainties of existence, its realization that there
is no finality in the continuing experience of living. To a great many
readers any novel that does not end happily is pessimistic; any novel
in which ignoble or sensual or ugly aspects of life are presented is
sordid. So "pessimism" and "sordidness" are the charges most frequently brought against the whole body of modern fiction, in a
confusion of values that makes no distinction between the impersonal, undogmatic reading of life's inexorable logic, the single-purposed documentation of social ills, and the cynical or clinical transcription of sensuality, vulgarity, and violence. It is true that the
general attitude toward life and the world today is a pessimistic one,

partly in deep awareness of social tragedies and human wastage that all our modern knowledge proves unable to avert; partly in panic presentiment that civilization cannot survive the rising forces of chaos and barbarism. In fiction every reaction to this attitude is registered: there is bitterness, violence, confusion, and bravado, as well as fortitude and a sense of common fellowship. But realism is not necessarily pessimism, and the realistic novel, in its better examples and in its full range, has not cast aside ideals or sunk into abysmal gloom. It approaches and deals with life in all the realities of circumstance, environment, and character; seeks to face facts with intelligent scrutiny, to weigh motives as well as actions, and to find the nobilities as well as the pettinesses of ordinary living.

Realistic fiction finds its oldest and still most popular expression in the straightforward biographic (often autobiographic) narrative of events happening in realizable time and space to people who are made real to the reader. *The Old Wives' Tale, The Forsyte Saga, Of Human Bondage, The Fortunes of Richard Mahony* are backlogs of modern realism: epitomes of the ordinary activities of ordinary people, in which minutiae of fact and a judicial impartiality of insight are fused in a steady glow of truth. Sinclair Lewis inspired one of the most powerful movements in the American fiction of the twenties when he focused realism in scathing satire on vulnerable aspects of American life. Booth Tarkington, from a less acrid, warmer realism, produced in *Alice Adams* a study of American girlhood that remains vital and undated. Ellen Glasgow's thoughtful, ironic realism has recorded the social history of Virginia through three generations, with inclusive grasp and keen yet sympathetic judgment. In continuing succession and variation of examples, the direct realistic narrative reveals how fine and powerful an instrument it can be in penetrating character and charting depths and shallows of ordinary human experience. The psychological element is as essential to its content as is the factual, the stream of consciousness is drawn upon, but the plain, direct narrative, uninterrupted by experimentation or expressionistic display, holds the appeal of comfortable familiarity to the ordinary reader.

In many divergencies the realistic narrative novel is carried into regional, historical, and biographical fiction. Indeed, its relationship to both history and biography is so close that in much recent work few lines of demarkation have been maintained. Like history and biography, the realistic novel strives to limit itself to the field of fact; but unlike them it is free to draw upon invention to attain verisimilitude. All three must assemble and arrange their facts and must organize from them a scheme of presentation that will sustain factual development and establish psychological reality in following out a situation or filling in the contours of character. The historian cannot recreate a period, the biographer cannot vitalize a personality, without exercise of the imaginative faculty; and the novelist, who has more latitude in bringing the imagination into play upon the same material, can often impart a more convincing radiation of reality. Zsolt de Harsanyi's novel, *The Star-Gazer*, gives to the ordinary reader a more intensive, more illuminating life of Galileo than does any biography that has yet appeared; it gives also an authentic, clearly focused recreation of that crowded age of the Renaissance when free scientific inquiry was rising in conflict with traditional, divinely constituted authority; and it presents fairly and impressively the dilemma of the human mind, rooted in moral and spiritual certainties and confronted with advancing forces that must inevitably destroy those certainties. There are many present-day novelists who in the practice of their own art are also historians and biographers of sound authority and valid import and whose work, in that specific relationship, has values that offset shortcomings in literary craftsmanship. Thus, Frank Hough's novel *Renown* is undistinguished as literary art; but its solid, absorbing narrative of the life of Benedict Arnold is an enlightening study, both objective and sympathetic, of one of the most complex and spectacular careers in American history. More expository than pictorial, lacking in flexibility of dialogue and in emotional magnetism, it nevertheless succeeds in rendering an individual human destiny in the terms of individual character.

The romantic novel in its traditionary formula has little place in fiction's modern domain. There are many popular survival patterns, such as the "light novel," smugly pursuing love's impeded course to ultimate beatitude, which flourishes in feminine borderlands, and its half-brother, the hairy-chested "Western," which stakes its claims in great open spaces of masculine mentality; but most of them are re-cut according to the realistic fashion of the day. The most saccharine sentimentalism is not immune to the infections of night life, jazz, alcoholism, and sexual indulgence. The heroics of "red blood" adventure are more heavily charged with raw brutalities and ribald profanities than were the earlier variations upon a similar theme devised by Zane Grey, Curwood, and their congeners.

In the great recent revival of American historical fiction the romantic pictorial-sentimental charm of earlier models—Robert Chambers, Paul Leicester Ford, Mary Johnston, Mrs. Catherwood—has been succeeded by unsparing chronicles of Indian torture, primitive ferocities, and physical extremities of pioneer struggle or military conflict. This is part of the novel's steady advance into the field of reality, and it means, not extinction of the spirit of romance, but abandonment of an older romantic form that had less genuine relationship to its own fundamental material. Romance is inextinguishable; and in some degree, in some manifestation—of idealism, or love, or loyalty, or simple or complex emotional release—it is fused into the substance of modern realism. *Gone with the Wind* derived its immense appeal from the completeness of this fusing. Romantic in spirit, realistic in substance, it combined dynamic vigor with an almost naïve simplicity; its creation of vital human characters and its immediacy of experience and intensity of realistic minutiae carried an impact of actuality that became a sweeping dramatic movement sustained at high emotional tension. These qualities offset defects of over-romantic artificiality, of unconvincing psychological development, of intense sectional bias. Indeed, the last characteristic deepens the book's essential truth, for it conveys with fundamental honesty the actual temper of the time and place and people that it records and interprets. Contrast it with *Anthony Adverse*—companion highlight in modern romanticism

—and its deeper fusing with realism is evident. Margaret Mitchell built her history romantically on a solid substructure of genuine human experience. Hervey Allen constructed against an immense historical background an elaborate fabrication of romanticism and allegory that, for all its wealth of varied historical fact, remains an imaginary epic adventure. Each represents a different type of fiction in values and relationships. In one we see the romantic historical novel as it evolves through realism to more complete reality; in the other we see a continuance of the traditional historical romance, bulwarked by realistic material, but held within its pristine channels.

Through much realistic and some romantic fiction runs the "stream of consciousness," most familiar of the modern art forms in which the novelist seeks to reveal and elucidate individual personality and to reproduce the actual sensation of living. The term is used broadly for a technique that has developed within a quarter-century and branched into many variations and extensions of method, all more or less experimental in their invention or adaptation of novel modes of expression, their endeavor by a different use of words to convey unformulated significances, to transmit states of consciousness, or to register sensory impressions.

Interpretation of character by means of modern psychology and the principles of psychoanalysis has become a basic element in contemporary fiction. Such interpretation has, of course, particular application to the detailed, subjective study of life experience, so that much fiction concerned with character analysis and with biographic narrative centers on the inner experiences of the mind, on the effort to probe and record the mingling of past and present—of what has been, what is, and what is becoming in the individual consciousness. In its full range this stream-of-consciousness fiction represents a threefold endeavor that may be carried out separately or in a combined manifestation. Most significant, perhaps, is the purpose to reveal the effect upon our conscious life of unconscious limitations, terrors, powers, impulses, that are stored deep down under our sentient selves: of this Thomas Wolfe discloses fragmentary glimpses in *Of Time and the River;* and Virginia Woolf, in *The Waves*, conveys delicate intimations of the fundamental, unchanging essence of personality. There is also involved, or implied, the endeavor to register that continuous flow of instinctive, emotional, and volitional sensation, which is the stream of consciousness itself: Dorothy Richardson's sequence of novels, *Pilgrimage*, set a standard pattern here; Morley's *Kitty Foyle* offered a popular cut-down model, streamlined and of much higher heart-power. And with this purpose to project continuity of experience is involved the endeavor to effect a visual and mental realization of the occurrence of many different events in the same moment of time; in other words to record "simultaneity," in a contrasting medley of impressions of immediate experience: colors, noises, smells, prismatic glimpses of scenes or persons, such as John Dos Passos produced in *Manhattan Transfer*. These three endeavors, and also virtually every other venture of stream-of-consciousness composition, conjoin in the work of James Joyce, whose *Ulysses* for twenty years has diffused its influence over the whole organic structure of fiction.

Origin of the phrase "stream-of-consciousness fiction" is not clearly evident. It has been attributed to Henry James and defined as the novelist's attempt "to portray life and character by setting down everything that goes on in his hero's mind; notably all those unimportant and chaotic thought-sequences which occupy our idle and somnolent moments and to which, in real life, we ourselves pay little attention." This, however, is a characterization that does not fairly indicate how greatly this type of fiction has strengthened the psychological values of the novel and enlarged its relationship to human experience. It would seem that the use of the term applied to it stems back, in this country at least, nearly half a century to the wide public recognition of William James's *Principles of Psychology*. Published in 1890, this was one of the transforming influences in education and in common life; and its chapter, "The Stream of Thought," offers a curiously exact description of the mental processes the stream-of-consciousness novel seeks to register. Consciousness, it affirms, is not composed of concrete bits joined together, but is a continuous, flowing current, and this current has five chief characteristics: it is personal, it is always changing, it is continuous, it deals with objects not itself, and it is always choosing among them, welcoming, rejecting, accentuating, selecting. Closely linked with this is the chapter, "The Perception of Time," in which again change and continuity are emphasized, and it is pointed out that in our immediate personal experience of time, the past, the present, and the future are all contained "in the specious present." Whatever foundation of acceptance was laid by James, it was the development of psychoanalysis by Freud and Jung (Freud's work was first published in the United States in 1915) that established the modern novelist's approach to interpretation of mental processes and emotional reactions and deposited the soil in which so many different types of experimental writing have germinated, flourished, and multiplied.

Perhaps the pervasiveness and variety of these types may be best indicated by a few specific examples. In the expressionistic type a time-focus on the simultaneous occurrence of different events and a technicolor visualization of exterior happenings often takes the place of direct continuity of individual consciousness. John Dos Passos, in *The Big Money*, produced a combined panorama and cross section of American life through the 1920's, that decade of "big money" that ended with the stockmarket crash of 1929. He mingled the expressionistic method with solid realistic narrative, setting dramatic episodes and sharp-edged character portrayals in opposition to interpolated "news reels" with glaring headlines, "camera eye" perspectives and close-ups, and nonfictional biographical sketches; all coalescing into a powerful composite evocation of a phase in contemporary social history. Richard Hughes's novel *In Hazard* represents application of psychological experimentation to sea adventure, linking in very interesting comparison of older and new techniques with Conrad's *Typhoon*. This is the presentation of a hurricane at sea, in which a turbine cargo vessel, the last word in streamlined power and complex equipment, is caught and held, her electricity killed, dead for five days, a helpless hulk, more helpless than the man-run ships of a less scientific age. Under taut, dramatic tension the movement runs in a parallel course: transmission of the storm in its immediate material effects; transmission of its effects on the minds and emotions of those subjected to it; the stream of consciousness running beside, over, and beneath the stream of hurricane—all conveying symbolic and ironic implications.

Different types constantly build upon one another. Older patterns are absorbed into the general mass, leaving their trace on its common substance, or contributing from their elements to some special re-emergence. Thus, the naturalistic type, as it was brought into being by Zola and given name and nurture in America by Frank Norris and Theodore Dreiser, has been largely absorbed into the later body of realistic fiction; but it still stamps its own impress on our proletarian fiction, re-emerges, as in Erskine Caldwell's grotesque, violent studies of subhuman existence, and holds its own against the stream of consciousness in *Studs Lonigan.* Of recent emergence in experimental fiction—natural, inevitable outflow from the stream of consciousness—is what Edwin Muir has called the "time novel," centering on the continuing cycle of living; on transition, not permanence. In Virginia Woolf's *The Years* time itself is the protagonist, and its flow through different lives during half a century is theme and substance and action. Kenneth Fearing's *The Hospital* focuses on a shorter time scale: a single day in a great New York hospital, its hours flashing simultaneous illumination of contrasts, paradoxes, and complexities of human circumstance. Both books represent a further development of the time element that permeates so many different types of modern fiction and that found its paramount expression in Marcel Proust's *Remembrance of Things Past*, in which the involuntary memory of a single individual, carried in an unending current of sensations, is made the focus for a three-generation unfolding of human experience. Perspective, or perhaps what might be more truly called an insistent time sense, has become more and more important in the novelist's art, as life is studied more analytically as a continuous flow of experience, never static, never finished. This explains why an "ending," in any sense of complete finality (except, of course, the finality of death) is so much less common today, even in novels of more conventional texture.

Of older structural forms, two that have long been familiar should perhaps have a word of comment, for they are still basic for much contemporary fiction. These are the traditional epic and dramatic forms that carry back through the whole history of the novel. In its name the epic novel still conveys a sense of grandeur, of heroic proportions and far-flung episodes; in its development it runs from early chronicles of chivalric conflict, through picaresque narratives of rogues' adventures, leisurely rehearsals of linked incidents (*Tom Jones* or *Pickwick Papers*), into the episodic romance and the full length realistic biographical novel of today. It offers a spacious structure in which events follow one another in loose or variable sequence; it admits excursions and extensions, which may be complete in themselves; it does not move in concentrated progression to a final culmination. The dramatic novel, on the other hand, builds precisely and compressively toward a dramatic climax; all its incidents are directed in logical, symmetrical plot development toward this climax; its bulk is less, its characters fewer and more continuously concerned in the central plot involvement: Hardy's *The Mayor of Casterbridge* is as basically dramatic as De Morgan's *Joseph Vance* is basically epic. One or the other of these forms may prevail in present-day novels of different types, just as Priestley's *The Good Companions* is an almost perfect example of the epic form, and in Daphne Du Maurier's *Rebecca* a solid old-style dramatic structure has been reconditioned and skillfully equipped with modern psychological accessories. Both epic and dramatic forms are combined in many of the finest novels of past and present —in *Vanity Fair* and *David Copperfield*, in *The Forsyte Saga* and *Nostromo*, in *South Riding* and *The Grapes of Wrath*. But while it is possible to trace what may be called hereditary strains, environmental influences, and acquired characteristics in the biological analysis of almost any novel, it must be remembered that the great body of fiction is constantly absorbing into itself different and conflicting elements and resolving them into an ever more expansive, more complex, more variable medium of expression.

Whatever its type may be, the novel itself's the thing: its content, its quality, its interest are the reader's chief concern. To experience joy in reading for its own sake and at the same time to gain clearer recognition of the values that exist in what is read are the simple processes—and the only ones—which impart that mysterious proficiency sought in millions of class rooms and study courses and known as "appreciation of literature." The term has been formalized and limited. To the average student it implies fixed rules and absolute values, expounded in bewildering contradiction, with controversial animus, by critics and teachers; or it represents tribute paid automatically to novels of the past by readers whose actual appreciation of literature is nourished by novels of the present. But it is, in fact, chiefly a matter of the individual growth of the mind that is fed by curiosity and that flowers in realization of an inexhaustible diversity of ascertained values. So perhaps it is worth while to consider briefly the ordinary reader's approach to a novel, some of the things to be looked for in reading it, and some of the ways in which, directly and indirectly, its reading may enlarge and enhance appreciation of literature.

Back of the reader's approach are the facts that fiction is an art, with a closer relationship to life than any other art; that its raw material is human nature and human experience; and that its existence and its meaning depend upon how successfully through its own medium—the medium of language—it shapes that material into semblance of reality and makes it alive, beautiful, or significant to the reader. The degree to which it justifies its existence and fulfills its meaning is the measure of its literary art; but in the ebb and flow of contemporary literature that measure has no fixed record. Only time will register a novel's permanence as art; current literary criticism, in a confusion of voices, will assign or attempt to assign its status in certain broad categories; but its values are relative, not absolute. What a novel brings to a reader depends on what the reader brings to the novel; and comparatively few ordinary readers bring to their reading any very strong interest in or clear perception of the qualities of literary art. Their approach is personal; intelligent, but not attentive; more prone to impatience than to enthusiasm, but actively responsive or aggressive when personal convictions are roused or emotions stirred. Readers' choice may be determined by popularity, by controversy, by curiosity, or simply by individual taste and expectation of enjoyment. Always individual preferences exist; and judgment is conditioned by those preferences and by the mental, moral, and emotional fibers of individual personality. Liking and disliking are instinctive human responses, unpredictable and violently contradictory as they affect the same subject. The final episode of *The Grapes of Wrath* was literally nauseous to many readers, moving and consistent to others, a false theatric device to some, a symbolic and beautiful finale to still others; readers offended by "indecency" in *The Constant Nymph* found acceptable entertainment in *The Nutmeg Tree; The Tree of Liberty* was informative but dull to many, of vital "human interest" to others. It is on liking or disliking that the reader founds his judgment of a novel; and that judgment is the test of that novel for that reader. This is a perfectly valid test, so far as it goes. Ford Madox Ford says: "For the judgment of contemporary literature, the only test is the test of one's personal taste"—and if a reader finds in a book none of the allure that others have discovered, then, as George Wither might have said:

> If it be not so to me,
> What care I how fair it be?

Taste and purpose are of first importance in the reader's approach to a novel. Bad taste, undeveloped taste, the taste that craves a single kind of sustenance and complacently refuses anything different, will block advance on higher levels. An approach that is confused and purposeless will shut off perspectives. Of course, all reading has some incentive: entertainment, retreat from reality, companionship, information, pursuit of a special interest or preoccupation, mental stimulation, enlargement of cultural background are main provocations; but many readers approach a novel without a clear idea of any purpose and never realize or follow out the paths it opens to some enlarged or different field of interest. Approach should not be hostile. Hostility may properly develop as the reader proceeds; it may legitimately be the final result of his progress; but at the outset fair play demands at least a spirit of co-operation and no malice prepense. An approach dictated by a stern sense of duty is also likely to be unfortunate; if the reader cannot muster some expectation of pleasure, some assurance of interest, he should at least make his venture in a spirit of curiosity or of hope. After all, there are no compulsions upon reading, and the world is wide. If a book successfully resists approach, it is better to turn aside: perhaps the effort is not worth while; if it is, the reader can in time forge a stronger key of purpose and understanding.

Reading a novel should not be the passive exercise that it too often is. Readers who never emerge from the borderlands of fiction —the flat regions of commonplace, synthetic romance and pious sentimentality, the mudbanks of vulgarity and cheap sensationalism —develop a kind of mental atrophy that makes them incapable of response to any different stimulus; and many others of more discriminating taste who read widely and with enjoyment accept novels as only casual entertainment and "like" them or "dislike" them without any understanding based on real knowledge. Entertainment is a legitimate demand; it is a superficial form of pleasure, and pleasure, in all its radiations into mind and heart, is the essential joy of reading. As Somerset Maugham says: "There is no need for pleasure to be unintelligent. One of the signs of culture is that you are able to extract pleasure from objects or events to which the ignorant are indifferent." Intelligent reading is an active exercise of the mind, directed at understanding a novel as a whole, extracting all the different values it may hold, and coming, for your own satisfaction, to some clear conclusion as to what you think of it and why you think as you do. Every novel worth reading presents some idea, which may dominate or be merely incidental. The reader should be aware of that idea, should consider its demonstration and its implications and should experience some reaction to it, through thought, or emotion, or memory. There is an incidental idea beneath the romantic melodrama of *Rebecca:* the change in personality that comes when a deep sense of inferiority is replaced by realization of being valued and indispensable. The reader who perceives this idea, who traces and tests it from experience or from remembered reading, has extracted a value lost to the mind that absorbs only a pleasing superficial thrill from Daphne Du Maurier's novel.

One of the most common reader reactions is the belief that if a novel proves uninteresting the book is at fault. Sometimes this is true: novels are often dull, or unconvincing, or overweighted; or a novelist's art, in skill and values, may be on a lower plane than is the reader's proficiency. But more often it is the reader's own limitations—intellectual immaturity, or prejudice or lack of imaginative perception—that are responsible. What a novel means *to me,* in my immediate personal reaction, does not necessarily mean that this is what that novel *is,* in its own quality or significance. There should be a more reasoned base of judgment: broader comprehension of a novel's content, clearer realization of the fact that a novel in which many intelligent readers find pleasure must possess qualities that are worth discovery. Any reader who establishes such a base of judgment is establishing also appreciation of literature.

Comprehension and appreciation involve definite mental operations. Determine, even if in broad generalization, what kind or type of fiction a novel represents, what is its subject, and what appears to be the point of view from which that subject is presented. Try to grasp the unity of the book as a whole; that is, its integration of different elements: descriptive (in background, incidental detail), objective (in action, dialogue, characterization), subjective (in purpose, implications, analysis). In doing this the reader in fact asks the questions: Where? When? What? Why? How? and finds their answer in the structure and substance of the novel. These are the simplest means to comprehension. Appreciation ranges from the instinctive response of unanalyzed pleasure to alert perception of a book's individual qualities of power, style, literary art, and to awareness of specific factual values;[1] but it depends upon sympathetic understanding even more than upon realization of pleasure conferred. Writer and reader should be in partnership with each other, one establishing communication, the other receiving and maintaining it; and if the kind and quality of the communication is the writer's responsibility, the strength and clearness of its reception depends chiefly upon the reader. Probably no reader, even the most appreciative, receives exactly the communication that the writer meant to transmit. For just as every writer puts his own temperament, his own view of life, into his work, so every reader's temperament and view of life affect his reception of the writer's work. Appreciation presupposes not simply the ability to experience pleasure but also a gusto for life, a spirit of mental and emotional adventure that seeks to enlarge vicarious experience and to develop new responses to beauty.

These are means to fuller participation in the values that fiction offers. By using them the ordinary reader may increase his enjoyment, clarify his taste, and ripen his judgment. They should serve, also, to make more evident the reading relationships that link novels not only with one another but also with every other kind of literature and that deepen and enlarge appreciation of life in all its expressions. It is true that refreshment and escape are instinctive cravings of the human spirit and that fiction in many of its manifestations satisfies those cravings. Novels of illusion and appeasement have their place as contributions toward the "great task of happiness." But our deepest interests lie in our own times, our own life experience; and the intelligent modern mind will find nourishment and incentive in the novels that vivify life, deepen awareness of its profundities, reveal its diversities, and interpret human experience.

[1] These points are more fully noted later, in relation to "Reviewing a Novel."

III. FROM MID-VICTORIAN ROOTS

He was occupied with the forming of a pattern out
of the manifold chaos of life.—SOMERSET MAUGHAM:
Of Human Bondage

ONE of the broadest, most familiar, and most highly cultivated
fields of modern fiction flourishes from the seed of the mid-
Victorian domestic novel. This is seed sown by Anthony Trollope,
whose belief, maintained in his works, was "that the novelist's chief
business is the creation of human men and women in whose existence one is forced to believe." His novels of English parishes and
politics, of social groups and domestic relations, even-toned, detailed,
so imbued with truth that they are Emerson's "journals of manners,"
carry their echoes into the work of many present-day novelists
whose patterns are woven of the substance of everyday living. Mrs.
Oliphant, now an almost forgotten name, was a seedsower, too,
with her practiced, weary craftsmanship, her underlying ironic
sadness. From the novels of Trollope and Mrs. Oliphant alone some
student of social history may some day compile a study of the origins, an explanation of the rise of the English militant suffrage
movement, going further back than Vera Brittain does in her novel
on that theme and striking more deeply into the roots of the long
struggle of English women for personal, professional, political, and
economic independence. Novels of Mrs. Humphry Ward, William
De Morgan, Archibald Marshall, Ethel Sidgwick come into the later
background, as Victorian domesticity felt the insistent prick of
modernity. Arnold Bennett invested that domesticity with inexhaustible minutiae of realism; May Sinclair probed it with neurotic
sensitivity and psychological ruthlessness; Hugh Walpole touched
it with intuitive romanticism; it is a continuing theme upon which
English fiction plays in every mood, grave, serene, and gay. English

novelists have been and still are masters in this field. In America, Howells set his stamp of delicate precision, of wistful illuminating humor, upon "domestic manners of the Americans," to use Mrs. Trollope's phrase. The later work of Mary S. Watts, with its sober, monotonous chronicle of everyday living; of Margaret Deland, instilling warm humanness into the sentimental and the ethical; of Tarkington, gleaning romance, drama, complacencies, and absurdities from the ordinary American home—all centered upon and amplified the theme. American writers are building here a structure of their own, less smoothly finished, but more varied in ramifications, more democratic in spirit, than is the familiar English type.

All these have been factors in the evolution of the novel that centers on family life, on domestic complications, on love, marriage, divorce, and children, in terms of group relationship, individual character, circumstance, and environment. We may call it the Family Novel; and if the term seems homely and genial, remember that the experiences of the House of Atreus and the House of Œdipus are Family Drama; that the family holds heredity, birth, life, death, frustration, and fulfillment all within its inescapable grip.

Henry Handel Richardson's trilogy, *The Fortunes of Richard Mahony*, gives us the family novel at its fullest tragic stature. This is one of the great contemporary novels of frustrated and unrelenting human experience; though it remains comparatively disregarded by the larger reading public. Perhaps it may be considered a biographical novel—as *The Old Wives' Tale* and *Of Human Bondage* are biographical; it has the attributes of regional fiction in its portrayal of Australian life during the middle and close of the nineteenth century; it impinges upon the "saga" in its life chronicle of a family group; but its core is the family, and its relationship to these other types makes it, I think, a basic example of the values that characterize the mid-Victorian domestic novel as it exists in the twentieth-century world.

The trilogy was published separately, with a ten-year interval between the first volume (in 1917) and the two volumes that followed; in 1931 it appeared complete in a single volume. It deals with the whole career of Richard Mahony (if you know him, you call him Ma-enny), a young Irish doctor of good family, who emigrates to Australia in the 1850's, the days of the first gold rush. He keeps a general store in the mining field near Ballarat and practices his profession now and then as accompaniment. Here he marries a girl, very young, sincere, capable, sweet, and unselfish. Polly—later, Mary—is a living and lovely character, consistent and deeply human, as we follow her through the ensuing years. Mahony himself is sincere, honest, capable, a competent physician, truly fine-spirited; far in advance of the people with whom he is thrown, in breeding, education, and intellect. But he is unmagnetic, unpopular, hot-tempered, prone to be critical and drastic in his judgments of others, and headstrong in his purposes; also he is sensitive and self-consuming, given to brooding and self-pity: qualities that deepen in misfortune and become tragic pathological forces, overthrowing the whole equilibrium of his being. Richard rises to success in his practice; a prosperous and respected professional career opens before him; many ties and associations develop, chiefly through his wife's family. One child born to him soon after marriage dies at birth, and Mary is said to be unable to have others. But she cares for the motherless babies of her harsh and wealthy brother, and loves them devotedly. There are a few happy years of well-being, and Richard's investments promise wealth. He is irked by the pioneer crudities of his environment, and his mind turns longingly back to England. Against Mary's unavailing grief and protest he sells his practice and they go together to England. With their departure the first volume (*Australia Felix*) closes.

The stay in England is short. Richard's investments prove uncertain, and he has losses through a dishonest broker. He resumes his practice twice in England; but all the environment is unfamiliar, unfriendly. There are none of the pioneer, democratic equalities to which they are accustomed; people are aloof, hostile, in long-established social strata, snobbish and contemptuous toward the colonials; the climate is chill and depressing; all seems crowded, dingy, petty, and irritating. He feels that his return to England has been a failure and turns back to Australia, disappointed and embittered, but never doubting that comfort and security are again within his reach. This is the second epoch of the chronicle: *The Way Home.*

Ultima Thule unfolds mounting, relentless, inevitable tragedy: an unforgettable transcript of the purgatory into which human experience can plunge. At first there is hope and unexpected compensation, for Mary becomes the mother, first of a son, then of twin daughters. Her children are her passionate devotion and delight; centered on them, her eyes are less keen to trace Richard's anxieties and brooding and the nerve-racking headaches that come with increasing frequency—all reflexes of his heavier responsibilities, his latent terror of being unequal to the family burden. Misfortunes follow: one of the little girls dies, in an episode of almost unendurable poignancy; Richard is progressively unsuccessful. His health fails; there is constant menace of cerebral stroke, though no one seems to recognize it; he endures agonies of concealed suffering, vertigo and fierce headaches in which he is violent with sudden almost insane rages. He drinks constantly to excess, and his practice grows less and less. They become poorer and poorer. Mary is torn to pieces by it all; her nerves are tensed; her patience worn out. On the surface she becomes embittered and hardened; husband and wife are caught in tragic revulsion against each other—a revulsion that is simply the distortion and agony of their deep and inextinguishable love. Mary meets the progressive fatality and despair. She faces everything and never admits defeat. When all is swept away, and Richard—so different, so tragic and terrible a figure—is violently and hopelessly insane, she carries the family burden as a country postmistress, a changed being herself: stern, gaunt, determined, a formidable creature, seizing for her young the necessities of existence. Richard she never ceases to love, to yearn over. As soon as she has food and shelter for her children and a livelihood for herself, she sets herself to take him from the miseries of the state asylum where he is confined; and somehow she accomplishes the impossible, overrides all rules and authorities, and brings back home the broken, helpless, demented creature who clings so pitifully to her protection. She rises above all difficulties and disasters. At the end she still has her two children; but we know that in the tragic flowing current of life all that has been endured and overcome is vague and unmeaning to those who have not yet lived through fatality and borne its burden. "Ultima Thule" is the name of the Mahonys' home in Victoria. But it has, I think, a deeper meaning than that: the ultimate realm of human tragedy; the land's end; life experience projected into the abyss.

Few family novels strike so sustained a tragic chord or devote so large a canvas to so small a family group. The old-fashioned Victorian surface of Henry Handel Richardson's novel is also rare today; but its minutiae of detail, its detachment of attitude, a certain grimness and muscularity in its strength (giving fitness to the author's masculine pseudonym), and its deep penetration into individual human nature are qualities that give it enduring dignity and significance and make it representative of the best contemporary realism.

On the solid substance of family experience are based many of the novels that are pre-eminently studies of social change or panoramas of history-in-the-making. These fall into the broad type-groups of sagas and regional fiction. Others, in spite of specific social theme, center on family life and individual character in a changing time scale. Evelyn Scott brought subtle insight and unflinching power of character portrayal into her compressed saga of an English family during two generations, from the late 1880's to the 1930's. In its title, *Breathe upon These Slain* conveys the underlying theme —for here, from the photographs left in an English home rented by Americans in England, is created a family group of characters whose lives are traced through decline to extinction under the deadly effects, the mental, physical, and spiritual frustrations, of a society dominated by resistance to change that throws the passions back upon themselves to consume within and grinds freedom of action between the millstones of convention. More intensive and specialized is the theme of Vera Brittain's novel *Honourable Estate*: the social revolution in the status of women that has been effected in England within the present century. Her title, from the English marriage service, refers not only to the three marriages in which she exemplifies the transition from Victorian repressions, but it stands also, she says, for "that position of dignity and respect which the world's women and the world's workers have striven for since the end of the eighteenth century and which within my own lifetime they have partly achieved." Upon a carefully planned framework of characters and events—firmly illustrative, accurately chronological—is built a solid structure of exposition, example, and dissertation. As a novel it is heavy-handed, without character "aliveness," devoid of humorous perceptions; but as a serious and sincere study of social forces behind the rise of woman suffrage and the labor movement in English political history it has distinct values.

Effort to demonstrate and appraise the influences conditioning the last three generations has been one of the dominant trends in the contemporary family novel, especially by English writers. It is inspired, of course, by that ever-recurrent conflict between what has been and what is that makes it impossible for the next generation to accept the previous generation's solution of life's problems. The enormous transformation, material, intellectual, and spiritual, that has come about in conditions and standards of living within the past half century has set most of the novelists whose working lives fall within that transition period to recalling, reassembling, the elements of that past experience, seeking to capture, to weigh and assess, influences and circumstances responsible for mutations, for failures, for shortcomings, for achievements. Thus we have socio-historical retrospect through the medium of family chronicle. Vera Brittain's retrospect is strongly feminist. In *The Balliols*, which begins in 1907 and closes in the 1930's, Alec Waugh offered a man's study of what he had observed in the life of two generations divided into three distinct groups: the men and women who were mature at the outbreak of the first World War in 1914; the youth of those opening war years; and the boys and girls of those years who became "postwar youth," casual, cynical, self-centered, but striking back to a more stable balance than could their war-shocked brothers and sisters. Good in its psychology and portrayal of men, shallow and uncon-

vincing in its depiction of women, the novel lacks flexibility and
vital reality, but it illuminates many phases of contemporary opinion
and traces many of the patterns that helped to shape the design for
living during those decades. Its theme is conveyed in the final scene:
the destruction of the old house that had been the Balliols' home;
spacious, clumsy, hard to heat and administer, now torn down to
give place to a fine block of flats with big garages—"modern, a
real modern home such as people want, a small place that they can
shut up week-ends and get away somewhere in a car." In other
words, the necessity for each generation to meet the demands of its
own day and hour, rather than those of an earlier day.

Broader in scope, more penetrating and complex, is Phyllis Bentley's family novel, *Sleep in Peace*, panoramic study of two English
families through three generations. In its title the same theme is implicit: the revolt of every generation against its predecessor, saying,
as in the lines from Feuchtwanger's *Ugly Duchess*, "Sleep in peace,
father! I shall be different from you." Here the setting is Yorkshire,
and the two families whose experiences we follow are joint owners
of a textile mill, in a partnership long established, broken by dissensions, then reunited, and at last merged by death and marriage. This
is a long and intricate chronicle, less concerned with the march of
time in events than with the changing contours of individual character, individual destiny, as these are shaped by time's more intangible
processes of erosion and accretion. The industrial expansion of the
nineties, the tragic ordeal and equally tragic aftermath of war, war-
time prosperity and ensuing collapse, strikes and depression years,
make the factual framework for the closely knit fabric of human
realities, warm loyalties, bitternesses, passions, conflicting reactions
and emotions. It shows the emergence of a new generation turning
to purposes and ideals entirely different from those for which their
predecessors struggled, contemptuous or indifferent toward the
standards those predecessors so passionately upheld in the cause of
what they believed must be a better world. And it closes on a note
of thoughtful retrospect, of questioning: "Was this a particular mo-

ment in the world's history, or did the generations always repeat this pattern of mutation?"

A similar transition is reflected against an American background in Margaret Ayer Barnes's novel *Years of Grace* which received the Pulitzer prize in 1931. Here retrospect of social history is combined with a well-balanced family novel, consistent in its truthful, even-toned reality. The era of transition is seen through the life story of Jane Ward, daughter of a prosperous Victorian household in Chicago, from childhood in the late eighties, to marriage amid the excitements of the Spanish-American War and during a long married life of security and ease in the comfortable suburban home from which she sees Chicago rise to ever-increasing power and expansion. It is in the development of her three children that Jane is faced by the modern age. She watches it and them with clear-eyed acceptance of changing standards, but at heart is never reconciled. To her the earlier years were the "years of grace." But there is fairness and understanding in the portrayal of the younger generation, with its light indifference to old-fashioned distinctions of "right" and "wrong," its cool logic and plausible reasoning, its matter-of-fact divorces and remarriages, which to Jane represent the shattering of all deep-rooted ideals of self-sacrifice and self-control in the conduct of life. The keynote of the novel lies in Jane's meditation on the problem:

But they had character. They had a code that was based—on what? Bravado and barbarism, or common sense? It was very perplexing. It was very complicated. They did not know what they had lost in life, these kindly, capable, clever young people who did not believe in worry. But she knew. Though it was difficult to define it.

The problem, however, is set for thoughtful consideration, not as moral warning. The younger generation encounters no carefully planned retribution for its hell-bent course; on the contrary, its self-satisfaction seems fairly justified, and the world no worse for modern behavior.

Lighter in touch, less retrospective, concerned not so much with social thesis as with the simplicities, absurdities, commonplaces, and cross currents that make the everyday flow of family life, is a body of fiction that represents the mid-Victorian domestic novel in its most popular and widely accepted twentieth-century survival. These are the books that May Lamberton Becker has called "solid solace," as being "interesting, amusing, clever without being silly, no war, no detective story, no promiscuous love affairs." Perhaps the last clause should be somewhat modified, for sophisticated and unconventional "love interest" tinges some of the novels—Margery Sharp's *The Nutmeg Tree* is one—that come within this company. English writers have a talent for these lively chronicles of family and social groups that hold charm, distinction, humor, sentiment and glinting satire; that open into the world of English households, gardens, tea tables, village streets, impish children, aunts, uncles, vicars, over which the spirit of Jane Austen hovers with smiling ironic scrutiny. For the influence of Jane Austen has been infused into this particular type of fiction for more than a century; she is still the idol and the model for the novelist who reflects life and interprets character through the medium of delicate but pointed irony, wit and lightness, that veil keen critical penetration. Women writers have especially revealed her influence; which is natural, for her gift was in its essence feminine, in perception and intuitiveness and in acceptance of things as they are.

The late Lady Russell, better known as "Elizabeth," is perhaps the foremost present-day exponent of the Jane Austen tradition; in her work, however, it takes on a different manifestation, more charged with emotion, less gayly unconcerned, and with a strong trend to the tragic and the psychological. Social comedy, of course, always carries tragic implications; it can give us poignant and agonizing experiences as well as gay and light-hearted enjoyment. "Elizabeth's" delicate brush is often tipped with caustic, as she delineates selfishness that drains or warps other lives, or conveys tyranny and insensitivity with merciless clarity and lightness of touch. *Mr. Skeffington,* her last, is also her most subtle piece of artistry. Here triviality is transformed to deep human significance, the undercurrents of life today are touched, as Lady Frances Skeffington—for years the most beautiful person in her world, adored and rich and free—facing her fiftieth birthday, finds her beauty passing, her empire withering under age and loneliness, her life utterly empty. In desperate quest of reassurance she turns to sift the ashes of her romantic past; and the story, with fleet delicacy, with shrewd, quizzical characterization, with a satire that is both probing and compassionate, follows that short, crucial quest to its moving and tender climax.

In direct succession to "Elizabeth" is E. M. Delafield, daughter of Mrs. Henry De La Pasture, who was a gay and graceful chronicler of domestic romance in a less realistic, more sentimental day. She has a similar skill in the probing of the egotist's nature, a kindred deft and witty contrasting of variant personalities, the same humorous perceptiveness that sees the absurdities and ironies of life's most painful moments and that carries its unfailing antidote for self-conceit or self-deception; but her background is more limited, her range more narrow, her artistry less perfect. In most of her novels character portrayal is the essential element; satirical, often relentless in its psychological penetration, it is almost entirely directed upon women. *Faster! Faster!* represents this aspect of her work: the story of a woman who runs a flourishing London business and supports a household of three children and an unsuccessful husband, it is a devastating yet compassionate presentment of the "martyr-complex" —that most deadly of feminine virtues, hiding its ostrich head of selfishness in sands of sacrificial assiduity. *The Diary of a Provincial Lady* remains her high achievement in the art of social comedy. For in this delightful record of everyday domestic happenings, sudden dramas of tea table, nursery, and fireside, veined with wit, sprinkled with alluring philosophic implication, there is a veritable texture of living, a weaving-in of types of character and fundamentals of experience that are universal. *The Provincial Lady in War-Time*, eight years later, has significance only as a pitiful unconscious gesture of disbelief before inevitable, incredible tragedy crashed upon the familiar English scene. That scene shines in the light of loving habitudes under the last and most serene ray of social comedy that broke through the thickening shadow of war. Jan Struther's essay-chronicle, *Mrs. Miniver*, like *The Diary of a Provincial Lady*, is a week-to-week record of normal, happy English family life, perhaps a little higher in the social scale. Graceful, witty, sensitive in mind and heart, beneath the apparent fragility of these quiet chapters of everyday home experience and meditative comment there is a firm sinew of strength, a clear essence of philosophic serenity. They close under the date of September, 1939, when the shape of things to come was still veiled against a dark horizon.

Thus, amid seismic tremors of social change and under the hurricane of war the Austen-Trollope tradition, serene, quizzical, amusing, is sustained by English writers. Angela Thirkell expresses it with lightness, humorous character depiction, and fundamental kindliness. Her novels of the gentry of the Cotswolds laugh at human foibles and fallacies, touch with satire rural controversies, neighborhood animosities, and everyday temperamental collisions of everyday people, and have made in their own county of Barsetshire a genuine extension of the old Trollope boundary line. Here is the country-house background of *August Folly, Pomfret Towers, The Brandons, Before Lunch;* the simple home setting of *Summer Half*, with its effervescent school holidays, its adolescent absurdities and domestic complications—all entertaining, sympathetic chronicles, neither sardonic nor sentimental. Even when, in *Cheerfulness Breaks In*, the familiar Brandon scene becomes a "Barsetshire war survey," these characteristics remain. Elizabeth Goudge brings a transcendental romanticism and a somewhat cloying sweetness to her novels of English domesticity and mellow traditions: *A City of Bells*, steeped in the reverent atmosphere of old cathedral precincts; *The Bird in the Tree*, in which the grim portent of war hovers over the spiritual sanctuary of an ancient paradisal garden on the Hampshire coast. Humphrey Pakington's gay comedies of village rectories and country homes were followed by *Family Album*, more serious and more significant, turning the pages of aristocratic English family life through the years from 1887 to 1938 in a vigorous, discerning presentment that mingles pungent satire with humorous but sympathetic understanding. Reginald Carter strikes back to a super-Archibald

Marshall Victorianism in *He and His*. *The Priory*, by Dorothy Whipple, follows the fortunes of an ancestral English estate and its owners, in a monotone of detail lightened by candid, indulgent humor; and D. E. Stevenson, in *Miss Buncle's Book*, more tenuous and less skillful, touches a fresh note of village comedy, mild but entertaining.

Social comedy is less dominant in Alice Rosman's novels, with their magnetic character portrayal and dramatic plot variations upon the family theme. Nor does it prevail in Susan Goodyear's thoughtful, well-integrated studies of life within the ecclesiastical circles of English parishes and cathedral towns (*Cathedral Close, Such Harmony*); these have a first-hand reality and a searching psychological insight, natural enough when it is remembered that this writer is the wife of the dean of one of the great English cathedrals. E. H. Young's family novels are also essentially studies of character and home relationships, in which the satirical touch is subdued to a quiet amusement at the inconsistencies, shortcomings, excitements, and compensations of everyday home existence. Her work shows its deftness and charm, its minute, veracious shading of character and conduct, in *Celia*, which in mild, uneventful, day-by-day chronicle brings to life not only Celia herself—middle-aged wife and mother, shrewd, sensible, inconsequent, and lovable, living in her own romantic daydream—but the whole family group with whose individual temperaments and collective problems her life is involved.

Novels such as these have for generations held a mirror to England's traditional way of life. Over its surface in clear or faint reflection have passed

> . . . the thoughts by England given;
> Her sights and sounds; dreams happy as her day;
> And laughter, learnt of friends; and gentleness,
> In hearts at peace, under an English heaven.

Whether that reflection is lost for the future, who can tell? The war, shattering familiar backgrounds, obliterating ancient paths, must leave different images before the mirror; but those older vistas, in their mellow securities, their smiling grace, are preserved in the long succession of novels, many of them minor and transitory enough, that with affection and raillery, with pride and humility, have chronicled an England "that Dread can darken not, nor Death destroy."

"Solid solace" receives no such representation in American fiction as in English. The type exists, but with a different range, a less traditional pattern. The satirical touch strikes more sharply at a thesis; there is less serenity and charm, less upwelling of spontaneous humor. The comedy of manners reached ironic perfection in Ellen Glasgow's *The Romantic Comedians*, its satiric wit sparkling over the familiar figure of the old man who cannot believe that at seventy he can no longer inspire romantic love in blooming seventeen; its epigrams and apothegms accenting the shrewd byplay of the feminine, the susceptibility of the masculine, nature. Anne Parrish struck the note of tragi-comedy in *The Perennial Bachelor*, a novel of real distinction in its unfolding of a half century of family history; of penetrating character study, in its rendering of the theme of egotism —the devotion of mother and sisters to the son and brother whose life is stultified by the sacrifices of which he is the object. Nearly all Anne Parrish's novels play on this theme of egotism, which receives its most original variation in *Mr. Despondency's Daughter*. This centers on the possessive, clinging mother, who strangles her children's lives with the proverbial silver cord; but it is skillfully handled as a woman's own self-study, in her late sixties, into the griefs that fate has brought her, the illumination that comes from old diaries and unglossed memory revealing her own selfishness, and her belated effort to make partial restitution. Slighter, less skillful in literary art, but with distinctive freshness and spontaneity of its own, is *Time at Her Heels*, in which Dorothy Aldis chronicles a single day in the drama of home life. Here, the mixture of tenderness and exasperation which infuses the family relationship is ever present, the reflection of character and environment is both entertaining and provocative, and for all its lightness the novel pricks below the surface, in modernity of spirit, in intelligent psychology.

Louise Kent's novels have a more traditional family flavor: detailed, smoothly sentimental, with a light touch of satirical and descriptive characterization. *The Terrace*, set in a group of century-old New England houses, has a pleasing preoccupation with antique furniture; the complacencies and futilities of "old Boston" give, in *Paul Revere Square*, background for a somewhat artificial romance. There is more solidity in *The Vantage Point*, chronicle of a family boarding house in suburban New York, which Hilda Morris has invested with romantic feeling and kindly humor. Margaret Flint's *The Old Ashburn Place* has firm substance and a warm homeliness that escapes sentimentality. These represent a type of domestic fiction that draws its readers predominantly from women: usually older women, not sophisticated in literary taste, who like a "quiet story," dealing with identifiable scenes and the kind of people they are familiar with. In its better examples this fiction offers mild reflection of common experience, valid interpretation of everyday life; in the descending scale it weakens, sentimentalizes, pietizes, or emotionalizes, and becomes a stereotype of the Grace Livingston Hill or Kathleen Norris pattern.

Every family relationship and every phase of domestic life have their radiations in this immense growth of fiction that rises from mid-Victorian roots. Marriage, husbands, wives, divorce; mothers, fathers, children; adolescence, youth, maturity, and age: all, in general or in particular, are studied by novelists of variant skills, seriously or lightly, with sympathy, tolerance, scorn, or anger, with every degree of candor, from every angle of diagnostic. These novels in their full range have values unrealized by the great majority of readers. Their obvious popularity lies in the fact that they are concerned with familiar experience and common problems of conduct that interest almost everyone, that they entertain, or satisfy curiosity, or reinforce standards of judgment. Their unrealized values are in extension of individual experience to new levels of personal response; in deepening or clarifying apprehension of influences that shape character or condition behavior; and in establishing common acceptance of factual physical actualities put into unglossed English. For the great American reading public still cherishing Victorian conventions, the age of reticence ended in January, 1907, when in the chaste columns of the *Atlantic* appeared the first installment of May Sinclair's new novel *The Helpmate*, opening with a conjugal conversation in bed.

Marriage is the focus of analytic study, copious chronicle, reflected phase, or flashlighted episode. Arnold Bennett's *Clayhanger* trilogy delved to the core of modern realism, as it disclosed in *These Twain* the unpredictable and baffling process of adaptation to married life, the friction of conflicting temperaments, and the ultimate compromise which accepts the fact that discontent is a condition of life and honestly endeavors to adjust conduct to an ideal. Various American women novelists pursue the theme in homely domestic chronicles, predominantly feminine in appeal. Among them, Dorothy Canfield upholds the stability of the family, the richness of home life, as gains offsetting drudgeries and sacrifices, in novels, earnest, moralistic, yet with warm human quality and an unfailing affectionate understanding of children. Helen Hull's novels (*Hardy Perennial, Frost Flower, Through the House Door*), more sophisticated in settings, present difficult marital situations with skillful craftsmanship and astute observation; her people have individual reality, their motives and actions emanate from within. Lights and shadows of the meridian of marriage are caught and held in the small clear mirror of Conrad Aiken's novel *Conversation*. Apparently slight and superficial, this episode of sudden, fierce quarrel between a young wife and husband—"as if a demon had got hold of us and jangled us"—carries subtle implications through individual character and personality into the whole complex marriage relationship. Vivid and delicate, the work of a poet even more than a novelist, in its swift flow of immediate speech and unspoken thoughts it projects the conflict of the artist's allegiance to his own original ideas, his own independence, against the wife's desire for security and social acceptability; until with insight and humorous tenderness the conflict dissolves in the deeper realities of the heart.

Divorce brings into present-day fiction significant studies, sensitive but unsentimental, of the effect upon children of disjoined

homes and divided family loyalties. *Nothing Is Safe*, by E. M. Delafield, reveals, from their own point of view, the unsettled minds and
broken habits of two English children, home from school for their
first holidays after their parents' divorce: the home in Hampstead
has been sold; their father is married to an unknown young woman;
their mother has a new husband, impatient and dominating. Brother
and sister are shuttled back and forth between these strange outposts, conscious of being an inconvenience or an irritation, shrinking and helpless under that consciousness and the haunting fear of
being separated from each other, yet with a resiliency and tenacity
of their own that is at once charming and appealing. There is painful neurotic intensity, but vital reality also, in *The Grown-Ups*,
Catharine Whitcomb's portrayal against American backgrounds
of a childhood and young girlhood tragically frustrated in its deep
craving for free and loving relationship with the father, mother, and
younger brother whose lives run their separate courses in mutual indifference or bitterness. Very different in its freshness, humor, and
individuality is Katharine Hulme's delightful narrative *We Lived as
Children* evoking—apparently from autobiographical reminiscence
—a gallant little divorced family of mother and three children,
bound in loyal confederation, who live proudly and pluckily in San
Francisco in the years before and after the earthquake, who adore
their debonair, libertine father, and who cherish the unfulfilled
dream that their parents will some day remarry and live happily ever
after. More familiar is the aspect given freshness and reality by Dan
Wickenden in *Walk Like a Mortal*, which is both distinctive family
chronicle on the most common plane of American living and also
sympathetic, valid study of youth confronted by a problem frequent
enough today, far more crucial and momentous than that favorite
adolescent problem of first love—the break-up of a boy's home under
the disintegration of his parents' marriage, his gradual understanding of causes and effects, and the necessity for him to work out his
own decision whether he will remain with his father or join the
mother who had been his childhood's adoration and dominating influence.

Childhood, adolescence, and youth give substance for many novels of everyday life. Fantasy does not belong here, though there are few illuminants of childhood as revealing as Richard Hughes's *Innocent Voyage*, or Christopher Morley's *Thunder on the Left*; neither does the fiction of full-length life experience, in which early years set the pattern for later development. Portrayals of childhood that link most closely to the family novel are complete in themselves and drawn from realities of experience and environment, even though they may be transfused with nostalgic memory or follow a design of deliberate inventiveness. English novels of childhood, more accomplished in artistry, more pervading in charm, are also more limited in range than is the work of American writers. Set, as a rule, on the upper levels of an established social order, they reveal that separate world of English childhood, so closely circumscribed in its material bounds of nursery and schoolroom, but so free and apart from the adult realm, so filled with its own independent activities, and so radiating the make-believe of imagination, playing over backgrounds of history, romance, poetry, sensitized by natural beauty, and woven into the warm, firm texture of home. Enid Bagnold draws from these roots of English living in *The Door of Life*, a single-purposed study, almost portentous in its seriousness, of the relationship of a mother to her children, the unborn and the born, in infancy and childhood years. Adrian Bell's *The Balcony* is essentially an intimate study of a child's mind, distilling recollection of an English childhood from the earliest conscious realization of color, movement, lights, and people to the first year of school, against a background of the adult world, as envisioned by a sensitive, imaginative boy. The unforgettable joys of childhood in country serenity and comfort live in Eiluned Lewis's *Dew on the Grass*, which captures the sparkling freshness of the magical dawn of childhood in the pristine old-world loveliness of the Welsh countryside.

American novels of childhood and youth have developed two more or less standardized patterns. One is the pattern set by Booth Tarkington, of kindly but burlesquing humor: an adult chuckling over the absurdities of "calf love," over the "growing pains" that find ridiculous and childish manifestation. The other is a pattern of emotional experience, psychological-physical intensities, unrelieved by perspective or normal adjustments. Frances Frost developed this pattern with grim and painful realism in *Innocent Summer:* powerful, sharply incised episodes during three months in the lives of a group of children in a small Vermont village. Of the two patterns, the latter seems to me the more truthful rendering of the inner confusions and turmoil that are part of the transition from childhood to youth; but its overconcentration leads to distortion, just as the amiable satire of the Tarkington pattern turns into artificiality. Fresher, more unified, and more complete in reality is the pattern that takes shape in Wickenden's novels of youth in everyday family setting; in Mrs. Rawlings's *The Yearling*, with its rich regional background, its sympathetic understanding of the painful transition from childhood to adolescence; in Steinbeck's tale "The Red Pony," more powerful and subtle rendering of the same theme; and in *Morning Shows the Day*, Evelyn Bolster's original, vigorous, unvarnished chronicle of one year in the life of three motherless children who live alone with their workman father near Olympia: untrained, primitive youngsters, "smart, but not handsome," inured to poverty, quarreling with one another, but presenting a united front to the world, their exciting existence centered on personal freedom and devotion to their father. All these patterns are indigenous, in their indifference to social distinctions, their inclination (practical rather than imaginative) toward experiment and adventure, and their realization of the many-layered foundations, the varied backgrounds, of the American scene.

Character depiction is, of course, implicit in fiction of everyday life and domestic relationships. Only human beings in whose existence one is made to believe can give vitality to group interplay or invest familiar problems of behavior with immediate significance. So the novel of family experience links to the more restricted novel of individual character study and merges into the full-length biographic novel that explores the character and follows in the footsteps of its subject from infancy to old age. The seven ages of man and woman, in all their phases and contrasts, are reflected in the looking-glass of fiction. The fleeting phase of girlhood is caught and held in crystalline perfection by Willa Cather in her short novel *Lucy Gayheart:* girlhood arrested in its own brief moment of time, light-moving, impulsive yet acceptant, just entering into awareness of the secret deeps of emotion. This is a study of youth infused with a sense of the whole of living, yet at the same time seizing and transmitting the freshness, the intense immediate bittersweet, of life's springtime. Girlhood, unworldly and ingenuous, stultified and betrayed in a hollow world of social artifice and febrile sterility, is revealed in Elizabeth Bowen's *The Death of the Heart,* coolly, with indirection, in a flowing current of thought, emotions, self-revelations, cumulative in its tragic irony. Girlhood, pitiful, absurd, and tragic in its struggle to bring daydreams to fulfillment by false pretenses, has its indelible record in *Alice Adams,* Booth Tarkington's masterpiece of sympathetic yet relentless realism. Girlhood, sharp-eyed, hardboiled, and tender-hearted, progressing through all the facts of life to a rather commonplace sophistication, is chronicled by Christopher Morley in *Kitty Foyle,* "the natural history of a woman" according to male research: ebullient, stream-of-consciousness retrospect, witty, often ribald, and warmly sentimental. There is greater depth and more penetrating reality in Mr. Morley's natural history of a man: *Human Being,* which must long remain an original, significant achievement in creative character depiction.

Motherhood is limned in varied aspects, possessive, parasitic, misguided, wise, inspiring. But not many readers know Frederick Niven's *Mrs. Barry:* a portrait firmly and delicately drawn, as true and living, though more shadowed, as the portrait of that earlier Mrs. Barrie (differently spelled) by her son, which stands in literature beside Whistler's canvas in pictorial art. Both mothers are Scotswomen, simple, everyday, obscure; but Margaret Ogilvy is set before us with the tender gayety of love, in serene life-fulfillment, while Mrs. Barry's short life chapter is a gallant, unregarded battle against grim necessity, made beautiful by high courage, selfless love, and the warm kindliness of human sympathy. For old age, envisioned as liberation from enforced conformities and insurgent emotions, there is *All Passion Spent*, Victoria Sackville-West's delicate prose epic of grace and quietude at the close of life's long day: "Youth has no beauty like the beauty of an old face; the face of youth was an unwritten page. Youth could never sit as still as that, in absolute repose, as though all haste, all movement, were over and done with, and nothing left but waiting and acquiescence."

The biographic novel, in the most specific application of the term, is the elaborate, personal chronicle that pursues an individual life through its full course and often carries detail to the microscopic vanishing point. Dr. Leacock called these the "Edward Endless" novels, which, he said, should properly be entitled "From the Cradle to the Grave, or One Thousand Pages for a Dollar." Samuel Butler, Theodore Dreiser, and Arnold Bennett set the pattern. J. D. Beresford deepened its trend to psychoanalysis. H. G. Wells turned it to social thesis, barbed with satire, weighted with an enormous mass of gathered and assimilated knowledge, and impelled by an inexhaustible gusto. Compton Mackenzie accented it with the emotionalism of youth in his *Sinister Street* trilogy, and after a quarter-century returned to follow a different progression in his panoramic life story, *The Four Winds of Love*. Here, in successive volumes (*The East Wind, The South Wind, The West Wind* are already published), he seeks to present the effect of the twentieth century upon a sensitive man's development. A sequence novel of the saga type, it is primarily a saga not of continuing generations, but of an individual quest for spiritual certainties, and it has a solid autobiographical quality that is more factual than fictional; its cumulative purport is that acceptance of the Roman Catholic faith offers the only appeasement of the conflict and upheaval of our present age.

Autobiographical realism is strong in much of this fiction of documentary self-revelation, of exploration below surface normality. Psychology and psychoanalysis reinforce the confessional urge. Sex is a dominant element; and the frustrations of sex repression, the excesses of sex release, have been disclosed in every possible physical and psychological manifestation. Whatever the monotonies, exaggerations, and egocentricities (and they are many) of these novels as they flourished in the literature of the twenties and thirties, they have unquestionably been a far-reaching, effective means of bringing the findings of modern psychology into public consciousness.

Biographic fiction has many other manifestations. Constantly expanding in range and finding new and varied forms of expression, it makes realizable all the factors of heredity, environment, character, temperament, and circumstance in their effect upon the processes of human development. The exact similitude to genuine biographical writing of a familiar kind achieved by J. P. Marquand in *The Late George Apley* gave final perfection to that subtle, satiric, keenly penetrating study of a social caste (not necessarily the Boston Brahmin alone), solidifying in complacent futility. Its companion piece in critical appraisal of the New England nature, George Santayana's *The Last Puritan,* was also framed as a memoir, subduing its quality as fiction to the philosophic reflection, the ironic commentary, of a scholar-philosopher. This simulation of the method of genuine biography, always a favorite mode in fiction, has taken on fresh popularity today. Hugh Walpole's *John Cornelius* is a skillful example: framed as the memorial tribute of a friend to a famous English writer, weaving in letters and excerpts from personal reminiscence, it invests an artificial character construction with oddly symbolic plausibility. Biographical fact is ingeniously mingled with romantic fiction in *Immortal Ease,* Kathleen Coyle's original, vital novel, presented as the memoir (in part autobiographical) of a famous Irish-American woman poet, Victoria Rising, and obviously reflective of the life story and personality of Elinor Wylie. There is beauty, sensitive perception, and appealing human reality in the portrait of the intense young poet that emerges from this complex intermixture of techniques; but the validity of the composition as a whole is destroyed by the melodramatic crudity of its conclusion.

The most significant present-day expansion in biographic fiction has been as a medium for serious biographical study of actual persons. Of course, since the day of Scott the historical novel has made portraiture of individual figures an important detail in its broad canvas of historic scenes. But it is only within the last quarter-century that the novelist has stepped at will into the role of the biographer, and the biographer has been moved to put on the habit of the novelist. The biographic novel gives us today valid, illuminating life studies of men and women famous in literature, in art, and in specific fields of achievement. Indeed, it may turn to more intimate memorials, as in Pearl Buck's novels *The Exile* and *Fighting Angel,* which with slight fictional disguise record the life stories and delineate the characters of the novelist's mother and father. Rachel Field, in *All This, and Heaven Too,* combined authentic history, family chronicle, dramatic murder mystery, and romantic love story, for this novel is, in fact, biography of the writer's great-aunt Henrietta, who, before she became Mrs. Henry Field, of New York and New England, was Henriette Desportes, the "Mademoiselle D." of the historic murder case of the Duchesse de Praslin, in Paris of 1847. There is close relationship between these novels and such biographical studies as Victoria Sackville-West's *Pepita* and Daphne Du Maurier's *Gerald:* family portraits by a member of the family, executed with imaginative insight, cool objectivity, affectionate but unsparing candor.

Only briefest indication can be given here of the richness and variety of this biographic fiction, as it brings to many readers a sense of personal relationship to great names of the past, not as names, but as human beings experiencing all the vicissitudes of common living. Against the background of English literature many figures are thus visualized. John Brophy's *Gentleman of Stratford* is probably the most ambitious of such endeavors, for it offers a full life story of Shakespeare, elaborate in detail and even more interpretative than factual, seeking to present, not the artist, but the human being. Based on assiduous research and conforming to the established facts of the life, it is dexterously carried out, a suggestive and interesting addition to Shakespeare literature, though as character creation it never takes on vital reality. In *Garland of Bays* Gwyn Jones has painted with solid authority, in heavy strokes and Teniers-like realism, the portrait of Robert Greene, one of the most complex and tragic figures of the Elizabethan age: poet, playwright, novelist, pamphleteer, contemporary and disparager of Shakespeare, associate of Marlowe, Peele, Nash, Lodge, and their fellows. Another novel that represents authority and research is Helen Ashton's beautiful, unusual narrative *The Swan of Usk*, which must stand as the first adequate biography of Henry Vaughan, the "poet of eternity," that has appeared in English literature. Early nineteenth-century English writers are studied in many novels: Emily Brontë in *Divide the Desolation*, Kathryn MacFarland's sensitively realized evocation of the genius that burned in that dark stone parsonage on the edge of the Yorkshire moors; the Lake Poets in Helen Ashton's quiet, reminiscent chronicle, *William and Dorothy*, built on closely-knit factual material, chiefly from Dorothy Wordsworth's journals; the Carlyles, whose lives receive faithful reconstruction against the background of their time by E. Thornton Cook, in *Speaking Dust;* Charles and Mary Lamb in *So Perish the Roses,* a penetrating character portrayal to which Neil Bell brought specialized research—a novel that links closely to the painstaking biographical record of Mary Lamb's later years by Ernest C. Ross, *The Ordeal of Bridget Elia*.

This is just a single subject field. There are many others. In modern art, Irving Stone's novel of Vincent Van Gogh, *Lust for Life*, is authentic, illuminating biography; in music, Henry Handel Richardson's *The Young Cosima*, is discerning character study of the early Wagner group; in science, Zsolt de Harsanyi's novel, *The Star-Gazer*, bringing Galileo to full-dimensional reality, has already been mentioned. In its many ramifications and continuing development the biographical novel is today establishing fundamental relationship to the whole literature of knowledge.

IV. LIVES, TIMES, AND PLACES

*. . . as he looked down on the world and on his past,
no matter what mean, ludicrous, or terrible effects
defaced the scene, his last impression of mankind was
one of splendor.*—JAMES BOYD: *Roll, River*

FAMILY novels and novels of biographic narrative give of their
substance to the broad interlocking type-groups of saga, panorama, and regional fiction. These groups merge and overlap, but
some lines of differentiation may be discerned. The saga, we may
say, is concerned with lives and times; it is the family novel extended through successive generations, recording and reflecting the
social backgrounds, the social changes, through which the collective
life-thread runs. The panorama—more pictorial, more historical—
is focused on times and places: a sweeping sequence of events and
scenes in which human figures have minor significance. The regional novel puts its emphasis on places and lives, in other words on
localities and the effect of environment on living; and the regional-
historical novel seeks to combine times and places and lives in a single compound, that differs from "straight" historical fiction chiefly
in being restricted to a single terrain. This whole body of fiction has
been enormously expanded and diversified within the last quarter-
century. Especially is this true as regards the American regional
and regional-historical novels, successors to the older "local color"
fiction, which in their full range represent, I think, the most significant development in our contemporary literature.

Varied as they are in scope and method, these closely related
groups have some characteristics in common. One of these is length.
Revival of the very long novel began with the biographical series-
novels of the immediate prewar years and came to its ultimate
achievement when *Anthony Adverse* launched half a million words

in a single massive volume, in 1933. *Of Time and the River* (360,-
000 words), in 1935, and *Gone with the Wind* (412,000 words), in
1936, set marks that have since been approached by many of the
most successful novels of the day. Of course, very long novels are
not new in English fiction. Richardson's *Pamela*, with 524,000
words, runs well ahead of *Anthony Adverse;* Tom Jones told his history in 340,000 words; David Copperfield, for his, used 390,000.
In England the standardized three-volume novel, the "old three-
decker," immortalized by Kipling, flourished for more than half a
century, from the 1830's to the 1880's, its average length remaining
about 200,000 words. The average individual length of Scott's
Waverley novels, it may be added, approximated 150,000 words, or
just about the length of Ernest Hemingway's *For Whom the Bell
Tolls*. But gradually the three-decker was submerged because of its
clumsiness and high price, and by 1890 the one-volume novel running from 80,000 to 100,000 words had become the ordinary fiction
form in England, as it had been for a much longer time in the
United States.

Physical compression of the very long novel into a single volume
has become more common as technical bookmaking methods have
developed; but another way of achieving length, especially characteristic of saga fiction, is by means of the series—or sequence—
novel, its successive volumes, each complete in itself, appearing at
intervals, yet building up a single more-or-less integrated chronicle.
Through such sequences the novelist seeks to establish an overview
from past to present, setting in relief a given environment, a particular human group, a phase of political or social history. Detail necessarily involves length. Elaborate descriptive and factual detail is
common to many of the novels in these groups. The conformation
of a region, its plants and trees and animals; the changing seasons;
growth or decay of a community; successive cycles in fashion, in
government, in standards of culture and of living—all are recorded
in a minute transcription of material detail that may become monotonous or repetitious, yet that establishes a sense of personal identification with place and time and kind of living. In treatment, a

realistic attitude prevails: romance expresses itself most often as wistful looking back upon earlier simplicities or acceptances, as sympathetic or poetic perception of natural beauty; rough speech, harsh drama, and primitive conditions are unsoftened; an objective or ironic spirit of social analysis is often manifest.

"Saga" fiction, in the present-day use of the term, stems directly from Galsworthy. *The Forsyte Saga* held the germ—its development later intensified by the play "Cavalcade"—that brought into being in the early 1930's a luxuriant growth of family chronicles that were at the same time panoramas of social and historical perspectives. Galsworthy's slowly rising epic structure was thirty years in the building, and it stands on an eminence of its own as one of the masterpieces of modern English literature. It epitomizes and universalizes individual lives as the expression of fundamental beliefs, prejudices, and traditions of Victorian England, but in doing this it also creates a living fabric of life drama and human personality. Through three generations its folk pursue their destinies—in kinship, in feud, in frustration—as the sturdy, confident nineteenth-century Victorians (so assured of Godship in heaven and rightness in a privately owned world) age and pass, and a new twentieth-century breed emerges, strange and unanchored amid postwar questioning and sophistication. Thackeray and Trollope and Hugh Walpole are probably the only other English novelists who have brought into existence so many human beings linked so intimately in so long a chain. Indeed, Galsworthy, as historian of late Victorian and later Georgian upper middle-class English life, seems to me the legitimate successor of Trollope, historian of the early and mid-Victorian period. He is as true a realist as Trollope, with the advantage of freedom from the conventional restraints that Trollope accepted. His history of the Forsytes is a miniature history of a class and of an era, reflecting life from myriad angles of philosophy, irony, art, and beauty. *The Forsyte Saga* focuses on lives and character and individual temperament more strongly than on the times of which those lives are the product; its historical perspectives are implicit rather than elaborated.

Akin to the Forsyte chronicle in its preoccupation with character and personality, but compressed into a closer time-frame and centered in historic world catastrophe, is Ford Madox Ford's sequence novel, the epic of Christopher Tietgens, "the last Tory in England," which opens in *Some Do Not*, continues in *No More Parades* and *A Man Could Stand Up*, and closes in the single day of *The Last Post*, with Christopher's brother, Mark, as the central figure. Christopher Tietgens is a quixotic figure, a sort of contemporary Chevalier Bayard; and his unswerving effort to live according to the traditional code of honor of his class in a world where traditions have been shattered and cast aside carries far-reaching tragic consequences, from prewar days in England, through the war years of 1914–18, into a peace time of troubled readjustment to a chaotic new order. This is a closely centralized chronicle, in spite of many sharply contrasted characters. Intensely self-sacrificial in theme (with Christopher Tietgens as symbolic, acceptant victim of the sins of the world), its attitude toward the war is epitomized in Mark Tietgens's vow "never more to speak word or move finger," because the Armistice terms closed hostilities before the war had been carried into Germany: "for the betrayal of France by her Allies at the supreme moment of triumph had been a crime news of which might well cause the end of the world to seem desirable." The whole work is an achievement in consummate, original craftsmanship that is often baffling or obscure to the uninitiated, for it uses an impressionism that combines entire realism and intense psychological individualism; that keeps the stream of consciousness flowing in many crosscurrents before the reader, and builds up human personalities in outward and inward completeness from intangibles of thought, impulse, and intention.

Family saga mingles with historical panorama in Hugh Walpole's ambitious novel-sequence that began in 1929 with *Rogue Herries* and was broken by the author's death in 1941, with three of its proposed eight volumes uncompleted. First designed as the history of an English family covering two hundred years and kept closely to the same setting, its range was widened as the chronicle went on, and in

1940 perspective was extended with the publication of *The Bright Pavilions*, which carries back to Elizabeth's day. Here, as founder of the Herries line, appears Nicholas Herries, elder of two brothers bound together in deep affection, but opposites in temperament: one, simple, lusty, practical, lover of life and action; the other, complex, emotional, idealist seeker of "the bright pavilions of God, the only resting place for the souls of blundering, weary travelers." About their contrasted natures is woven an elaborate mesh of tragic romance, sinister drama, and colorful adventure, all drawn from the stuff of the age itself—its intensities of religious passion, its brutalities, superstitions, and hardihood, its physical and spiritual energies. The mortal struggle between Catholicism and Protestantism pulses through the narrative and reaches its climax in portrayal of Mary Stuart brought to her doom in Fotheringay. In the contrast of the two brothers is disclosed the curiously mixed Herries temperament that is a continuing heritage: "fact and poetry—the two strains in the family blending to cover the whole round of life." Vital human reality in individual character portrayal is lacking, however; the novel's significance is rather in its depiction of the teeming, many-sided life of Elizabethan England, of smiling Sussex manor lands, and of the moors and rugged hills of the Cumberland country; its effect is of an intricate design, rich in detail and in color, carried out on a smooth enamel surface.

Nicholas Herries's life story runs into the early seventeenth century. Three succeeding volumes were to have carried the Herries chronicle to the opening of the eighteenth century, thus filling out a visualization of English backgrounds, natural, social, political, and literary, sweeping down nearly four centuries. *Rogue Herries*, first published volume in the sequence, covers almost the whole of the eighteenth century in the stormy life of Francis Herries, great-grandson of Nicholas, a strange mixture of ruffian and dreamer, whose divided nature is never quite convincing. Here, again, character portrayal and plot consistency are of less value than the vigorous, graphic picture of eighteenth-century England—a picture that may well stand beside the prologue to Lord David Cecil's biography of Cowper, *The Stricken Deer*, which in twenty pages evokes the whole spirit of that age. Indeed, *Rogue Herries* and *The Stricken Deer*, read in conjunction, will establish in any responsive mind a memorable vicarious experience of eighteenth-century living. Judith, Rogue Herries's daughter, born as her father dies, continues the succession. *Judith Paris* carries her through the first fifty years of a life no less stormy, though less violent, than her father's, centered in Sussex and Cumberland (especially heedful of the Lake District and its poets), deflected to glimpses of London and of revolutionary Paris. A genealogical chart shows the ramifications of the Herries family through three generations, bringing in the Trenchard stock by marriage, and opening prospective relationship to characters made familiar in Walpole's novels of modern setting. In *The Fortress* Judith, matriarch of the clan, is brought to her hundredth birthday; and *Vanessa*, romantic love story of Judith's granddaughter, closes the saga, carrying the family history down from the 1880's to the early 1930's. The Herries chronicle is probably one of the most distinctive examples in contemporary English fiction of a saga structure capable of indefinite extension and enlargement that conveys both factual and symbolic representation of national life and character through the continuing annals of a family—"not a very important family," as Hugh Walpole says, "but scattered about England and Scotland, through centuries doing its part and paying its way, having a certain spiritual history, preferring its own birth and begetting to any other." Whereas the men and women of the Forsyte saga live as human beings in their own right, the members of the Herries clan are more obvious embodiments of heredity or temperament, of vice or virtue.

In all the varied work that English novelists have done in the field of saga-panorama fiction, L. H. Myer's sequence-novel, *The Root and the Flower*, stands by itself in exotic interest, in qualities of philosophic imagination and literary art. Under the collective title three of the books in the sequence were brought together in a single volume in 1935; these are *The Near and the Far* (published separately in 1931), *Prince Jali* (published separately in 1933), and *Rajah*

Amar, which had its first publication here. In 1940 *The Pool of Vishnu* added another volume to the work, but brought no obvious conclusion. The setting is India in the time of the great Mogul emperor Akbar, which is the Elizabethan period in England; each of the four novels is linked in close sequence of event; each deals with the same central figures, about whom move a varied array of keenly visualized, distinctive characters, all brought into changing, complex relationships. *The Root and the Flower* is essentially a study and an evaluation of life in some crucial or unusual phase of experience that shapes the destiny of an individual. It has affinities with Pater's *Marius, the Epicurean*, though, of course, on a much enlarged scale; also, and more evidently, with Proust's great work, though it comprehends heroism and individual nobility that are not within Proust's range; also, particularly in exotic and delicate background and oriental aspects of living, with Lady Murasaki's *Tale of Genji*—indeed, Mr. Myers himself says that his incentive came in a measure from that exquisite chronicle. This is a rich, crowded, profound, and unusual work, in which a deep substratum of philosophic thought on the meaning of life is basis for an interweaving of drama, romance, passionate feuds, tyrannies, cruelties, fanaticisms, ritual and pomp, hate and love, that makes a tapestry of life at the Mogul court, yet holds implication and similitude for man's ageless problems. A continuous thread of philosophical discussion runs through the whole: varying aspects of life's mystery as it is seen by Christian, by Buddhist, by philosopher and mystic; conflict between the active life and the contemplative life; illusion dissolving in disillusion; strange contradictions and oppositions in human nature—all these phases of experience appear and disappear, arresting thought in any reflective mind. Intellectual and philosophical perceptions are throughout stronger than are the elements of plot and of action. *The Root and the Flower* is not intended as a historical novel, "fact and fancy," Mr. Myers says, "are intricately mixed up"; nor is it an attempt to portray specifically oriental modes of thinking and living. It is concerned with the penetration of character and with the analysis and appraisal of the rival claims of moral and aesthetic sensibility.

These three novel-sequences, each so different in treatment, in scope, and in substance, are impressive achievements in this particular form of present-day fiction. They indicate the trend to expand the novel of historical or social perspectives, of continuing time-flow, into what is virtually the old-fashioned serial, "continued in our next"; but this is still the trend of a minority. There are many more in which the saga is told, the panorama unfolded, in a solid single-volume chronicle. Doris Leslie's *Full Flavour* telescopes English backgrounds from the Indian Mutiny and the Crimea to the opening of the World War in 1914, into the life story of Catherine Ducrox, who inherited an old London tobacco shop and presided over its evolution to commercial supremacy through the rise of the cigarette. Her *Fair Company*, still more compressed, covers 130 years in the experiences of four generations of one family, unfolding in successive panels the story of the four women of the house, whose lives run from 1796 to 1934. Kate O'Brien, in *Without My Cloak*, Hawthornden Prize winner of 1932, through the family saga discloses the organic human structure of middle-class Catholic mid-Victorian Ireland. This chronicle of an Irish family runs through only seventeen years, but it is built on the beginnings of the clan seventy years before, and in its development may be traced those subtle, inescapable influences of inheritance, environment, compulsion, and circumstance that produce both the race type and the individual human being. It is a fine example of the centralized saga: a firmly built, strong, and complex structure, sustained in human interest and beautiful in its renderings of scene. The comfort, well-being, and solidity of the Victorian life it depicts are much like those made so familiar through English fiction, but with the crucial difference that here Irish Catholicism molds character and influences experience. This aspect is presented with remarkable detachment and clarity, showing the unrelenting rule of spiritual authority over conduct, the conflict of passions never recognized in their true nature, and the ultimate surrender—more fatalistic than devout—to compulsions that sacrifice the individual self to the traditional sanctities of the family and the home.

In American fiction the saga that is primarily the plain family
novel seldom runs to sequence length. Perhaps the most notable ex-
ception is Canadian: the *Jalna* novels (eight in number, in 1941), in
which Mazo De La Roche, since 1927, has carried on the chronicle
of the Whiteoak family. Jalna is the East Indian name of the Canadian estate of the family: a boisterous clan of men, women, and
children, living on the ancestral acres and for years dominated by a
tyrannical matriarch grandmother. Essentially a family chronicle
from the woman's point of view that narrows upon home detail and
emotional interplay, the Whiteoak annals represent an individual
group that is almost a feudal survival. Backgrounds shift at intervals
from Canada to England and Ireland, music and religion and the
stage contribute to dramatic action and character development, and
in time the World War lets fall its thunderbolt. There is, however,
no inwoven mesh of different threads of a diverse social fabric; but
a self-contained communal existence of a group of intense individ-
ualists, sharing certain genetic characteristics and all in constant
mutual reaction and ebullition. Written with ease and vividness,
with play of humor and frequent touches of melodrama, the chief
quality of the *Jalna* sequence is the consistent, individualistic, dramatic character portrayal, which has endued the Whiteoak people
with a flesh-and-blood reality of their own.

Foremost among American novels of the saga type must stand
James Boyd's *Roll, River*, which combines family chronicle with
panorama of American life. As with Thomas Wolfe, the stream of
life is the "river" of the title, but the novel gives it an actual symbol
in the river (implicitly the Susquehanna) which flows through the
Pennsylvania town (implicitly Harrisburg) in which the saga chiefly
runs its course. Here the Rand family had lived for several generations; here is unfolded the life experience of Clara Rand and her
nephew, Tommy Rand, as, dying in a hospital, his mind turns back
through his own fifty years and his aunt's lifespan, seeking to understand "what principle controlled the ever-flowing stream of life or
the ever-elusive mystery beyond." Beginning in 1880 and running
into the 1930's, through four generations, the chronicle has an

integration that fuses the different elements of personality, of time, of environment, and holds wisdom, strength, and tenderness under its quiet-toned detail. The community in its changing social and economic phases has the genuine substance of the American scene, the intrinsic quality of American life and character. There is more solid American reality here than in the two linked novels of Thomas Wolfe's tumultuous epic of self-revelation. *Look Homeward, Angel*, for all its fiercely intensified regional background, and *Of Time and the River*, despite its panoramic sweep of sense impressions, its evocation of vast, changing vistas, have not the collective nature of the saga, but constitute a closely focused autobiographic chronicle of enormous vitality, inexhaustible magniloquence, and passionate megalomania.

Most American saga fiction has definite regional associations and draws heavily upon historical perspectives. There are many variations, as in *The Long Way Home*, where Sylvia Chatfield Bates follows the life-course of women in a single family, beginning in colonial Connecticut and closing in twentieth-century New York; and in Stephen Longstreet's *Decade, 1929–39*, which like a modernistic highly colored newsreel flashes over decadences, disasters and portents of the 1930's and concentrates on the dominating figure of a rugged old industrialist, a survival, in his nineties, of the age of giants in America's money-power era. The pictorial panorama touch is frequent. Thus, Michael Foster's *American Dream* makes a panoramic sequence of what are virtually three separate novels linked by family descent, depicting aspects of American life from the pioneer wilderness of the eighteenth century to the Irish famine migration of 1848, the Boston of the fifties, the western Indian fighting of the seventies, the middle west of the nineties, the spy hysteria of the First World War days; and the unrest and pessimism of the 1930's. Saga-panorama on a thesis is a variation common with both English and American novelists. The thesis may dominate a closely knit family chronicle, as does feminism in Vera Brittain's *Honourable Estate*, or the saga form may be the device that gives the thesis cumulative expression. Thus, Beatrice Kean Seymour, in *The Unquiet Field*, carries her thesis of the abolition of the slave trade in England through varied experiences of a shipowning family, from 1720 to 1841; and in much cruder fashion, propagandist rather than thematic, Taylor Caldwell's elaborate sequence-novels, *The Dynasty of Death* and *The Eagles Gather*, melodramatize the sinister annals of a family of Franco-American munitions makers from the 1840's to the present.

So we approach the domain of regional fiction. There can be no close delimitation of boundaries here; the sagas and the sequences run their course within these borders; historical novels germinate and flourish in abundant outgrowth. In its name this group denotes its character, as the descriptive or pictorial evocation of the natural attributes and human associations of a specific region, in imaginative but essentially authentic portrayal. Places and lives in intimate inter-relationship are its concern. Closer definition would apply the term to novels that concentrate on provincial or remote or highly specialized local settings rather than to novels that center on character study and dramatic plot development, even though these are set against a distinctive background. In the United States the regional has become one of the most extensive fields of modern fiction: a medium for the observation and depiction of natural scene or human habitat, in fauna, flora, topographical characteristics, folk backgrounds, customs, speech, influences of environment, tradition, and processes of growth, in all sections and many localities of the country. There has been no such development elsewhere, in mass and variety, although regional novels exist in almost every part of the world. England, Scotland, Wales, Ireland, France, Spain, all the countries of Europe and the western hemisphere, many of the orient, have novelists whose work, rooted in their own soil, helps to compose in literature a mosaic of the common life of man upon the earth.

In English fiction the regional element is more often infused into the art of the novel as a whole, as with Hardy, whose Wessex is regional background for complex, ironic tragedies of human passion and mortal circumstance that, however deepened by environment, might in their essential nature have been played out against almost any setting. But Hardy's are regional novels (think of Egdon Heath and the Dorset rustics of *Under the Greenwood Tree*); and English regional fiction, though less expansive and elaborate than the American variety, is rich in substance and diversity, sending radiations deep into literature, history, and common experience. We need think only of Mary Webb's Shropshire countrysides, where men's destinies blend with the fields and skies, as they do in Housman's Shropshire poems; of Sheila Kaye-Smith's Sussex farmlands; of Coppard's tales of the Cotswolds; of Winifred Holtby's and Phyllis Bentley's Yorkshire ridings and mill towns. Among present-day English regional writers Constance Holme holds a place of her own. Her roots lie deep in the Westmoreland region of valley farms, moorlands, lakes, and mountains, between the Yorkshire border and the Cumberland country, with its Lake District, where so many of Hugh Walpole's novels have their setting. In this region her eight novels, published from 1913 to 1930, all center. Diverse in range, they have unity of perfection, in their calm, clear beauty of expression, their serene integrity of spirit, and their subtle penetration into hidden depths of feeling. All are short novels; nearly all are tinged with some flavor of folk superstition lingering in portent or tradition; each gives in simple reality a different aspect of the life of Westmoreland gentry and farm folk: a single market-day trip of two old people, an old woman's effort to adjust herself to a new home; an Elizabethan legend, still living in its present-day heritage.

From Wales comes one of the memorable later contributions to English regional fiction: *How Green Was My Valley*, Richard Llewellyn's beautiful chronicle of his green Welsh valley through the years of childhood, youth, home, family life, work and joy and pain. Of the past, not of the present, it is tinged with sadness for the passing of a golden day, but holds neither pessimism nor bitterness; rather the understanding that life-fulfillment lies in being part of life itself, its deep earth-roots, its changing winds, its storm and sunshine. Told by Huw Morgan, Welsh in heritage and environment, this is the story of his family, whose lives, ingrained in the life of a little mining community, are carried along the currents of change from the 1880's to the turn of the century. Back of the tumultuous flow of living, in its gusto, humor, gayety and violence, love, frustration, tenderness and anger, is the passing of the old order. Deeper conflicts arise between miners and owners; as unions grow, strikes become more complex; poverty increases; the great slag pile back of the pits mounts and spreads, the clear streams are polluted, and the green valley shrinks into desolation. Drama, comedy, and tragedy mingle in this chronicle of flesh-and-blood people whose lives touch and cross and intertwine in varied and intense relationships. While there is no central plot-thread, there is a pristine vigor and reality of emotions, of circumstances, and conditions that give dramatic unity and deep human appeal. One of the finest values of the book is as revelation of the Welsh character, in its sense of nationality, its pride, its narrowness and intensity of religious faith, its inborn gift of music, its brooding self-constraints and volcanic temper. Caradoc Evans, Rhys Davies, and other regional novelists deepen and enlarge realization of the Welsh scene. Intense social consciousness dominates Rhys Davies's novel, *A Time to Laugh*, with its graphic depiction of two great strikes, its abundant factual detail of economic conflict and disintegration in the Welsh coal mining industry from 1899. There is homespun simplicity and earnestness in *Bidden to the Feast*, by Jack Jones, himself the son of a Welsh collier, who as a boy worked in the pits and knew neither schooling nor decent living: a quiet, moving, deep-veined narrative of life in a grimy Welsh mining district in the 1860's. Brutal realism, starkly compressed into a few hours' action, has tragic impact in Howard Clewes's short novel, *Sailor Comes Home*, set in a little mining seaport near Cardiff. An old man's memories of peasant life on the Welsh coast, primitive, God-fearing, filled with poverty and toil and fleeting pleasures, are given poetic, warmly sympathetic expression by Wyn Griffith in *The Wooden Spoon;* and Francis Brett Young, in *The House under the Water*, sets against the beautiful background of an old Welsh estate a complex novel of mingled, antagonistic family strains. In these half-dozen novels regional fiction makes evident its concentration and its variety.

Canada offers logical entrance to the continental expanse of American regional fiction. There are, however, few contemporary Canadian novels that possess mature literary art and regional significance. The *Jalna* novels are concerned much more with individualistic drama of character and temperament than with scenic or social backgrounds; and little of the indigenous fiction that reflects French-Canadian life comes to English readers. More than a quarter-century ago *Maria Chapdelaine* became the accepted classic in this particular field, and its influence has strengthened a traditional, poetic, religiously idealistic, rather than a realistic, treatment of peasant and pioneer life. But Louis Hémon's beautiful novel deserves and will long hold its primacy. Himself a Frenchman, not a French-Canadian, he had lived and worked with the people of whom he wrote; and his idyl of the farms and forests of the wild Lake St. John country beyond the Saguenay River is a true masterpiece of limpid simplicity, delicate charm, and deep human reality.

The most important present-day regional novel of French Canada is *Thirty Acres*, published in Paris in 1939 and brought to English readers in translation the following year. It is a first novel, the work of Dr. Philippe Panneton, who is a native of the Three Rivers district of Montreal, where the scene of his book is laid, and whose writing is done under the name "Ringuet." One of those peasant epics of the soil that exist in every country's literature, it turns from the romanticism of *Maria Chapdelaine* to more ironic realism, to thoughtful social documentation, as it records the life story of a Habitant farmer, bound to the land by the instinctive passion of his race, in a quiet chronicle that is yet packed with incidental detail and redolent of the life and character of the sturdy French peasant stock that remains unchanged from its ancient matrix of Normandy and Artois. Few sociological treatises could so graphically disclose the different elements of feudal and religious and peasant heritage that make both a separate racial culture and a continuing political problem in the French-Canadian province of Quebec. A lighter, gayer refraction from this racial culture sparkles in *The Habitant-Merchant*, J. E. Le Rossignol's genial tale of Jovite Laberge, prosperous Quebec merchant, erstwhile farmer, with his shrewd bargaining, his gusto, his humor and warm generosity of temper, his family, and his innumerable relatives. And these contemporary studies of the French-Canadian race group are balanced by faithful, vigorous portrayal of the different English-Canadian culture, as given by Frederick Philip Grove in his novel *Two Generations*, which, like *Thirty Acres*, is a family farm chronicle, but set in the English province of Ontario.

In the United States regional fiction has so increased in volume, so expanded in range, that no summary can do more than dip and hover over the surface of its vast domain. American novelists of an earlier day, letting memory and imagination play upon familiar environment, set background patterns for the local-color fiction that was its precursor and that first opened to the common reader unrealized vistas of the American scene. Only those whose reading runs back through many decades know how diverse, how vivid in color and authentic in outline, is the long succession of American novels that paint local scenes, portray local types of character, and record aspects of life past and present in almost every state and every geographical section of the country. Look back over that succession, and unfading pictures rise in mind and memory: Huckleberry Finn and Tom Sawyer, boy spirits of the historic days of slavery and flatboats; Howells, with his gallery of careful, eventoned etchings of eastern city and country life, his shadowy pictures of pioneer Ohio; Mary Wilkins Freeman's cool, precise embodiments of New England villages; Churchill's heavy, sturdy compositions focused on New England politics and industry; Owen Wister's cattle country; the old South of Thomas Nelson Page, romantic, stately, undefeated in spirit, however broken in substance; George W. Cable's deeper black and white patterns of old New Orleans; Mary Murfree's powerful studies of Tennessee mountain life, hinting of a later realism; and John Fox's revealing though overtenderized presentment of Kentucky mountain folk. Upon these, other pictures crowd and multiply, not yet so timeworn, changing in technique, using different mediums for the artists' purpose: Willa Cather's unforgettable portrayals of the windswept plains, the solitary farms of Nebraska, her lucent sun-steeped backgrounds of New Mexico's mesas and many-colored desert, her drypoint of the great citadel looming on its rock in old Quebec; the drab and ugly Midwest hamlets that Sherwood Anderson recalled from boyhood memories; the stone-walled pastures and green hills of Dorothy Canfield's Vermont; DuBose Heyward's deep-toned etchings of Charleston's Negro hives and alleys; Edith Wharton's clear steel engravings of New York in different eras and phases; Elizabeth Roberts's green expanse of Kentucky, past and present. This recital might go on indefinitely. Perhaps it may be summed up in saying that through the regional novels flourishing and multiplying today America's infinitely varied material aspects, her myriad diverse human components, are receiving a memorable, colorful, essentially faithful presentation that illuminates and interprets the historic processes of the nation's evolution in time, the nature and the life of the land and the people.

The regional fiction that has superseded the older local-color novels has not only taken on different dimensions but also has established closer and more complex relationships with literature in historical, sociological, economic, and other fields. For "regionalism," in the specific meaning of the term, has become the study of the different elements in a national culture with the purpose of maintaining their individual values, yet integrating them into a unified pattern of ideals and achievement. "Localism," "sectionalism," "provincialism" carry implications of separateness and antagonism; "regionalism," their opposite, implies an organic unity, and the development of a regional-national culture should bring all the rich and varied materials of tradition and folk heritage, old and new, all the distinctive contours of distinctive areas, into a national pattern at once disparate and interdependent: a pattern of unity in diversity. The movement toward regionalism, as Lewis Mumford has noted,[1] tends, consciously or unconsciously, to pass through a regular cycle: "It begins with a revival of poetry and language: it ends with plans for the economic invigoration of regional agriculture and industry,

[1] Lewis Mumford, *The Culture of Cities*, New York, Harcourt, 1938, p. 360.

with proposals for a more autonomous political life, with an effort to build up local centers of learning and culture." The part that contemporary fiction plays in this movement is indicated in Odum and Moore's encyclopedic volume, *American Regionalism* (New York, Holt, 1938), where more than 2,000 regional novels published during the past two decades are cited as evidence of the "rich regional heritage" which is transmitted in our national literature.

Perhaps some further indication should be given of specific values and relationships that differentiate present-day regional novels from most of the older local-color fiction. Their scope has been much enlarged by the use of historical perspective: currents of the nation's life are thus traced through successive political, social, and economic cycles; moral and ethical influences—especially in the postwar period and the depression years—are analyzed; and a sort of birdseye evolutionary presentment is given for a region or a community. Harold Sinclair, in three linked novels, writes a history of the town of Bloomington, Illinois: *American Years* runs from the founding of the town in 1830 to the eve of the Civil War, in 1860; *The Years of Growth* carries the chronicle from 1860 to 1893; and in *Years of Illusion* it runs from 1900 to 1914. Sioux City, Iowa, in the 1930's is protagonist of J. Hyatt Downing's novel of that name. Family and state history are focused on Stonington, Connecticut, from 1812 to 1822, by Lucile Grebenc in *The Time of Change*. August Derleth paints a detailed canvas of his native Wisconsin in his sequence of Sac Prairie saga novels, which run, in varying perspective, through regional annals of nearly a century. Comprehensive state histories take fictional form, as in Lella Warren's massive novel *Foundation Stone*, which tells the story of Alabama, from the pioneer struggle against the wilderness, in the 1820's, through the ample, patrician life of the great prewar plantations and the dark blight of the Civil War, into the heartbreaking task of rebuilding from the wreckage; and the two full-bodied chronicles of Texas, in which Laura Krey tells of the birth of the Lone Star state (*On the Long Tide*) and of the later Civil War and Reconstruction era (. . . *And Tell of Time*). These, of course, represent a merging of the regional and the historical novel; but the regional element is predominant. Nowhere has this coalescence had such remarkable manifestation as in the body of Civil War fiction which has come into being since 1930 and has carried radiations into the whole field of contemporary study of the economic and social problems of the South.

As vehicles for historical reconstruction of national and regional backgrounds many of these novels convey authentic detail of an almost antiquarian exactitude and recreate settings and "atmosphere," particularly of the pioneer past. Such is Merle Colby's *All Ye People*, so rich in antiquarian detail that it has become standard school reading for American history classes. On the thread of the experiences of a youth who set out in 1810 for the Ohio wilderness, it weaves a tissue of incident, detail, and background information that reveals manifold aspects of the epoch: farms, inns, turnpikes, crossroads, and ferries; cities growing up from villages; the continuous procession of pioneers with Conestoga wagons, barges, coaches, riders, and walkers; camp meetings, remote settlements, and outposts in the wilderness; landseekers, and woodsmen, and lingering Indians. There is deeper primitive quality and more pervading natural beauty in Conrad Richter's short novel *The Trees*, which fuses detail of research into the perfection of creative art and brings to living reality the still earlier forest wilderness in which lay the seeds of America's future. Sensitive, clearcut, moving, it is the story of a family's march from tamer Pennsylvania settlements, where the woodsmen's axe was driving the game away, to the virgin woods of Ohio, "the wild trees," where bird and animal were still undisturbed by man; and of the gradual making there of community beginnings. Minute detail of daily life as it existed in southern Michigan in the early 1830's is the essential substance of Della Lutes's novel, *Gabriel's Search*, with its sedulous descriptive information on the houses, the "Michigan beds," and the other common accessories of living. The whole domestic economy of life on a great New York estate in 1850 is set forth in *Artillery of Time*, Chard Powers Smith's 375,000-word regional-historical-family novel: what of their own subsistence these people produced, and how; how and what they cooked;

the clothes they wore; how they traveled; their household, family, social, and community relationships: an enormous mass of factual detail welded into a complex chronicle of the political, economic, and social transitions of the Civil War era. Such detail may be applied to a specific phase of living as well as to period or natural environment. Thus, the life of a small community of the Amish sect in Indiana is pictured in Ruth Dobson's *Straw in the Wind*, unvitalized as a novel, but of value as a careful, evidently first-hand, presentation of Amish folkways, the clothing of the sect, its religious services, its marriage customs, its food, its funerals, and its speech; while Maurine Whipple's novel *The Giant Joshua* offers elaborate minutiae of Mormon family living in pioneer Utah in the years when polygamy prevailed.

In point of view, as in treatment, the regional novelist's handling of his material differs greatly from that of the earlier local-colorists. Romanticism, sentimentality, mildly humorous bucolic philosophizing, circumspection in incident and language, once so pervasive, have faded out under the stronger dyes of concentrated realism, corrosive analysis, and undiluted folk speech. Especially is there an earthiness, a rough and primitive physical vigor, in the depiction of the breed of American pioneers and backwoods settlers, that dissipates cherished tradition. D. H. Lawrence, in his introduction to Edward Dahlberg's novel *Bottom Dogs*, said:

The real pioneer in America fought like hell and suffered till the soul was ground out of him. That is why pioneer literature which contains the amazing Odyssey of the brute fight with savage conditions of the western continent, hardly exists and is absolutely unpopular. Americans will not stand for the pioneer stuff, except in small, sentimentalized doses. They know too well the grimness of it, the savage fight and the savage failure which broke the back of the country, but also broke something in the human soul. The spirit and the will survived, but something in the soul perished; the softness, the floweriness, the natural tenderness.

The work of many regional novelists through the decade of the 1930's, with its emphasis on crude violence, variegated profanity, matter-of-fact sensuality, obscene or bawdy or brutal episodes, has given us this harsh, unvarnished rendering of grim realities. To illuminate contrasted modes of pioneer portrayal applied to the same region the reader need only take Bess Streeter Aldrich's *Lantern in Her Hand* and set it down on the threshold of Marie Sandoz's *Slogum House*. Both are pioneer family chronicles of Nebraska. Mrs. Aldrich gives a simple, homely narrative of early settlers, especially of Abbie Deal, in her adjustment to new conditions of living, to such calamities of nature as drought, locusts, blizzards, and floods, and her unflagging purpose to give her children advantages she could only dream of; it deals with the everyday cycle of living— birth, death, marriage, grief, happiness, toil, community bonds of mutual help and mutual welfare; with little literary art, sentimentalized and somewhat monotonous, it yet holds its own place as a valid reflection of typical American experience. Marie Sandoz gives a later pioneer chronicle: the fierce, melodramatic narrative of a single family whose history is of violence, crime, ill-gotten gains, and savage dominance, under the rule of Gulla, grim, ferocious mother of the brood, who is the moving spirit in all the villainy; it runs from the outlaw era of horse stealing, arson, and murder, through the years of settlement, development of community and social stability, the boom years, and the depression, into the new currents of conflicting political doctrines. That both novelists drew from authentic material can hardly be doubted. Deals and Slogums alike have played their part in our pioneer annals; but it is certain that in those annals the Abbie Deals far outnumber the Gulla Slogums.

Each mode has its truth and its exaggeration. The pattern of exaggeration prevailed for a decade in many of the novels concerned with the life of the soil and the mores of remote rural communities. Sinister farmhouses inhabited by imbeciles, perverts, drunkards, and ferocious tyrants; somber hamlets, sunk in apathy, but not too apathetic for hidden depravities and orgies of fanaticism; these are common materials of the regional fiction of the 1930's. They are, of course, genuine materials; but they cannot fairly be extracted alone from the whole amalgam of human living into which they are welded. As this fiction develops, it must broaden and mellow, merging extreme contrasts into a deeper substance of universals of human experience: fulfillments as well as frustrations, joy as well as anger, simple decencies as well as complex sensualities, kindness stronger than cruelty.

This is but a partial and fleeting glance at the extent, the values, and the varied relationships of regional fiction as it flourishes today. For fuller, more specific, consideration, the list that follows may be useful. It offers a gleaning of one hundred regional novels, using the term in broad application that includes the historical as well as the immediate local aspect, arranged under twenty-one states, and designed to bring out contrasts in treatment and variety in specific phase. No novels published before 1930 are included, and most of them come within or after the late years of the decade. States not represented are omitted only because it was desired to indicate different regional aspects by grouping several titles under a state, which, with a limitation to one hundred titles, would not have been possible, had all the states been included; also, it is apparent that certain states—Maine, Louisiana, California are examples—have had an unusual development in regional fiction within the last few years. The long-range historical aspect is perhaps less fully represented in this list than are specialized perspectives of scene and experience. Social, economic, industrial, and racial phases of American living are especially reflected as they have unfolded through half a century in familiar regions and in little-known corners of our country. But the panorama that is rolled out from these novels runs from the post Revolutionary and Civil War periods, through the pioneer era, into the life currents of the immediate present. Some of these novels are of minor literary quality; there is weakness, crudity, absence of creative vitality; but there is also freshness of approach, firsthand knowledge, laborious research, keen observation, serious purpose. Whatever their shortcomings as literary art, their values are definite, for they represent an immense store of factual information, descriptive, social, and historical, they illuminate physical backgrounds of America and visualize the complex strands that weave the human fabric of the nation.

One Hundred American Regional Novels Published since 1930
(Arranged by states)

ALABAMA

Gaither, Frances. Follow the Drinking Gourd. New York, Macmillan, 1940.
Norris, Helen. Something More Than Earth. Boston, Little, 1940.
Rayford, Julian L. Cottonmouth. New York, Scribner, 1941.
Vines, Howell H. This Green Thicket World. Boston, Little, 1934.
Warren, Lella. Foundation Stone. New York, Knopf, 1940.

ARIZONA

Edgerton, Lucile Selk. Pillars of Gold. New York, Knopf, 1941.
Gillmor, Frances. Fruit Out of Rock. New York, Duell, 1940.
Kelland, Clarence Budington. Arizona. New York, Harper, 1939.
La Farge, Oliver. The Enemy Gods. Boston, Houghton, 1937.

ARKANSAS

Hamilton, Harry. Watch Us Grow. Indianapolis, Bobbs-Merrill, 1940.
Lee, C. P. The Unwilling Journey. New York, Macmillan, 1940.
Simon, Charlie M. The Sharecropper. New York, Dutton, 1937.
Williamson, Thames. The Woods Colt. New York, Harcourt, 1933.

CALIFORNIA

Dana, Julian. Lost Springtime. New York, Macmillan, 1938.
Fisher, Anne B. Cathedral in the Sun. New York, Carlyle, 1940.
McKee, Ruth Eleanor. Christopher Strange. New York, Doubleday, 1941.
Miller, May Merrill. First the Blade. New York, Knopf, 1938.
Steinbeck, John. Tortilla Flat. New York, Viking, 1935.
Stewart, George R. East of the Giants. New York, Holt, 1938.
Van der Veer, Judy. November Grass. New York, Longmans, 1940.

COLORADO

Gardiner, Dorothy. Snow-Water. New York, Doubleday, 1939.
Waters, Frank. The Dust within the Rock. New York, Doubleday, 1940. Concludes sequence: (1) *The Wild Earth's Nobility* (New York, Liveright, 1935); (2) *Below Grass Roots* (New York, Liveright, 1937).

THE DAKOTAS

Downing, J. Hyatt. A Prayer for Tomorrow. New York, Putnam, 1938.

—— Hope of Living. New York, Putnam, 1939.

Kramer, Horace. Marginal Land. Philadelphia, Lippincott, 1931.

Lane, Rose Wilder. Let the Hurricane Roar. New York, Longmans, 1933.

FLORIDA

Bell, Vereen. Swamp Water. Boston, Little, 1941.

Faherty, Robert. Big Old Sun. New York, Putnam, 1941.

Hurston, Zora Neale. Their Eyes Were Watching God. Philadelphia, Lippincott, 1937.

Rawlings, Marjorie K. The Yearling. New York, Scribner, 1938.

GEORGIA

Caldwell, Erskine. God's Little Acre. New York, Viking, 1933.

Ethridge, Willie Snow. Mingled Yarn. New York, Macmillan, 1938.

Hanna, Evelyn. Blackberry Winter. New York, Dutton, 1938.

Miller, Caroline. Lamb in His Bosom. New York, Harper, 1933.

ILLINOIS

Engstrand, Stuart David. They Sought for Paradise. New York, Harper, 1939.

Peattie, Donald Culross. A Prairie Grove. New York, Simon, 1938.

Sinclair, Harold. Years of Illusion. New York, Doubleday, 1941. Continues sequence: (1) *American Years* (New York, Doubleday, 1938); (2) *The Years of Growth* (New York, Doubleday, 1940).

IOWA

Aldrich, Bess Streeter. Song of Years. New York, Appleton-Century, 1939.

Corey, Paul. County Seat. Indianapolis, Bobbs-Merrill, 1941. Continues sequence: (1) *Three Miles Square* (Indianapolis, Bobbs-Merrill, 1939; (2) *The Road Returns* (Indianapolis, Bobbs-Merrill, 1940).

Downing, J. Hyatt. Anthony Trant. New York, Putnam, 1941. Continues *Sioux City* (New York, Putnam, 1940).

Engle, Paul. Always the Land. New York, Random, 1941.

Stong, Philip. The Long Lane. New York, Farrar, 1939.

Suckow, Ruth. The Folks. New York, Farrar, 1934.

KENTUCKY

Chamberlain, W. W. Leaf Gold. Indianapolis, Bobbs-Merrill, 1941.

Hergesheimer, Joseph. The Limestone Tree. New York, Knopf, 1931.

Roberts, Elizabeth Madox. Black Is My True Love's Hair. New York, Viking, 1938.

Seifert, Shirley. Land of Tomorrow. New York, Mill, 1937.

Skidmore, Hubert. Heaven Came So Near. New York, Doubleday, 1938. Sequel to *I Will Lift Up Mine Eyes* (New York, Doubleday, 1936).

Still, James. River of Earth. New York, Viking, 1940.

Stuart, Jesse. Trees of Heaven. New York, Dutton, 1940.

Warren, Robert Penn. Night Rider. Boston, Houghton, 1939.

LOUISIANA

Bristow, Gwen. This Side of Glory. New York, Crowell, 1940. Concludes sequence: (1) *Deep Summer* (New York, Crowell, 1937); (2) *The Handsome Road* (New York, Crowell, 1938).

Godchaux, Elma. Stubborn Roots. New York, Macmillan, 1936.

Huggins, Clelie B. Point Noir. Boston, Houghton, 1937.

O'Donnell, E. P. Green Margins. Boston, Houghton, 1936.

St. Martin, Thaddeus. Madame Toussaint's Wedding Day. Boston, Little, 1936.

Saxon, Lyle. Children of Strangers. Boston, Houghton, 1937.

MAINE

Carroll, Gladys Hasty. As the Earth Turns. New York, Macmillan, 1933.

Chase, Mary Ellen. Silas Crockett. New York, Macmillan, 1935.

Coffin, Robert Peter Tristram. Lost Paradise. New York, Macmillan, 1934.

Kempton, Kenneth Payson. Monday Go to Meeting. New York, Farrar, 1937.

Muir, Emily. Small Potatoes. New York, Scribner, 1940.

Williams, Ben Ames. Come Spring. Boston, Houghton, 1940.

MINNESOTA

Krause, Herbert. Wind without Rain. Indianapolis, Bobbs-Merrill, 1939.

Wise, Evelyn Vose. As the Pines Grow. New York, Appleton-Century, 1939.
—— The Long Tomorrow. New York, Appleton-Century, 1938.

MISSISSIPPI

Faulkner, William. As I Lay Dying. New York, Smith, 1930.
Hamill, Katherine. Swamp Shadow. New York, Knopf, 1936.
Kroll, Harry Harrison. The Keepers of the House. Indianapolis, Bobbs-Merrill, 1940.
Rylee, Robert. Deep, Dark River. New York, Farrar, 1935.

NEBRASKA

Aldrich, Bess Streeter. Spring Came On Forever. New York, Appleton-Century, 1935.
Davis, Claude Brion. Nebraska Coast. New York, Farrar, 1939.
Ostenso, Martha. The Stone Field. New York, Dodd, 1937.
Sandoz, Marie. Slogum House. Boston, Little, 1937.
Thomas, Dorothy. The Home Place. New York, Knopf, 1936.
Winther, Sophus K. This Passion Never Dies. New York, Macmillan, 1938. Third in sequence: (1) *Take All to Nebraska* (New York, Macmillan, 1936); (2) *Mortgage Your Heart* (New York, Macmillan, 1937).

NORTH CAROLINA

Dargan, Olive T. Call Home the Heart. New York, Longmans, 1932.
Green, Paul E. This Body the Earth. New York, Harper, 1934.
Hannum, Alberta Pierson. The Gods and One. New York, Duell, 1941.
Harris, Bernice Kelly. Purslane. Chapel Hill, Univ. of N.C., 1939.
Lumpkin, Grace. To Make My Bread. New York, Macaulay, 1932.
Wood, Charles. First, the Fields. Chapel Hill, Univ. of N.C., 1941.

OKLAHOMA

Aydelotte, Dora. Full Harvest. New York, Appleton-Century, 1939.
—— Trumpets Calling. New York, Appleton-Century, 1938.
Covert, Alice Lent. Return to Dust. New York, Kinsey, 1939.
Ferber, Edna. Cimarron. New York, Doubleday, 1930.

TEXAS

King, Mary. Quincie Bolliver. Boston, Houghton, 1941.
Krey, Laura. . . . And Tell of Time. Boston, Houghton, 1938.

Krey, Laura. On the Long Tide. Boston, Houghton, 1940.
Lanham, Edwin. Thunder in the Earth. New York, Harcourt, 1941.
Perry, George Sessions. Hold Autumn in Your Hand. New York, Viking, 1941.

UTAH

Ertz, Susan. The Proselyte. New York, Appleton-Century, 1933.
Fisher, Vardis. Children of God. New York, Harper, 1939.
Sykes, Hope W. The Joppa Door. New York, Putnam, 1937.
Whipple, Maurine. The Giant Joshua. Boston, Houghton, 1940.
Woodman, Jean. Glory Spent. New York, Carrick, 1940.

WISCONSIN

Derleth, August. Bright Journey. New York, Scribner, 1940. Fourth in Sac Prairie sequence: (1) *Still in the Summer Night* (New York, Scribner, 1937); (2) *Wind over Wisconsin* (New York, Scribner, 1938); (3) *Restless Is the River* (New York, Scribner, 1939).
Ferber, Edna. Come and Get It. New York, Doubleday, 1935.
Havighurst, Walter. The Winds of Spring. New York, Macmillan, 1940.
North, Sterling. Plowing on Sunday. New York, Macmillan, 1934.

V. THE WORLD WE LIVE IN

. . . it's all one flow, like a stream, little eddies, little waterfalls, but the river, it goes right on. . . . We ain't gonna die out. People is goin' on—changin' a little, maybe, but goin' right on.—JOHN STEINBECK: *The Grapes of Wrath*

THE NOVEL has long been an instrument of social purpose, ethical, humanitarian, economic, and political. Our present-day fiction concerned with social problems, so immense in range, so various in kind, has its heritage from Dickens, father of humanitarian fiction; from the Christian socialism novels of Charles Kingsley; from Charles Reade's sincere, melodramatic championship of prison reform, of proper insanity laws, of industrial fair dealing; from the compassionate, courageous novels of Mrs. Gaskell that recorded miseries of industrial oppression in Lancashire cotton mills during the "hungry forties" a century ago. Changing, succeeding, currents of a hundred years have flowed into its expanse. Through the last quarter-century we see new standards rise, new issues emerge, earlier valuations change, former realities disappear. In English and American fiction alike, humanitarian zeal was succeeded by proletarian militancy, the conflict of labor and capital enlarged into the problem of industrial control and socialization, poverty and unemployment assumed economic as well as human aspects. For more than twenty years war novels poured out in a continuing current of emotional power, swelling bitterness and distrust toward world politics and creating an intense, pervasive sentiment of pacifism. Postwar disillusion and the harsh impact of the depression strengthened radical political doctrines and made communism and Marxism accepted groundwork for novels of social import. As barbaric forces of world conquest rose to submerge Europe, emerging revolutionary idealism was checked or bewildered, and with the advent of 1940 hopes and illusions were transfixed by immediate realities.

Proletarian fiction, novels of social revolt, pessimism, and protest reached their peak in the decade of the thirties, with a growing emphasis on documentation and factual accuracy and on detachment of attitude, and at the same time with an inflowing of broader sympathy and more impartial psychology. The element of propaganda, of course, is strong in all literature of reform or of controversial theme: it may be pointed out in the work of poets, dramatists, satirists, and novelists through the whole course of world literature. What propaganda is has become difficult to define. Broadly, I suppose, it denotes any effort or scheme, organized or individual, to instill acceptance of a specific doctrine or a system of principles; in its fusing of emotional and intellectual conviction, it finds expression in the finest creative literary art as well as in the exhortations of the doctrinaire or the cultist. Application of the propaganda label to almost every utterance of opinion and belief is so common today that its use may well foster a mental state of confusion and indifference rather than develop clear thinking or sound judgment. For the element of propaganda that is infused in the fiction of the last decade is primarily sign and expression of the turmoil of the period itself, with its changing, intensifying social consciousness and its deepening conflict of political dogmas. In spite of many obvious shortcomings—exaggeration, mechanized characterization, violent and unreal contrasts of the evils of capitalism and the virtues of revolution—this fiction has been one of the most far-reaching and powerful influences in evoking popular realization of the crucial problems of our day.

In American fiction concerned with social problems the work of Negro novelists holds a place of its own. These novels are uneven in literary quality; but in their firsthand knowledge, their psychological intimacy, they are a pristine source of true understanding of Negro life and character and of the Negro problem in the United States. That problem is imbedded deep within our national structure: the problem of twelve million native Americans who are an

unprivileged minority people, subject to continuing social and economic restrictions and to sustained racial discrimination. Among
white and Negro Americans alike there is a growing consciousness
of this problem and an increasing effort toward its solution; but it
is from the younger Negro writers, artists, and musicians, from the
steady inflow of intelligent, talented young people who are products
of democratic education and who have pride and purpose for their
race, that the problem will be clarified and its solution slowly take
shape. Negro life as it is reflected in American fiction still gives us
chiefly an image constructed by white observers. Often it is an image
reflected with truth and sympathy—as in DuBose Heyward's *Porgy*
and *Mamba's Daughters,* or Robert Rylee's *Deep, Dark River* or,
though with narrower vision, in Mrs. Peterkin's *Black April.* As reflected in Carl Van Vechten's *Nigger Heaven,* it brought to many
readers their first realization of the night life of black Harlem as
parallel to the night life of white New York. Negro life as portrayed
by Negro novelists is less generally familiar; but it has more authentic value and much deeper significance. Often it has followed too
closely the pattern of white novelists, in emphasis on sensational
aspects of sexual promiscuity or of vicious living, and often it is
thrown out of balance by a violence of tragic bitterness that is natural and inevitable, but crude and repellant in effect. Negro life,
I believe, must be portrayed by Negro writers if it is to be rendered
in full truthful reality; it must reflect not only tragedy and frustration, but simplicities and achievements of everyday people, patient,
hardworking, warmhearted, with fine ideals and standards and truly
heroic qualities, as well as excesses and abnormalities.

Not until the 1920's did the work of Negro novelists rise to appre-
ciable proportions. The gently wistful, conventionally humorous
stories of Paul Lawrence Dunbar and the grimmer, more realistic
novels of Charles Chestnutt came at the turn of the century, fore-
runners of James Weldon Johnson's powerful, expository *Autobiography of an Ex-Colored Man* and of Burghardt Dubois's symbolic,
melodramatic fantasies of race oppression. Then, with the novels of
Jean Toomer and Jessie Fauset, began the succession of present-day

Negro novelists, whose books have visualized tragic, simple, and complex aspects of common Negro experience and have revealed with power and understanding the nature of their own people. In range these novels are extremely varied, and their values as studies of environment, of race consciousness and race prejudice, of economic conditions and of different social levels in Negro community life should have some specific indication here.

Jessie Fauset's novels, although their dramatic elements derive from illegitimacy and the heritage of mixed blood, are usually set in northern cities, in Philadelphia and New Jersey, and deal with normalities of conventional middle-class life: people who are self-respecting, industrious, absorbed in all the activities that make modern living. Walter Turpin tells of Negro life on Maryland's eastern shore, in Baltimore and Philadelphia, and in Chicago's south side. He pictures Negroes of every degree and every disposition, poor, struggling, destitute, prosperous; working in many different occupations, as field hands, farmers, stevedores, teachers, lawyers, in kitchens, in theaters, in business; his treatment is realistic, sympathetic but objective. More limited, more warmly human and magnetic, is Langston Hughes's novel, *Not without Laughter:* simple chronicle of the life of a Negro family in a small Kansas town before and during the years of the first World War. Its texture of truth is manifest: it is appealing, often poignant in tragic implications of race discrimination, in matter-of-fact record of poverty and privation and toil; it is never violent and never artificial. There is no sustained plot structure, no dramatic development, no sentimentality, and no sensationalism. Mr. Hughes knows and loves his people and pictures them with sympathy and understanding in their individual personalities and differing characters; some are lazy and lovable, some hardworking and uncomplaining, some embittered, some ambitious, some talented, some vicious; but all are fighting the same foes: poverty and prejudice. A hard and unending fight, with all odds against them, in an indifferent or hostile white world, it is waged bravely and "not without laughter."

Most distinctive of present-day Negro novelists are Zora Hurston and Richard Wright. *Their Eyes Were Watching God* is Zora Hurston's second novel, but her third work of fiction, for one of the two books that preceded it was a collection of Negro folk tales (*Mules and Men*). In this novel—vital, unified, rooted deep in race —the folk element is strong; so is the quality of earthiness, of simplicity, of elemental human instinct. It has a pristine rhythm in expression, a poetic savor a little like the imagery of the spirituals; and it uses the unpurified speech, the common, gross naturalism of phrase, that is the natural utterance of the people it depicts. With this naturalism mingles the rich imaginative gift of the race, warmth and humor and pristine simplicity. Most Negro novelists in their work evince a close relationship to white culture; it is evident that this is the source of their method, though they may go deep beneath the surface in depiction of their own people. But Zora Hurston seems to draw all she presents, in manner and in substance, from undiluted race instinct and race experience. The story of a woman's life from childhood to middle age, this novel is regional as well as racial; its Florida backgrounds—the town founded and populated by Negroes; the Everglades, where a seasonal Negro community of bean and cane pickers work on "the muck"—are invested with an almost tangible actuality. Throughout there are many flashes of poetic beauty; much that is amusing, light with racial gayety, and a pervading reality of Negro nature and Negro living.

Very different is the novel in which Richard Wright launches with horrifying impact his attack upon the injustice of the racial code. *Native Son* (the bitter irony of the title hints of the passion hidden beneath the stark objectivity of treatment) invites comparison with Theodore Dreiser's *An American Tragedy*, for both books deal with maladjusted youth conditioned to crime by environment and character. In Dreiser's novel, however, character disintegration is gradual and progress toward crime hesitant. Clyde Griffith, but for moral weakness, might have been a satisfactory enough citizen. But Richard Wright shows us, in Bigger Thomas, a Negro youth who is sullen, furtive, and brutal, whose sudden appalling plunge into crime is precipitated by fear and circumstance, but who in any event would have inevitably followed a criminal course. The thesis is that in his own nature Bigger Thomas is the product of segregation and race discrimination; his hatred of white people is rooted in fear and in an unconscious psychological struggle against imposed inferiority; in the fury and excitement of crime he finds self-fulfillment and emotional release. It is a grim thesis, and it runs through a narrative of mounting dramatic intensity that carries Bigger from unintentional murder to terrified atrocities, to attempted blackmail and a second murder, to flight from mob pursuit over Chicago rooftops, to capture, trial, and the death penalty. Objective and compelling throughout in its drive of events, its freedom from exposition, the book is yet infused with an intense spirit of revolt, born of Mr. Wright's acceptance of the communist doctrine that only through organized resistance can oppressed minorities throw off their chains. In *Native Son* and in his preceding volume of short stories, *Uncle Tom's Children*, Mr. Wright brings the Negro problem under the shadow of the extreme left wing. As a proletarian and a revolutionist, he indicts our civilization for the criminality and the human wastage that its evils and its blindness produce. His influence may be discernible in William Attaway's short novel *Blood on the Forge*, stark in realism, violent in intensity, which fuses the triple problem of race antagonism, of the southern sharecroppers, and of labor conflict in a harsh, tragic tale of three Negro brothers, sharecroppers, starving on a worked-out Kentucky farm, lured by strikebreaking agencies to work in a northern steel mill, hated by white workers, scorned by union organizers, destroyed by the conditions of their existence.

Proletarian fiction is the most significant type-group in the present-day fiction that centers on social, economic, and political problems. The term has various shades of meaning. It has come to its dominance in the work of contemporary novelists only since the 1920's, but it has a long lineage. George Sand, passing from socialism to communism amid the revolutionary enthusiasms of France in 1848, declared that she had always been a proletarian, and in her preface to the verses of the young Provençal mason-poet, Charles

Poncy, she urged: "Go, proletarian poets, to your work: find the social, religious, and political laws that will unite all interests in one." But her novels, for all their ardent challenge to bourgeois standards, their humanitarian idealism, and political utopianism, conveyed no proletarian gospel. It is to Emile Zola that the development of modern proletarian fiction is traced, outgrowth of the colossal cycle of naturalistic novels in which he sought to display a panorama of French life from 1852 to 1870, studying vice and crime in minutest detail, recording the sordid, the gross, and the bestial with "enormity and totality." *Germinal*, thirteenth in the Rougon-Macquart cycle, published in 1885, is considered the first milestone on the road to the proletarian novel of today. Zola himself was no proletarian. He saw himself as the scientist, the analyst, working with entire objectivity on complete and precise data in the laboratory of human living. His purpose was to demonstrate heredity as the controlling force in human development, and to show what was wrong with the world in the hope that evils might be reformed. *Germinal* is a novel of life in the mines of northern France, where under socialist leadership a strike registers protest against starvation wages and unjust fines; bitter conflict ensues, and the miners meet with defeat and fall back into their old servitude. Here is made manifest the class struggle that is the underlying theme of later proletarian fiction; the spirit of the book's final prophecy is revolutionary, and the title itself may be regarded as a curious portent of the growth that was to germinate and flourish from the seed here sown. Gorky's *Mother* and Nexö's *Pelle the Conqueror* are famous later milestones; and in America the novels of Upton Sinclair and Jack London mark the opening path.

In strictest definition a proletarian novel is, according to Marxian doctrine, a novel about people of the working class which is motivated by the "class conscious" point of view; and "class consciousness" is the revolutionary tenet of communism that conceives the working class as the dominant class of the future and seeks through collective purpose and action to attain this dominance. A novel is not proletarian because it is about proletarians. The novels of Dickens, of Charles Kingsley, and of Mrs. Gaskell are novels of social problems, social protest, but they are not proletarian novels in the strict meaning of the term. Class conscious workers are those who are conscious of their class interests as opposed to the interests of other classes of society, or who can be roused to such consciousness and to collective or revolutionary action to establish their class interests. In some proletarian fiction the class struggle in its full communist meaning is the central or underlying theme; in more, I think, the class consciousness depicted is rather the workers' personal realization of injustice and oppression that turns to collective action through unionization or strikes as the only effective remedy. Naturally a great many of these novels center on labor strikes, on the struggle to bring union solidarity to unorganized and helpless workers, and on employer warfare directed against unionization. Fundamentally they represent championship of human welfare and social justice. The strike novel, it has been said, has had two functions: it has restored the evangelical note to our literature and it has acted as a seismogram of the tremors beneath the social surface. Certainly it has brought to public knowledge conditions and effects that are a major national problem and has visualized, for the remote and the indifferent, lives of millions of workers in mines, in lumber and textile mills, in automobile factories, in commerce, and in agriculture. Proletarian fiction in its full range finds human beings, however poor and humble, however illiterate, ignorant, distorted by poverty or degradation, worthy or inspiring subjects for the novelist's art. It has meant the extension of democracy to literature on a scale never known before.

Undue partisanship is the chief defect of this fiction: the propagandist ardor that sees capitalism all black, labor all white; that depicts only luxurious and dissipated living for employers, sordid and embittered living for workers. Other defects are unrelieved profanities and vulgarities of language, extreme preoccupation with sex, an overflow of doctrinaire preachment, lack of plausible characters, vital and actual human beings. These defects are evident in many strike novels; but they are defects of exaggeration, of inadequate artistry, that do not necessarily invalidate the authenticity or significance of the essential subject matter. In much social problem fiction developed during the successive moods of postwar disillusion and depression bitterness there is a high-tension violence, a strain of sadistic cruelty, an untempered presentation of brutality and depravity unprecedented in our literature. These characteristics are more evident in regional novels than in those that are primarily proletarian; they were strongest in the earlier work of the 1930's and reached their ultimate expression in Faulkner's Mississippi nightmares of degeneracy. In this whole field of fiction an uncompromising realism prevails that is often intolerable to readers who shrink from scenes of violence, from grossness of speech, from the grim and painful impact of opposed social forces. But it should be added that much of the protest directed upon profane and obscene language found in proletarian fiction is an expression either of the conservative moralism or of the conventional good taste that are both outraged by flagrant realities of inadmissible experience. This was particularly true of *The Grapes of Wrath*, which was attacked with a violence of epithet far exceeding anything in its own pages. In Steinbeck's novel the speech recorded is the spontaneous utterance of the speakers; there are ribaldries and profanities, but they are part of the common idiom of primitive folk who are neither animals nor monstrosities, but flesh-and-blood people, self-respecting, honest, and decent, closely bound in family loyalties. There is more obscenity (though not obscenity of language) veined throughout Aldous Huxley's satiric tale, *After Many a Summer Dies the Swan*, than in any proletarian novel of the decade that I can recall.

A large group of proletarian novels center on the South, as "America's number one economic problem." They have illuminated that problem in nearly all its aspects: race discrimination, tenant farming, sharecropping, land ownership, cotton and tobacco growing, agricultural and industrial labor conditions, the vicious undertow of hopeless poverty and subhuman degradation of living—and it may be doubted if any other medium of public enlightenment has had so vigorous and far-reaching an influence. Grace Lumpkin and Olive Tilford Dargan, among the earliest and still among the best of the present-day novelists who have made this their field, both published their most important novels in the same year, 1932. Both deal with North Carolina millworkers, picturing the mountain people, of old American stock, who in speech and living have carried the eighteenth century into the twentieth, driven by deepening poverty from the independence of their native hills into the dependence, the more hopeless poverty, and the dehumanized toil of the textile mills in the cities. There is a moving human quality in *To Make My Bread*, Grace Lumpkin's simple, earnest narrative of a mountain family thus forced by economic conditions to become millworkers and brought by intolerable pressures into violent strike conflict and revolt against the established order. This novel was dramatized as the proletarian play, "Let Freedom Ring."

Mrs. Dargan's novels have more sustained power and finer art. Written under the name of Fielding Burke, they are the work of a southern poet, whose quality of classic dignity is combined with deep feeling for nature and for man. Her gifts are evident in two novels that stand out for their idealism and their warm human vitality. Inherently, they are propaganda, in championship of the cotton-mill workers, in endeavor to organize them for better labor conditions and to stir them out of apathy to rebellion against injustice and oppression. To Mrs. Dargan communism is the gospel that offers labor hope and confidence and points the way out of the competitive jungle of industrial conflict to a firm and fertile ground of co-operation and mutual well-being. No one can read these books without knowing that in them an idealist is speaking, not in hatred of capitalism, but in conviction that the capitalist system must end, and in all-embracing sympathy for the lives that are sacrificed to it. Closely linked, both novels tell the life story of the mountain woman, Ishma, a heroic figure who might be incredible in her courage and idealism, but who is somehow made simple and living and real. *Call Home the Heart* shows her first, as a girl of eighteen, born and reared in the North Carolina mountains, carrying the burden of a large family that has sunk from comfortable farm living to shiftlessness and penury. She loves and marries, but toil and childbearing and unend-

ing poverty become intolerable to her. Her babies die. Her husband
seeks work elsewhere. Stirred to anger and bitterness, she leaves for
the mill town, in the piedmont region, between mountains and low-
land. Here is different toil, more grinding in its ruthless exploitation
of the workers. A communist-led movement of revolt, in which
Ishma is enlisted, seeks to organize the millworkers; she shares in
strike-leading, barely escapes mob violence, undergoes danger and
frustration, and finally goes back to her mountains, her husband, and
child. *A Stone Came Rolling* carries her back again to mill-town
conflict: to strikes, picketing, and violence, the incitations of communist speakers and organizers, the poverty and exploitation of
workers. Here Ishma's husband is a central figure; his death, a sacrifice to the class struggle. More didactic, more expository, than *Call
Home the Heart*, the thesis is the pressure brought upon liberal-
minded millowners by other millowners and by inescapable reac-
tionary influences that defeats honest effort toward fair dealing.
These novels show (as did Ellen Glasgow in *Vein of Iron*) the cleavage between the old farm and rural life, hopelessly impoverished as
the depression years opened, and the more bitter, complex struggle
for life in the industrial towns, where exploitation of labor was fostered by oversupply of helpless, unskilled workers.

In all these novels the regional element is strong. While the rise of
industrialism in the southern states is shown, the dominating problem here (next, perhaps, to the race problem) is agricultural, just
as in proletarian novels of Chicago, Detroit, and other urban environment, the situation is apt to be one of industrial conflict and
of the effect of the machine in dehumanizing life. Paul Green's
novel, *This Body the Earth*, penetrates into the whole tenant-farmer
system of North Carolina, especially in relation to the penal system
and to "poor white" and Negro living: a powerful, somber chronicle, painful and earthy, of a sharecropper foredoomed to failure in
his life struggle to own a few acres of land. The same subject in different regional environment receives more limited and very different treatment by Charlie Simon in *The Sharecropper*. Earnest,
simple, sincere, this has the effect of a case study rather than of a

well-wrought novel; but it appeals to readers who would be repelled by the harshness and brutality of Paul Green's recital, and it has definite values of authenticity and sympathy. Set among share-croppers of Arkansas, in the region near the Mississippi, it is an elementary narrative of two young people—children of tenant farmers, entering into the same life their parents have known—from their marriage through the next twelve or fifteen years. Both are stoical, ambitious, hardworking. Their hearts are set on possessing a home of their own; yet they are inextricably held in the grip of unremitting poverty and virtual serfdom; forced to borrow of landlords at exorbitant interest, forced into debt at the commissary store, constrained to move only in a hopeless, vicious circle. Efforts to reach the evils through unionization result in terrorism and more immitigable frustration; the tragedy of the parents is the continuing tragedy of the children. Edwin Lanham enlarges the sharecropper problem, deepens its complexities, and presents it with harsher, more powerful dynamic in *The Stricklands*, chronicle of eroded Oklahoma land, of tenant-farmers crushed in penury, helpless under moneyed oppression, and of a fierce, tragic struggle to unite white men, Negroes, and Indians in one body to fight for the right to decent living.

The Grapes of Wrath, John Steinbeck's tragic epic of America's second great migration, shows the social significance and factual value of the novel as a medium of public enlightenment, an instrument of remedial action, at its highest contemporary level. Here is the record in terms of human experience of a crucial national problem of our immediate day. Inextricably entwined with the problem of the southern sharecroppers, it is a triple problem, of land conservation, of land tenure, and of human rights. Erosion, exhausted soil, depredations of man and nature alike, have taken the soil from those who owned it, who drew from it an ever more pitiful livelihood, and who through their poverty have seen its ownership pass to the banks and the great land companies. Like the mountain people driven to Carolina and Georgia mill towns, these victims of economic change are of old American stock, rooted in the land for generations in primitive and retrograde living. Dispossessed, nearly penniless, they are the "dustbowl" nomads, fleeing westward in a great tide of migration that rose under the impact of the depression in the early 1930's, reached its peak in 1938, and continued its flow through succeeding years. Steinbeck's novel tells the story of the Joads, Americans of seven generations, thus driven from their farm in Oklahoma, of their flight to the golden land of California, whose orange groves and fruit ranches needed agricultural labor, and of what happened to them after they got there. With power and beauty and high creative art it fuses all the elements of Steinbeck's previous work—simplicity, depth, coarseness, humor, pity, tragedy—into a single current of human nature and human destiny that sweeps the reader through the pristine stream of life. It strikes to the heart; it kindles a spark of anger that does not die; perhaps it may affront with unglossed, vulgar speech; but it comforts and inspires in its realization of the dignity and courage and honesty and plain goodness with which ordinary men and women face the fearful odds of fate. These are high qualities of the art of fiction. But *The Grapes of Wrath* is also an authentic sociological document for the subject it deals with. It was built on Steinbeck's firsthand record of his own experience in the autumn of 1936, when he followed the people who followed the crops in California, to see their working and living conditions, and published his findings in a San Francisco paper and later in a pamphlet with the title "Their Blood Is Strong." A companion piece to Carey McWilliams's study of migratory farm labor in California, *Factories in the Field*, many of its scenes, episodes and characters are identifiable by those familiar with the migrant camps and the great corporative ranches during the middle and later years of the decade; and it links with such books as Stuart Chase's *Rich Land, Poor Land*, Paul Sears's *Deserts on the March*, and Lange and Taylor's pictorial documentary record, *An American Exodus*.

Strictly speaking, *The Grapes of Wrath* is not a proletarian novel. The Joads have no class consciousness; the struggle in which they are engaged is not that of opposed classes, but of plain men and women in desperate encounter with personal catastrophe. The revolutionary note is here only as an undercurrent, running through disastrous, pitiful realities, as the dispossessed and miserable, fear hardening into anger, move blindly toward a dimly visioned goal. Steinbeck's earlier novel, *In Dubious Battle*, however, carries the dynamic impact of the class struggle and remains, I think, the most honest, courageous, and penetrating proletarian novel of high literary craftsmanship that has so far come from an American writer. The story of a strike among migratory fruitpickers in the apple orchards of northern California, it deals with the conditions and characteristics of the migratory workers, the activities of labor organizers among them, the communist fomentation and under-leadership of revolt and strikes; vigilante violence, repression, tragedy, futility; and the constantly renewing spark of communist incitation that is fed by poverty, by intolerable conditions of living, and by suspicion and intransigence of both workers and employers. How communist propaganda among workers at a low economic level is carried on and why it meets response are made clear in a narrative of cumulative dramatic movement, deep intensity of feeling; often raw and painful; powerful in its vivid character outlines.

Industrial rather than agricultural conflict finds record in the majority of proletarian novels. Meyer Levin's *Citizens* exemplifies the actual source-experience and the factual authority that are strong elements in their content, and its supplemental "Note on Method" gives exposition and justification of this incorporation of reality in fiction. The novel itself centers on the Chicago steel works strike of 1937, with the killing of ten men in a police attack on the picket line on Memorial Day (changed in the text to Fourth of July). Its chief concern, however, is the tracing of causes, the study of personalities and of individual experiences, beliefs, and purposes involved in the whole complex skein of events. Thus, the greater part of the narrative is devoted to the investigation conducted in Washington by the La Follette Committee (here, the Gottschalk Committee) and at times follows the official record verbatim; with this is interpolated separate life stories of nine of the ten men killed, in which elicited facts furnish suggestion for imaginary character creation. In the commentary upon his method, Mr. Levin answers the question, why, instead of a novel, he did not write precise history: "I did not do so," he says, "because the form of the novel appeared to permit me the most effective interpretation of events and the conditions which gave rise to them." He adds:

There may be some question as to why I changed the names of certain individuals and institutions. The change is not for the sake of disguise, but as a constant reminder that this, in the final analysis, is not a report: it is not history; it is a novel. It is not written as an exposure, but as an interpretation. It may be asked why was it necessary for the writer to go so close to actuality for his material, without stepping into the realm of history? I believe modern writers are impelled to this method by a sense that the inner human truths of motive and compulsion can be found by examining experiences of reality. By using only actual, attested events as materials, the writer reduces the possibility of arriving at false conclusions.

This fusion of the factual and the imaginative is the factor that gives the novel today its immense extension of range and makes it the most effective public medium for diffusion of knowledge and stimulation of intelligence. It is time that critics and educators revise the familiar dogma of literary criticism that the values of fiction are purely aesthetic (as Mortimer Adler remarks, "there are novelists who do not know the difference between fiction and sociology"), and give recognition to its practical values of exposition and information.

Ruth McKenney's volume *Industrial Valley* is one of the most notable examples of proletarian fiction that is dominantly factual. A narrative of the great strike at Akron, Ohio, through its whole course from January, 1932, to its close with C.I.O. victory in March, 1936, it is authentic labor history, depicting actual persons, scenes, and events (though with one imaginary family), using some dialogue, and following the Dos Passos "movie pattern" of interjected newspaper headlines, posters, and similiar visualized documentation. The proletarian note is strong in *Out of This Furnace*, Thomas Bell's impressive, carefully built three-generation saga of a family of Slavic steel workers, laboring in the Homestead mills from 1881, when ten cents an hour was the wage of the newly arrived "Hunkie" for his twelve-hour day through a seven-day week, to the early 1930's, when that Hunkie's American grandson, electrician in the same mills, helps organize his fellow workers for the C.I.O. And it is on a more tragic base of contemporary fact that Hubert Skidmore sets *Hawk's Nest*, deeply moving, poignantly real novel of a West Virginia mountain tunnel project, carried on without protection from silicosis, from which 80 percent of the workers met death. In this, as in Meyer Levin's novel, official records of a Senate investigating committee bulwark the novelist's detailed, dramatic, closely factual presentation of a major crime in the annals of industrial exploitation.

From industry, labor, and business in different phases a ceaseless inflow of novels draw theme and substance: Detroit, in the tension of the C.I.O. struggle for unionization of the automobile industry, with its conflict of communism and fascism, in 1936 (*The Underground Stream*, by Albert Maltz); high-speed organization and regimentation of great automobile factories (*F.O.B. Detroit*, by Wessel Smitter); the rise of the garment-workers' union from a Chicago sweatshop (*Tomorrow's Bread*, by Beatrice Bisno), and, conversely, union racketeering in the same industry that brings ruin to the small manufacturer (*Seventh Avenue*, by Dorothy Meyersburg); labor relations in a New York department store, depicted in what is probably the first novel used as a means of organizing the workers whose story it tells (*A Time to Remember*, by Leane Zugsmith); everyday management and routine of a department store in a smaller city, following the year's succession of selling events with a detail that presents virtually a manual of method (*The Customer Is Always Right*, by Anne Pence Davis); mechanized, fast-paced routine of a great mail-order house, under the driving compulsion of "big business" competition and overexpansion (*The Chute*, by Albert Halper); life and labor of New York's Italian bricklayers, in their primitive intensities of poverty, toil, struggle, joy, well-being, and hardship (*Christ in Concrete*, by Pietro di Donato). Such novels as these, quite apart from their individual qualities as literary art, are valid factual and interpretative materials of social study. There is less difference between fiction and sociology than Dr. Adler realizes.

Only a few of the other economic and social problems that concern contemporary novelists can be noted here. Mining is one of them. Dr. Cronin, Richard Llewellyn, and other English and Welsh novelists have visualized conditions that change little through the years and have recorded issues of nationalization and unionization that are still unresolved. An American novel on the subject, without literary quality, but of solid factual value, is Thomas Tippett's *Horse Shoe Bottoms*, the story of an Illinois mine through two generations, from the 1870's, chronicling with honesty and simplicity the same unequal struggle that Dr. Cronin depicted in *The Stars Look Down*. More ambitious and comprehensive is Sarah Atherton's historical novel of the mining industry in Pennsylvania, *Mark's Own*, a family saga of four generations of mine owners in the Wyoming Valley anthracite region, which, in spite of sentimental alloy, has genuine factual significance, as it carries the story of a great mine through increasing industrialization and labor complexities from its opening in 1840 to its shutdown in 1929.

Unemployment and relief, grim offspring of the depression years, are reflected in novels of kindred grimness—in studies of disintegrating morale, of economic insecurity sapping youth and hope, of blind alleys which open no way out to worth-while living. This is not the "recreational reading" that fiction is commonly believed to offer: it is social criticism, social record, of immediate phases of contemporary living. Thus, futilities, inconsistencies, and inadequacies of social welfare and relief administration are probed relentlessly, from long experience, in Caroline Slade's two novels: *The Triumph of Willie Pond*, ironic tragedy of a man who finds death his only practicable means of providing for his family's necessities; and *Job's House*, in which the humiliations and harsh restrictions that hedge old age pensions are set forth in the story of an aged couple faced with destitution, who maintain their own independence and win a victory over circumstances.

Achievement and advance in social endeavor find reflection, too. Jerome Ellison's dynamic, short novel, *The Dam*, invests with courage and self-respect the task of a WPA project, on which men beaten down by misfortune and humiliated by the dole regain their dignity in honest and useful work; and in *Another Morning* Wessel Smitter builds a solid, truthful, heartening narrative—realistic, often poignant, but rounded and satisfying—of the Matanuska colony, that "New Deal" experiment in pioneer living, by which 200 destitute farming families were transplanted by the Government from their submarginal land to the virgin soil of Alaska, to work out for themselves an independent yet co-operative living that offers freedom, dignity, and opportunity. In the social field Winifred Holtby's novel *South Riding* holds a place of its own, as a concentrated, vital presentment of the organized means, the official structure, by which the community seeks to establish a first line of defense against its common enemies—poverty, sickness, ignorance, isolation, mental derangement, and social maladjustment. Within the framework of an English county council (typical of the governing body of any English or American local political unit) and under its different administrative divisions, such as Education, Highways and Bridges, Public Health, Public Assistance, Mental Deficiency, Housing, there unfolds drama of everyday experience that shows below the frustrations, selfishnesses, and blindnesses of individual aims and actions a slow but progressive effort toward human brotherhood and social justice.

World problems surging far beyond local and regional boundaries leave their changing impress on the fiction of the day. For some twenty years the mounting stream of war novels poured out its powerful, fresh-flowing current. *All Quiet on the Western Front, The Case of Sergeant Grischa, Farewell to Arms, Paths of Glory* crystallized the destruction, suffering, futilities, and stupidities of war into universal human tragedy. Novels of Sassoon, Tomlinson, Dos Passos, Aldington, and many others registered, each in a different key, but with mastery of literary art, the reaction of individual temperaments to the experiences of a war generation. Emergent political doctrines, the rise of communism, fascism, and nazism, in the deepening, ever more complex conflict between opposed forces of democracy and dictatorship, find record and interpretation in later fiction that reflects the course of history-in-the-making. Spain's civil war, epochal prelude to the nascent world conflict, has had no more illuminating background study than Ralph Bates gave in *The Olive Field*, which set events of the years from February, 1932, to December, 1934, in their basic relation to fundamental political and social conditions. Its immediate stark intensities of passion and despair, its fierce reprisals generating ever fiercer resistance, were projected in hammering emotional impact from Ernest Hemingway's *For Whom the Bell Tolls.*

In the literature that enlarges and clarifies understanding of the far-flung human tragedy now playing on the world stage, novels have vital, influential place. Phyllis Bottome's *The Mortal Storm* gives tempered, penetrating presentment of the rise of Nazi loyalties in German youth, of the inculcation of race hatred, and the mounting tide of Jewish persecution. Other phases of the Jewish tragedy are touched with dramatic power in Otto Schisgall's *Swastika;* with compassion, beauty, and terror in Louis Golding's *Mr. Emmanuel;* with sympathetic understanding in Margaret Sothern's *Chosen Races;* with sensitive perception of the self-sacrifice and love that are stronger than fear of death, in R. C. Hutchinson's *The Fire and the Wood.* What Thomas Mann calls "the lust for human degradation," that finds expression in the ruthless, deliberate policy of extermination of a race and in development of a brutal terrorism that paralyzes its victims and corrupts its instruments, is brought poignantly to immediate realization in many of these novels, which draw their material from facts more terrible than fiction could ever invent.

Thus, Peter Mendelssohn's *Across the Dark River* presents in simple, objective narrative an episode that furnished brief dispatches to the American press in 1938: the experience of some fifty Jewish victims, driven from their Austrian villages when that country came under German mastery, robbed, abused, herded on a barge in the Danube and left there, helpless, to be shot down in any attempt to land on either bank. Based on firsthand personal observation, deep in background knowledge, well integrated, comprehensive, and significant is Maurice Hindus's long, deeply moving novel, *To Sing with the Angels.* The story of a Moravian village in Czechoslovakia, it runs through only a few months in 1938–40, but in essence it is the history of the whole of that country—of any country in Europe —when Nazi rule settles upon it in ruthless despotism, despoiling, degrading, strangling hope and well-being, and kindling underground fires of consuming, inextinguishable hatred. There is longer perspective and wider range in Storm Jameson's *Europe to Let.* Also built on firsthand material, on immediate personal relationships, this is intrinsically hardly a novel, but a sequence of four separate episodes, linked only as opening and culminative steps in Europe's progress toward doom, narrated by an observer helpless to avert or to mitigate the tragedy. There is no protagonist, except, perhaps, Europe, no central plot except the rise and march of the Nazi terror: presaged in a group of young Germans encountered in Cologne in January, 1923, who have been linked in bitter fellowship of defeat, privation, outraged national pride, and searing hatred of the French; brought to manifestation in Vienna fourteen years later, with the Anschluss and the first impact of German rule; and carried on through the annihilation of Czechoslovakia, in 1938, and by the spreading poison of Jewish persecution as it sweeps across other national borders. Even in the minor fiction evoked by the world conflict there are often definite values of personal observation or specialized information. Martha Gelhorn's slight novel *A Stricken Field* gave firsthand portrayal of the city of Prague, tense and despairing, just after the Munich "appeasement"; Nevil Shute's *Landfall* is at once a simply told English love story and an authentic, illuminating presentment of the Royal Air Force at war, by a writer who is also an expert aviator and airplane technician. In *The Sun Shall Greet Them,* David Rame's novel of the heroic British drama of Dunkirk, is the accent of unforgettable personal experience.

To chronicle in fiction this whole era of world conflict is the ambitious purpose of Upton Sinclair, who in 1940 launched a novel-sequence of which three massive volumes appeared within two years. *World's End,* first of the series, surveys prewar Europe through the eyes of adolescent Lanny Budd, protagonist of the whole chronicle, and closes with the outbreak of the first World War. *Between Two Worlds* deals with the years from 1919 to 1929, in Europe and America. *Dragon's Teeth* centers on Hitler's rise to power in Germany from 1930 to 1934; and the author's intimation is that the narrative will continue until the careers of Hitler and Mussolini are closed. Predominantly descriptive and homiletic, patterned to the specifications of socialist liberalism, there is ingenuity and dramatic skill in this facile, if superficial, "processing" of the history of the last three decades, which will take its place as the climactic expression of Upton Sinclair's lifelong social evangelism.

How fiction will be affected by the present world convulsion no one can tell. The novels noted here are not great novels. But as they rise to the surface and pass in the flowing stream of current literature they convey refractions, interpretations, visualizations of the incredible realities of immediate experience. They are part of the documentary record of world catastrophe, as were the war novels of the first World War, and they have values of personal observation and factual commentary, of moral and spiritual stimulus. No masterpiece has yet emerged among them, nor is one likely soon to do so. A great novel is rarely born under the stress of mass catastrophe and mass emotion. Concentration, detachment, perspective, are necessary to creative literary production; the repercussion of continuing agonies and terrors must numb the powers even of writers who are not in direct relationship to them. From the flooding tragedies, dramas, horrors, crises, perils, escapes, and survivals that in a single year engulfed human existence, fiction through years to come will draw inexhaustible materials. A great novelist may in time bring to the recreation and interpretation of this world epoch the moral conviction, the realism and vitality and immense imaginative vision that Tolstoy brought to the recreation of an earlier epoch in *War and Peace*. In the meantime many novels that are not masterpieces, but that have truth, power, and insight, will widen realization and deepen understanding of the fates and sufferings of fellow-beings, the crucial issues of destiny, that confront the world we live in.

Twenty-five Novels of Negro Life by Negro Writers

Attaway, William. Blood on the Forge. New York, Doubleday, 1941.

Bontemps, Arna. Black Thunder. New York, Macmillan, 1936.

—— Drums at Dusk. New York, Macmillan, 1939.

—— God Sends Sunday. New York, Harcourt, 1931.

Cullen, Countee. One Way to Heaven. New York, Harper, 1932.

Dunbar, Paul Lawrence. The Best Stories of Paul Lawrence Dunbar; selected and ed. with introd. by B. Brawley. New York, Dodd, 1938.

Fauset, Jessie. The Chinaberry Tree. New York, Stokes, 1931.

—— Comedy American Style. New York, Stokes, 1933.

—— Plum Bun. New York, Stokes, 1929.

—— There Is Confusion. New York, Boni & Liveright, 1924.

Fisher, Rudolph. The Conjure Man Dies. New York, Covici, 1932.

Henderson, G. W. Ollie Miss. New York, Stokes, 1935.

Hughes, Langston. Not without Laughter. New York, Knopf, 1930.

Hurston, Zora N. Jonah's Gourd Vine. Philadelphia, Lippincott, 1934.

—— Their Eyes Were Watching God. Philadelphia, Lippincott, 1937.

Larsen, Nella. Passing. New York, Knopf, 1929.

—— Quicksand. New York, Knopf, 1928.

McKay, Claude. Banjo. New York, Harper, 1929.

—— Home to Harlem. New York, Harper, 1928.

Toomer, Jean. Cane. New York, Boni & Liveright, 1923.

Turpin, Waters Edward. These Low Grounds. New York, Harper, 1937.

—— O Canaan! New York, Doubleday, 1939.

White, Walter. Fire in the Flint. New York, Knopf, 1924.

—— Flight. New York, Knopf, 1926.

Wright, Richard. Native Son. New York, Harper, 1940.

VI. HISTORY IN FICTION

*He doesn't allow enough for the future. In his idea
there is thought in the past and action in the present,
but he does not show you the future pressing on me,
on all of us, more or less, like an unborn babe, forcing
us to action for its sake, not for our own.*—NAOMI
MITCHISON: *The Corn King and the Spring Queen*

PERSPECTIVES open into the past from novels concerned with
contemporary experience. Such perspectives converge and cul-
minate in the particular body of fiction that concerns itself with
bringing the experience of the past to contemporary realization. The
historical novel, cross-fertilizing history with fiction, has established
a genus of its own. Within its order may be found many of the
different forms, variant types, nearly all the divergencies of purpose,
defects and qualities of performance that exist in the whole structure of contemporary fiction; but there is also an organic relation
to history which gives this fiction a somewhat equivocal place in
two great departments of the literature of knowledge. That the historical novel may legitimately stand beside the work of the historian
and the biographer is still matter of argument, although its value
as an aid and incentive to historical study has long been recognized.

More than forty years ago Henry Morse Stephens, writing as a
historian, pointed out the particular service that the historical
novel rendered "to the cause of historical truth," because, being
confessedly fiction, its factual inaccuracies are allowed for by the
reader, while its reproduction of the atmosphere of the past is essentially veracious. "Readers of Scott and Dumas and Kingsley and
Weir Mitchell," he said, "are much more likely to approach history
with stimulated imagination and a longing to discover the truth than
readers of Froude and Carlyle and Bancroft." Through succeeding

years historical fiction has strengthened steadily in authority, developed in richly varied content, and so widened in significance that Sir Archibald Wavell, in his lecture on the art of generalship, delivered at Cambridge in 1939, could say: "When you study military history don't read outlines on strategy or the principles of war. Read biographies, memoirs, historical novels, such as *The Road to Glory* or *Schoenbrunn*. Get at the flesh and blood of it, not the skeleton." The influences of this fiction are far-reaching; its appeal has been continuous, among English readers at least, from the advent of Edward Waverley, in 1814, to that of Scarlett O'Hara, in 1936; and as its range widens, it becomes more and more concerned with aspects of history that have meaning for us today, depicted with realistic precision rather than with romantic glamor.

Entertainment and instruction are the most commonly emphasized values of historical fiction. That readers seek escape from the exigencies of the present by turning to romance or conflict or adventure in the past is the explanation usually advanced for the immense popularity of the American historical novels that have poured out through the depression decade and the years of advancing world tragedy. This, though valid, is only partial explanation of a trend that has much greater significance. In the same way, a good historical novel is more than a pill of history, sugar-coated for mass consumption, as it is often regarded. Of course the factual and informational values of history in fiction are obvious. Obvious, too, are the reading relationships that radiate from almost any historical novel, major or minor, into vistas of history, biography, travel, drama, or poetry. But there are other, different, values, less generally perceived.

The continuing preoccupation of American novelists with our historic past and the unabated interest of readers in the novels that depict that past represent, I think, not a surface wave of escapism, but a deep, unconscious movement toward national homogeneity. It is part of the revival of interest in American things that became manifest as the fight against the depression got under way and recognition of evils and weaknesses in our social structure brought clearer vision of the American heritage and stronger purpose for its fulfillment. Vision and purpose deepened as world civilization plunged toward catastrophe. All people must meet adversity from resources within themselves; and it was inevitable that Americans should turn instinctively for reassurance and inspiration to the American past, rooted in conviction of the dignity of man; to the American scene, in its continental richness and variety; to America's power of welding human diversity into unity. Thus, American traditions, resources, ways of living, achievements, opportunities, were made, more fully than ever before, common substance of current literature. The "American Guide Series," begun in 1935, by 1941 had covered the forty-eight states, Alaska, Puerto Rico, and the District of Columbia in a thorough, vigorous expository panorama of fifty-one massive volumes; and the WPA Federal Writers Project, which fathered it, produced during the same time more than 700 local guides and works of historical or regional interest. American rivers, American cities, American seaports, American folkways, and other aspects of life in America were celebrated in distinctive series; while American historical novels, in unprecedented number and diversity, fitted many-colored, changing, contrasting figures from three centuries of the American past into a kaleidoscope of evocation and interpretation. The present intensity of this "American renaissance" will undoubtedly wane, but its influence must be more than transitory. Our historical novels have gained a maturity of art and method never possessed before; they are producing, in their own measure, the background-making values that English historical novels have so long held, creating that strong sense of a common past that integrates a people and making the heritage of American memories a test of the present, a quickening power for the future.

Interpretation of the past that becomes commentary on the present is conveyed in much historical fiction; so also, though more rarely, is transmitted realization of the future as taking shape through forces of past and present. Thus, similitudes to the rise of dictatorships in modern Europe are implicit in *Freedom, Farewell*, Phyllis Bentley's novel of the disintegration of the Roman republic and the rise of imperialism under Julius Caesar. From Naomi Mitchison's magnificent pageant of *The Corn King and the Spring Queen* emanates a sense of forces of the future dimly shaping in the ancient world—a sense that more strongly permeates Harsanyi's envisionment of the Renaissance age, in his novel of Galileo, *The Star-Gazer.* These are fundamental values of history, and fiction possesses them only in different and more limited degree. For the historical novelist cannot, like the historian, record, interpret, and appraise from a vantage point above and outside the events he depicts. He must present those events from within the experience of his characters and must keep his characters, in their own experience, motives, actions, understanding, within the immediacy of their own moment in time. In this limitation, however, is the greatest value of the historical novel: its visualization and actualization of the past in terms of individual human lives imbedded in the realities of their own day. Here lies the continuing appeal to the reader, whether in romantic adventure against a historic background, or in realistic mass drama of historic event, or in minor threads of everyday living weaving a pattern of their own on history's loom.

Through more than a century of its existence the historical novel bore the impress of its originating genius, Walter Scott. Rooted in the romantic tradition, Scott's work nevertheless combined romanticism and realism. He made a romancer's use of the historic past, but he also invested his materials with plain human reality and dealt with flesh and blood and individual experience. Probably few readers today are fortunate enough to turn in memory to the noble procession of Scott's novels that opened in 1814 with publication of *Waverley*, its author's identity not revealed for ten years. There are the novels of Scotland's recent past, his own land, his own people as he knew them: *Rob Roy, Old Mortality, Redgauntlet, The Heart of Midlothian;* those of a more remote historic day, *Ivanhoe, The Talisman, The Fair Maid of Perth, Quentin Durward, Kenilworth, The Abbot, The Fortunes of Nigel;* those later forced into existence by compulsion of hand and brain, *Count Robert of Paris, Anne of Geierstein*, more monotonous, heavier, yet with richness and power, too. In the abundance of his work is the fecundity of the great crea tors—Balzac, Dickens, Jokai. His novels have dignity, picturesque color, warm human feeling, salient characters, shrewd humor, dramatic and tragic power, nobility of theme. His portraits of historic persons, like Shakespeare's, are stamped on the coinage of literature. Scott's defects are easily enumerated. He has partisanship and prejudice (less virulent, perhaps, than that of Kenneth Roberts); redundancies of expression, diffuseness of detail overweight his narratives (in avoirdupois, however, they yield to *Anthony Adverse* and many other modern productions); anachronisms are often evident; psychological insight is inadequate or superficial; there are sentimentalities and artificialities. Grant all this; but the fact remains that Scott is one of the great romantic writers and that he furnished inspiration and example for most of the historical novelists who followed him. Cooper, his immediate successor, who set the mold in which American historical fiction was to be poured for a century, accepted Scott's ideals and was guided by his method; he wrote *The Pilot*, first American novel of the sea, it may be remembered, to prove that his seamanship was superior to Scott's in *The Pirate*. Dumas built faithfully on Scott; so did Sienkiewicz; Jokai, the Hungarian novelist, was always his loyal disciple. His influence, however unrealized, is still latent in the historical novel of today, which in the spirit and with the equipment of the modern age carries on the reconstruction of the past that he initiated.

Within the last few years the historical novel has turned uncompromisingly from romance to realism. Hereditary traits that still persist derive less from the magnificences of what Scott himself called his "big bowwow" mastership than from his characterizations of humble folk, his recreation of ordinary living. Emphasis is not now so much upon the heroic in terms of individual gallantry and man-to-man combat as upon personal endurance, mass conflict, and collective endeavor. Romantic love, picturesque adventure, and a "happy ending" still hold their lure, but they are minor elements, especially in the work of the novelists who are building a structure of American history in fiction from unvarnished factual materials. Partisan violence, rivalries and complexities of internecine conflict, barbaric cruelties of Indian warfare, harsh actualities of pioneer experience are ingrained in the substance of many of these novels. In unglossed language they depict primitive crudities and common sensualities. They apply modern psychological study to interpretation of character, indicate motives and compulsions arising from economic and political conditions, and convey social judgment by seeking to express the spirit of the times in its own terms. Realism, psychology, and social awareness are the transforming factors in present-day development of historical fiction.

Biographic novels, family sagas, regional novels, all merge so variously into historical fiction that border lines are often indistinguishable. Novels that visualize and actualize phases of the first World War undoubtedly have historical significance today; but a perspective of more than a generation seems necessary to make a novel historical in the specific meaning of the term. Novels that mirror truthfully and vividly aspects of the present world conflict are materials of our own history-in-the-making, with values of direct illumination; but they are novels of contemporary experience, not reconstruction or interpretation of history in fiction. One of the definitions of the historical novel is that it is a novel which depicts actual periods, persons, or events of history in such a manner that they are readily identifiable. This definition is, perhaps, unduly broad, but it allows for the many variations in scope and method that prevail in this genre of fiction. Depiction of the past may be comprehensive in range, elaborate in detail: it may evoke a civilization, as in Thomas Mann's recreation of ancient Egypt; or reconstruct a period in a nation's history, as Hugh Walpole does in *The Bright Pavilions;* or, like *The Tree of Liberty,* it may conscientiously set forth the evolution of a nation's structure. Or the scale may be reduced, the frame narrowed, to an event, an episode, a locality, or simply to a segment of life in the past. A period and a region may be depicted in some fundamental aspect without presentation of any specific historical event or any historical person, as was done in James Boyd's novel of the Tennessee wilderness trapper, *The Long Hunt.* "Atmosphere" alone can make a novel historical, in the evocation of background—a place, a time, a way of living—that brings to life the historic past. Willa Cather's *Sapphira and the Slave Girl* does this on a miniature scale, recapturing everyday country living in rural Virginia before the Civil War and probing more deeply, with more delicate precision, into the nature of slavery in its effect upon human beings than do any of the full-length novels of historic southern background. The atmosphere of a period is successfully sustained in the gusto and humor of *Chad Hanna*, Walter Edmonds's slight, picaresque tale, set in upper New York state in 1836; it permeates in romantic iridescence *Here I Stay*, Elizabeth Coatsworth's gentle idyl of a solitary winter in a remote Maine hamlet in 1817; it envelops with compelling immediacy *Beckoning Ridge*, Emerson Waldman's powerful novel of plain country people caught between the hammer and anvil of war in the Shenandoah Valley in the 1860's. In their nature these may be considered regional, rather than definitely historical; but they indicate how much of the immense field of regional fiction falls within the domain of the historical novel.

Certain patterns have gained special popularity in present-day historical fiction, and from them many different yet closely related types have developed. Foremost, perhaps, among American novels is the pattern of robust realistic record, turning up the foundation soil of the American dream in its virility and pristine earthiness. Here the work of Kenneth Roberts represents a familiar type development: massive narratives of period scope, bulwarked by factual authority, abounding in pictorialized detail, with variety in characterization, highly colored dramatization of incident, and an impact of violent action that carries the reader over long stretches of monotonous groundwork and mitigates crudities in literary quality. For novels of this type the whole field of American history has been drawn upon: not only the Indian wars, the Revolution, and the War of 1812, which have been the special concern of Kenneth Roberts, Van Wyck Mason, and others, but phases of migration, settlement, and expansion in all regions of the country, from the colonial era to the winning of the West. Subsidiary types may be more restricted in time-frame, more centralized in theme, more tempered in treatment, but they maintain the basic characteristics of realism, detail, and historical authority. Predominant also is the Old South pattern that has shaped much present-day Civil War and Reconstruction fiction. Here a different realism prevails: historical authenticity is thoroughly maintained, detail is skillful, vivid, and accurate; but realistic substance is often enveloped in a partisan romanticism, in a loyalty to the "lost cause," that enshrines a single traditional aspect and obscures other aspects equally fundamental. The pattern of romantic adventure keeps its perennial lure, but older designs are modified by solid realistic detail, and rationalism underlies glamor.

In character depiction of historical persons there are many patterns, intricate and simple—from the formal full-length biographic portrait to the intuitive, creative evocation of a vital personality, from the carefully worked out portrait group (like the steel engravings of an earlier day) to the lightly sketched profile likeness, from the silhouette to the caricature. Psychological study has emphasized motive as the key to action; a quiet inflow of stream-of-consciousness reveals character more subtly and realistically than does extrinsic analysis; but as a rule character depiction in this field of fiction is more objective than subjective. The plain third-person narrative which is a heritage from Scott remains the favorite medium of expression, but it is closely rivaled by the autobiographical memoir, with its flavor of personal intimacy, its flexibility in conveying the manner and speech of a bygone day. Always two pitfalls lie in the novelist's path: undue antiquarianism, smothering flesh and blood under historic costume and antique furniture, turning speech into timeworn archaic jargon; and undue modernity, seeking to inject vitality into the past by the use of present-day idiom, entirely inconsistent with the period and persons portrayed. Both, however, are becoming more avoidable. Within recent years there has been a great improvement in developing a smooth and lively technique that conveys thought and action suitably to the modern reader, but is neither oppressively antiquarian nor preposterously modern. Evan John's brilliant study of James I of Scotland, in *Crippled Splendour*, the Elizabethan scene in Gwyn Jones's *Garland of Bays*, Helen

White's treatment of French Revolutionary figures in *To the End of the World*, Iola Fuller's portrayal of Indian life and character in her novel of old Mackinac, *The Loon Feather*, show in very different compositions how skillfully and harmoniously the colors of the past can be blended for its depiction and interpretation.

Factual accuracy based on sound historical data has become an accepted responsibility; it is no longer, as Henry Morse Stephens thought it, of negligible value to the reader of historical fiction. Many histories and biographies that receive wide acceptance are less well documented, less carefully grounded on authoritative material, than are the historical novels of Kenneth Roberts, Neil Swanson, Esther Forbes, Naomi Mitchison, Gwyn Jones, and many others. Kenneth Roberts's methods of research for his sequence of American historical novels that began in 1931 with *Arundel* are well known. He reads, collates, if possible annotates, all available source material, makes copious notes and careful summaries, draws or collates maps and battle plans, and visits the terrain his novel deals with for firsthand observations. His collection of source material for *Rabble in Arms* was deposited in the library of Dartmouth College for use by English classes studying construction of the novel. Elizabeth Page brought the background and experience of a teacher of history to her novel *The Tree of Liberty*, designed to make vivid through a three-generation family chronicle the democratic processes by which the American nation developed out of the colonial conditions of the eighteenth century. Her research covered five years of study in special collections, collaboration with scholars and specialists, and visits to places described. The nine-page bibliography appended to her book records such special material as court records and manuscripts, important primary sources, and secondary material that includes work of 121 historians and writers of standing. Frederick Niven's novel, *Mine Inheritance*, builds on a similar authoritative base its chronicle of Lord Selkirk's settlement of Scottish families, in 1811, on the Red River, in western Canada. Essentially a narrative of fact, there is here close historical accuracy and sequence in events; actual words of historical characters are used as dialogue; and the whole course of this heroic struggle for existence is vigorously conveyed. Fictional creation is limited to a few characters; the novelist's function has been to establish personality for his narrator, whose experiences integrate the historical material, and by means of a stereotype love plot to centralize emotional appeal.

The structural method these novels represent is commonly used today. It does not assure a living recreation of the past; that depends on the novelist's sensitivity, imagination, insight, and power of expression; but it does establish a basic substance of history that gives genuine and continuing value to many novels that would otherwise have little significance. Not many readers realize how much care is taken to verify incidental details and guard against anachronisms. *Gone with the Wind* was subjected through eight months before publication to a rigorous checking of facts, a systematic recording of proof for specific statements. Kinds of firearms, fashions and dress materials, music and songs of the South before the Civil War were among the details traced and authenticated. An English reviewer who thought he had found an anachronism in a reference to the use of iodine in the Civil War learned that this and every other statement of specific fact had been verified from four sources before being incorporated in the text.

Research and factual accuracy, however, have little relation to a novelist's theme and point of view. They assure authoritative raw materials, but in the use of those materials they do not eliminate bias, partisanship, intention to prove a thesis, to vindicate or condemn a person or a cause. Robert Graves says: "All that readers of an historical novel can fairly ask from the author is an assurance that he has not wilfully falsified geography, chronology, or character, and that the information contained in it is accurate enough to add, without discount, to their general stock of history." It is true that in its nature the historical novel is fiction, not history: a work of imagination, not a record of fact. It seeks to recreate, not to transcribe; and the novelist is free to choose any subject that interests him and to write about it from any point of view that he wishes to take. But it is also true that his concern is with history in fiction and that he is under certain obligations to historic fact. He may "debunk" heroic figures, confute long-cherished popular judgments, transpose time or reshape minor events to fit into his plot scheme; but he may not falsify history's fundamental record. A novel on Christopher Marlowe, written today, may no longer depict his death as tragic love drama, for the facts are now established; a novel that exalts Aaron Burr has justification, for it deals with conflicting evidence and still existent controversy; but one that presented John Hay as a co-conspirator in Lincoln's assassination would be fantastic. Good historical novels satisfy broad requirements of historical truth and probability; they have narrative power and perceptive characterization; they interpret as well as recreate the past; they have been an unfailing source of entertainment to successive generations of readers, but their value as history is stronger and more continuing than their value as entertainment.

No survey of the full field of present-day historical fiction can be attempted here. The "American renaissance," however, in its far-reaching development and the values it holds for American readers, demands at least partial summary and characterization. From novels in a few representative groups it may be possible to trace dominant trends, to observe relationships and divergencies, note characteristics of treatment, and indicate the rich and varied materials of American history incorporated in current fiction.

The panorama unrolls through three centuries, from the colonial period to the Civil War and beyond, with the pioneer advance in successive phases and varying perspectives as a continuous accompaniment. Esther Forbes, in *Paradise*, brings seventeenth-century New England to life, in its conflicting manifestations: the social, political, and religious tensions, the contrasts of culture and primitive living, of pioneer crudities and aristocratic distinction, the struggle on the one hand to maintain and on the other to break down barriers of English caste rule; and always the dangerous relations with the Indians, despised and oppressed when brought into subservience, yet feared and distrusted in the ever-present possibility of Indian warfare. There are picturesque glimpses of the colonial town of Boston, but the scene centers on the little village of Canaan, twenty miles inland from Boston, and especially on the great estate (partly farm, partly gentleman's great house) of Paradise, founded in 1639, by Jude Parre, scholar and individualist, who left England to escape civil war and to set up a family dynasty in the colonies. Here is no romantic or sentimental portrayal of colonial life. Roughness, violence, pioneer coarsenesses, rigidities of Puritan fanaticism, heavy drinking, primitive living conditions, and the toil of redeeming a wilderness all find record in a narrative that concentrates essential elements of the place and time it deals with.

The Deerfield massacre, long echoing down New England's history, is the kernel of Grace Zaring Stone's novel *The Cold Journey*, which evokes the French and Indian wars and the struggle of England and France in the New World. It was in February, 1704, that the Indian allies of a small French command attacked the little palisaded settlement of Deerfield, in the Massachusetts Colony, killed fifty of the inhabitants, and made captive a hundred more who surrendered. Narratives of such Indian captivities form an early American literature of their own and offer materials of history for fiction that are only beginning to be appreciated. The Deerfield captives were taken through forests and rivers into Connecticut, through the Green Mountains to Lake Champlain, and on to Canada and Quebec: the "cold journey" of the hapless band whose experiences the novel follows. Names have been changed, but facts are accurate and many of the incidents are unaltered. Essentially, the novel is a study of three contrasting races and ways of living: the Puritans, narrow in faith, ascetic, harsh, pioneers without amenities or ease, but of an unflinching determination; the French, bringing into the wilderness the graces and suppleness of Latin culture, the warmth and color of Catholic ritual, the assurance and indifference of an aristocratic order of society; the Indians, with their aboriginal folkways, their own life pattern of animal vigor, of elemental nature. In its cool, balanced, slightly ironical study of the interplay of human relationships among these men and women of different mold this novel touches the social-psychological note that is deepening in historical fiction; in period, background, and delicate precision of outline it links with *Shadows on the Rock,* though it has not the crystalline perfection of Willa Cather's mirror-image of old Quebec.

Colonial rule in New France gives background and theme for many novels. Arthur Pound's *Hawk of Detroit* centers on the foundation of Detroit in 1701, by Antoine de la Mothe Cadillac, in a lively chronicle, mingling romance and adventure. There is historic value in the picture of Indian forest life, with its tribal enmities and precarious relations with the French, and in the glimpses of problems of colonial administration: demands, pressures, and dissensions in dealing with the home government, conflicting interests of church, traders, soldiers, and settlers, and the weakening effect on colonial development of the government-controlled monopolies that were a basic colonial policy of the time. Evelyn Eaton drew from Nova Scotian archives the materials for a successful reconstruction of the story of Louise de Freneuse, which runs through the last eleven years of French rule in Acadia and finds its climax in the capture of Port Royal by the British in 1710. Her novel, *Quietly My Captain Waits,* is firm-fibered in historical substance, graphic and vigorous in its backgrounds of Quebec and of pioneer Acadian life, surrounded by vast, desolate recesses of forest and menaced always by Indian terror. Romantic in spirit, with imaginative insight in character portrayal, it has warm, magnetic vitality, but is nonsentimental, touched instead with the light ironic objectivity that is so strong an element in fictional art today.

The vast frontier that was America is reflected in an increasing flow of novels that range through its various historic phases and perspectives. Indian warfare, the French and British struggle for power, Spain's stake in the new world, the rising currents of the Revolution and the changing tides that set the course of the young republic, the fierce battle for existence waged by settlers in remote outposts, the vicissitudes and exploits of traders, wilderness hunters, voyageurs, the whole epic adventure of the fur trade, all are components in a structure of fiction that, however uneven in quality it may be, is establishing more general foundational knowledge of our early history. The time scale of *Not without Peril*, in which Marguerite Allis reconstructs one of the famous New England chronicles of Indian captivity, is of a single life span, but it runs from colonial to post-Revolutionary times, and covers much of the stormy history of the New Hampshire Grants, from which the state of Vermont came into being. It is the story of Jemima Sartwell, who was born in 1723, in what was then the New Hampshire wilderness, and died in 1805; who married three times, had two husbands killed by Indians, was herself captured, separated from her seven children, taken to Canada, and sold as a servant in Montreal; who later recovered her sons from the Indians, and with five of her children restored to her returned to her wilderness home, where she lived through territorial discords, Revolutionary conflict, and the long and difficult birth struggle of the state of Vermont. This is solid substance of historic American experience: a life story, powerful, veracious, and moving, rooted in pioneer simplicity, dauntless courage, and incredible endurance.

Neil Swanson, in *The First Rebel*, reshapes as a novel the narrative of Colonel James Smith, published in 1834, which is one of the early American sources on Indian captivities and pre-Revolutionary campaigns. Smith, born in a log cabin on the outmost fringe of the Pennsylvania frontier, was eighteen in 1750, at the opening of Braddock's French and Indian campaign, when he was made prisoner by Indians near Fort Duquesne. For five years he was a captive, experiencing perils and hairbreadth escapes that now seem fantastic melodrama, but that were common realities of the pioneer era; and later he was leader of the Pennsylvania uprising against British troops that ten years before Lexington foretokened the Revolution. Reconstruction is well done; in its sound historical material, its successful evocation of the atmosphere of the time, its vivid depiction of scenes of violence and danger, the novel links with Edmonds's *Drums along the Mohawk*, and Roberts's *Northwest Passage*. But its more immediate relationship is to the long series of interrelated historical novels in which Mr. Swanson seeks to present a saga of the middle border from colonial days to the Civil War: the advance of the American frontier from Delaware to the Jerseys, Maryland and Pennsylvania, across the Ohio country to the Mississippi. *The Judas Tree, The Forbidden Ground,* and *The Silent Drum* take their place in this series, each dealing independently with a phase of the subject, yet more or less related to one another in characters or time sequence. To this ambitious undertaking (six volumes had appeared by 1941) Mr. Swanson brings careful research, graphic and dramatic narrative facility; his tendency to stereotype plot patterns, to superficial characterization, and to over-exuberance of expression are weaknesses that make many historical novels which are valuable as reconstruction of history negligible as creative art. Creative art, however, combines with historical value in two different yet closely related novels of pioneer America that have held their primacy for more than a decade: one, man's advance upon the adventure of the wilderness depicted in James Boyd's *The Long Hunt,* evoking the life of the Tennessee trapper who followed forest trails with gun and powder horn, matching his skill against red man and wild creatures; the other, woman's share in that adventure, as it is brought to luminous yet tangible recreation in *The Great Meadow,* Elizabeth Madox Roberts's novel of the Kentucky wilderness, set against Revolutionary backgrounds.

Novels concerned with the American Revolution are legion. They deal with its foreshadowings and its aftermath, its conduct on land and sea, its effects on trade and social life, the personality and behavior of many of its leaders. Their emphasis on historical research, factual accuracy, and realistic technique have been noted. Their most salient recent trend has been the turn from the traditional "patriotic" pattern, long stamped upon our school history textbooks and ingrained in the work of earlier novelists, to the "revisionist" design, established by the intensive critical research, the objective and rationalizing attitude of present-day historians. The cherished popular concept of the Revolution is represented by what Bernard De Voto calls "the Parson Weems picture," of heroic patriots united against tyranny and injustice, embattled against forces of mercenary troops, and achieving victory against heavy odds through Washington's leadership and their own determination, self-sacrifice, and resourcefulness. Throughout the revival of American historical fiction that flourished at the turn of the century this concept remained virtually intact. The aristocratic flavor was strong, nobility was the American role, villainy a British prerogative, the lower orders played a minor part, the complexities and discords of class interests were rarely touched upon. Now, however, more mixed and seamier aspects are brought into view. The Revolution is seen as a fragmentary, uneven conflict, carried on, not in united patriotic fervor, but in local and regional enmities, in the embroilment of neighbor with neighbor, in flares of economic and social revolt, its military history characterized by the blunders and confusion of raw colonists and the blindness and lethargy of the British, which stultified superiority in numbers and resources. Common folk in homespun living, independent settlers on small farms or forest clearings, small tradesmen, artisans, rascals and vagabonds are now more familiar figures than the graceful heroines, the dashing heroes, of a more romantic day. In Walter Edmonds's *Drums along the Mohawk* the everyday living of common people fighting for their homes and lives is solid substance of history, kept to ordinary, obscure human materials, but transformed into flesh and blood and bones. James Boyd's *Drums*, one of the earlier novels in which this realistic treatment of the development and effect of the Revolution prevails, still remains one of the best. Solid in substance, balanced and thoughtful, it is one of the few novels that bring to creative realization the democratic ideal living below rough and ugly surfaces. Far more comprehensive in range is the enormous canvas on which Van Wyck Mason paints his panorama of the maritime aspects of the Revolution not only in the war at sea but also in effect on the life of the thirteen colonies. *Three Harbours* and *Stars on the Sea* are the first two of his proposed sequence of four novels. Norfolk, Boston, and Bermuda are the three harbors of the opening novel; for the second, the field of action stretches from Rhode Island to Charleston and the West Indies. Both are massive in bulk, crowded with characters, ranging over sea and land in a clamorous, kaleidoscopic projection of historical events and melodramatic adventures. Akin to Kenneth Roberts's novels in general character, they are somewhat rougher in workmanship, with less personal intensity in point of view.

One effect of the "revisionist" trend is seen in a rising wave of sympathy for the Loyalist rather than the Revolutionary cause, an upwelling of hero worship for Benedict Arnold, and an accentuation of demagoguery, corruption, and self-seeking on the part of the rebel political and military leaders. From the older image of the "ragged Continentals," withstanding starvation and lack of arms with unshaken purpose, the pendulum has swung to the spectacle of a "rabble in arms," lawless and cowardly, plundering, burning, and spreading terror among decent citizens. Basically, presentation of the Loyalist side of the Revolution has strong values, enriching the substance of fiction by important historical material and establishing much more general realization of the divided loyalties that did, in a measure, give to the Revolutionary conflict the nature of a civil war. Ties of blood, a common heritage, bound the colonies to the country of their ancestors. America was as much a part of Britain as England, Scotland, Wales; the breaking away from the mother country involved bitter division of judgment, distortions of fact, fierce economic cleavage, and uprising against privilege, and rendered counsels of moderation, patience, and tolerance as ineffective as they have always been in intensities of family feudism.

These long-unregarded realities of the past are illuminated in many recent Revolutionary novels. The illumination, however, is at times so focused that its effect tends to distortion rather than to enlightenment. Kenneth Roberts achieves this effect in *Oliver Wiswell*, Robert Graves in *Sergeant Lamb's America* and its successor, *Proceed, Sergeant Lamb*: novels that set highwater mark in championship of the Loyalist side, in denigration of the Revolution and its supporters. *Oliver Wiswell*, like *Northwest Passage*, is an immense scene painting of an era: it covers actively only the seven years from 1775 to 1782, but it compasses the full range of the Revolution, and it is the first of Mr. Roberts's novels to be the vehicle for an intensely partisan presentation of the historical material it deals with. Formidable in bulk as in momentum, the 830 pages of crisis, conflict, brutality, adventure, excitement, and disquisition that make up Oliver Wiswell's autobiographical narrative constitute a battering ram driven in continuous hammer attacks upon the rebel cause. The Revolution is regarded as conceived in iniquity and born of evil, directed by conscienceless political tricksters, rabble-rousing demagogues, and crazy theorists, "turning all our colonies into madhouses," supported by brutal mob violence, and carried on by a shambling, pockmarked, cowardly rabble that ran like rabbits whenever firmly encountered. All virtue, all intelligence, all ability belong to the Tories; and the deplorable conclusion of the miserable conflict stripped the country of its best, sanest, and most loyal citizens. Publication in 1941 of Carl Van Doren's memorable compendium of documentary source material, *The Secret History of the American Revolution*, should, however, go far to modify the *Oliver Wiswell* pattern in our Revolutionary fiction. The hero worship of Benedict Arnold that finds extreme expression in Kenneth Roberts's novel is unlikely long to survive the overwhelming weight of historical fact here presented. As Mr. Van Doren says: "Traditional guesses about Arnold, either that he was a villain out of melodrama, or that he was a disillusioned hero honestly converted to the enemy, give way to facts which show him to have been bold, crafty, unscrupulous, unrepentant: the Iago of traitors."

Robert Graves's attack is as uncompromising as Kenneth Roberts's, but less venomous and more limited. Ostensibly based on the genuine narrative of a British soldier of the period, it reproduces so perfectly, in style, form, and essential nature the eighteenth-century autobiographical memoir that the artificial plot thread and the lack of sustained dramatic development are of minor importance, for the effect on the reader is of a serious personal record, rather than of a novel. Sergeant Roger Lamb takes on a flesh-and-blood reality in this explicit unself-conscious chronicle of his experiences during the British campaign in Canada under Burgoyne, to and after the defeat at Saratoga, and in its continuation through the campaigns in New

York, the Carolinas, Maryland, and Virginia to the close of the war. His exposition of the causes and conduct of the Revolution is devastating enough, but it is a natural expression of the bias to be expected of a British soldier holding firm and honest allegiance to his country's rule. More temperate consideration of the Loyalist cause, truer understanding of the Revolutionary struggle, are found in Frank Hough's novel *The Neutral Ground*, concerned with the divided loyalties that prevailed in the no-man's-land of New York's Westchester county; *Renown*, his earlier biographic novel of Benedict Arnold, though strong in admiration and sympathy, keeps a fair-minded attitude. So does *Trumpets at Dawn*, in which Cyril Harris follows the fortunes of a Patriot-Loyalist divided family through the whole course of the war. *Tory Oath*, by Tim Pridgen, is a romantic adventure tale of the gallant, tragic struggle waged by the Loyalist-Scottish clansmen of North Carolina against the "Boston cause"; and in North Carolina (background of James Boyd's *Drums*) Inglis Fletcher sets her novel *Raleigh's Eden*, with its clear-sighted, graphic, yet thoughtful presentation, from a side unseen by Oliver Wiswell, of the Revolution in its emerging issues, its rise, and its culmination.

Many forgotten bits of history are brought to life in novels concerned with post-Revolutionary years. Hortense Lion's *Mill Stream*, centering on Providence in 1814, deals with the beginnings of the clothmaking industry in New England and the change of what had been a thriving seaport to a manufacturing city. *The Loon Feather*, by Iola Fuller, tells the story of the great Tecumseh's daughter, from 1806 to 1834, in a warm and vital recreation of Indian life and character, of the fur trade at old Mackinac, and the beginnings of the Black Hawk war. A *cause célèbre* of the 1840's—the case of the Cuban vessel "Amistad," manned by Negroes who mutinied outside Havana, seized the ship, and tried blindly to sail back to Africa—is recorded with historical accuracy and imaginative impressionism by Blair Niles in *East by Day*, a novel that reflects New England's rising moral fervor against slavery. Such themes as industrial and regional expansion, continuing conflict with the Indians, the darkening shadow of secession, westward migration, the Argonauts' quest, the Mormon epic run through scores of regional-historical novels that build from materials of the past their chronicle of America in the making.

With the great inflowing of Civil War novels during the decade of the 1930's American historical fiction registered its finest achievement, in valid imaginative rendering of historic fact, transmitted through intelligence as well as through emotion. However different in tinge of idea and opinion, these novels are based on the findings of history; carefully documented, they possess close factual accuracy, and, as a rule, they manifest more finished literary art than do the novels that depict the Revolutionary period. Realistic method dominates, though often strongly infused with romanticism, and always there is the modern vision that pierces through the age-old panoply and glory of war to the torn human flesh, the agonized human soul, beneath. Whitman, forerunner of the present, in "Drum Taps" sounds the muffled note that rolls in full resonance through this reconstruction of America's most tragic drama: "I play not marches for accepted victors only."

The greater part of this Civil War fiction has come from talented Southern writers, whose early environment, inherited memories, and personal background of experience give to their recreation of the War between the States (their preferred and now familiar designation) an intensity of partisan conviction and a nostalgic sublimation. Its effect has been to focus popular sympathy upon the Southern cause and to establish a dream image of the Old South as a civilization of ease, culture, aristocracy, swept to destruction by rising forces of industrialism. The crucial issue of slavery receives little attention; the usual attitude toward the Negroes is of protective, kindly possessiveness toward those "good" and "faithful" ones who found life fulfillment in servitude, of distrust or scorn for those who welcomed freedom; the Union cause shrinks into political corruption and fanatic unreason; the Confederacy becomes the union of men and women joined in defense and support of a way of life built for them by their own generations, that represents beauty, harmony, dignity, and continuity. This, like the pro-Loyalist Revolutionary fiction, is "revisionist" reading of history; but it is more deeply tinged with romantic tradition. Its values have been to give to non-Southern readers a clearer understanding of the Southern side of the war, deeper realization of the ruthlessness, greed, and blindness of Reconstruction, and of the long struggle to rebuild a structure of living from disintegration and devastation; its weakness lies in suppression of the crucial immediate issues which inspired the ideals of the Northern cause.

Allen Tate's *The Fathers* is essentially a study of the traditional culture of the Old South, stable, gracious, and disciplined, challenged and destroyed by the incursion from without of violence determined to possess what it had not inherited. Presented in terms of character, clash of opinion, complexities of human relationship, set in Virginia just before and after the beginning of the war, its theme is subtly conveyed in a tragic family melodrama for which the war furnishes only remote background. Concrete historical substance is molded with factual accuracy and imaginative insight into DuBose Heyward's novel of Charleston in the first dawning of the war. *Peter Ashley* opens on December 20, 1860, when the ordinance of secession was passed in Charleston's convention hall; its climax is the all-night vigil of April 12, 1861, when from every roof and vantage point Charleston watched through the darkness the flames that opened the bombardment of Fort Sumter. The novel is of romantic pattern, old-fashioned in flavor; its continuing value lies in the careful step-by-step tracing of the severance of North and South, in the vividness and precision with which it conveys the detail of Charleston's immediate life. Mr. Heyward's theme is the passing of an aristocracy, established in power of race and high traditional standards of conduct. Slavery he takes for granted, from the aspect of kindly, legitimate authority exercised according to an intricate code of "good form"; yet there are implications of a more sinister realism, in which this aristocratic conviction may be discerned as tragic illusion; and from the novel as a whole there rises a sense of nostalgic enchantment rather than of flesh-and-blood reality. More warmth and charm pervade *So Red the Rose*, Stark Young's evocation of the Old South civilization of culture, ease, and class domination, as opposed to the professional, mechanical, industrial civilization of the North. In its main events this novel is set in Mississippi, on the estates and plantations lying about Natchez and in Natchez itself. Covering the years from 1859 to 1865, it is concerned with a group of intricately related families, whose ties of kin reach into Louisiana and Virginia. Long, slow-moving, simple, yet involved, threaded on unending conversations, the narrative imparts somehow a sense of intimate reality, and takes on the dignity of a memorial of the heart, as it rises slowly into a crescendo of war devastation, of tragedy and devotion, brutality and kindness, rage and pity.

Gone with the Wind stands by itself in Civil War fiction; indeed, it is likely to long remain a phenomenon in the history of the American novel. Published in June, 1936, it had sold a million copies by the end of that year, and a million and a half more had been added to the record by 1940. Critical opinion has clashed violently over Margaret Mitchell's first and only book. Overpowering success brought the familiar reactions of indiscriminate eulogy and contemptuous disparagement; time alone can pass ultimate judgment; but in any fair-minded consideration it must, I think, be recognized as one of those rare novels that in sheer storytelling quality commands absorbed interest and spontaneous emotional response. Closely localized, it covers the Civil War and early Reconstruction era in Georgia, and offers a commentary on Sherman's march "from Atlanta to the sea" in terms, not of military history, but of tragic human experience. There are psychological unrealities in character development; high-colored romanticism, deep-dyed sectionalism, tinge the fabric; but it is a fabric of flesh and blood reality, of genuine historic substance, in which dynamic energy is combined with almost naïve simplicity. Here, under all make-believe of plot, unfolds the drama of the rising Civil War, entered upon with gay confidence by gallant Southern youth, eager to "whip the Yankees"; here, the tragedy of inevitable defeat, met with unconquerable courage and inexhaustible devotion; here, woe to the conquered, in the burning of Atlanta, the ruthless devastation of the country; here, bitter humiliations and fierce reprisals of "carpet-bag" rule; thus, the whole sequence of Georgia's experience through the twelve years that saw the passing of the Old South—"gone with the wind" of the mighty storm sweeping down from the North—and that left a heritage of hatred enduring into the fourth generation.

Notable in authority and epic quality, is Caroline Gordon's *None Shall Look Back*, a broad-scale, heroic treatment of the war in the Cumberland Valley from 1862 to 1864, centering on the figure of General Nathan Bedford Forrest, dashing Confederate cavalry leader. There is a flavor of *So Red the Rose* in its portrayal of old plantation estates and its traditional attitude toward Southern aristocracy; but it is essentially a concentration and visualization of campaign annals, opening with the battle and surrender of Fort Donelson, reaching its climax in the battle of Chickamauga, where Forrest died; and conveying, often in almost unendurable intensity, the terrors and desolation of war. Its touch throughout seems more that of a man than a woman. As a novel, its weaknesses are confusion and lack of the converging dramatic tension that is so strong in *Gone with the Wind*. The battle-ringed, war-torn Atlanta of Margaret Mitchell's novel has its parallel in *Bugles Blow No More*, Clifford Dowdey's stirring, harrowing presentment of life in Richmond during the four years of the war, with its climax in the siege and fall of the city; and there is broad relationship of theme and treatment to *Gone with the Wind* in *By the Dim Lamps*, Nathan Schachner's novel of the war and Reconstruction in Louisiana, centering in New Orleans and building its vigorous melodrama on sound historical foundations.

There is much Civil War fiction not of Old South pattern, rich in variety and significance. No other novel, I think, equals in transfiguring imaginative power the one that strikes the prelude to the whole conflict: Leonard Ehrlich's novel of the life of John Brown, *God's Angry Man*, which, published in 1932, waited nearly ten years for the fuller recognition it deserved. Based on Oswald Garrison Villard's life of John Brown, moving scrupulously within the frame of historical fact, this is a profound and thrilling evocation of personality, an infusion of the raw substance of life with the burning essence of that life's passion, delusion, purpose, and tragedy. The nature of the fanatic is penetrated, in its surging currents of exaltation, despair, anguish, ruthlessness; the color and movement of the time is transmitted—the contrasting backgrounds of North and South, the "dark and bloody ground" of fierce reprisal and unslaked vengeance, the tragic climax, with its portent of greater tragedy to follow; and the narrative, keyed to poetic intensity, is full of instantaneous portrayals (such as the brilliant twelve-line etching of Thoreau) and fleeting, powerful gusts of emotion and insight.

Unflinching realism in graphic, harsh detail renders an unforgettable picture of the three-day battle of Gettysburg, in MacKinlay Kantor's novel *Long Remember*. Solid in bulk, meticulous in historical exactitude, painful, sometimes hideous, in its portrayal of wounds, suffering, and death, the underlying note here is that of the detached observer, seeing ideals of human unity defeated under the clash of opposed convictions meeting force with force. Realism blended with love interest is focused upon the fortunes of a Union private soldier in the Cumberland Valley campaigns by Royce Brier, in *Boy in Blue;* its particular interest, however, is not as expression of any Union viewpoint, but for comparison, from a different angle, with the same phase of the war as it is presented in *None Can Look Back*. More comprehensive in scope, tempered and thoughtful in treatment, is James Boyd's *Marching On*, which, published in 1927, still holds its place as one of the finest Civil War novels. In a sense it continues the thread of *Drums*, for the central figure, James Fraser, is a descendant of the Johnny Fraser of the earlier book, and his experience is a similar one of emotional development. The theme lies in the breaking of caste lines by upheaval of civil conflict and in the essential kinship of man, however he may betray or deny it by cruelty or passion. There is dignity and beauty all through the book; a restraint that invests its essential drama with power and reality. A similar tone prevails in *Action at Aquila*, Hervey Allen's novel of Sheridan's Shenandoah Valley campaign in the last year of the war.

Restricted though it is in locale, the novel is not sectional, but rather a synthesis of war itself, in its tragedy, its devastation, baseness, and nobility, and also in the lure and challenge of its immediate excitement and tension. Constructionally and emotionally its relationship to *Anthony Adverse* is evident, in color and minutiae of pictorial backgrounds, in vigor of dramatic exposition, in flavor of the "grand style," insistence on the obvious, two-dimensional character portrayal, pervasive philosophic communings, and old-fashioned sentimentality. Presented as reminiscence, this is essentially an "overview" of the war, with fairness and sympathy for both sides, yet with realization that dissolution of the Union meant disintegration of the nation: "wars, endless Gettysburgs, implacable angers and growing hatreds, reprisals for generations to come." This realization, smothered under the Old South tradition and the "economic forces" doctrine, so dominant today, gives continuing value to Hervey Allen's tale; but there is need of a further rendering of the Union cause in fiction that will revitalize its ideals and reinforce its basic principles.

Outside ordinary categories stands *The Wave*, Evelyn Scott's unique contribution to Civil War history in modern fiction. Impressive in creative energy and dramatic intensity, this is hardly a novel; but rather, as the subtitle states, "narratives of the Civil War." It consists of a sequence of poignant or tragic or dramatic glimpses of human beings in some crisis of mind or body involved in the process of the war, presented in seventy-two separate scenes, assembled in twenty groups. Sometimes, instead of scenes, there are extracts from letters, a pro-slavery sermon, paragraphs from Northern or Southern or English newspapers, or excerpts from army orders; some scenes are merest glimpses, some full-fledged short stories. As in the opening scene we hear the first shot fired on Sumter, so in the final one we watch the victory parade of the Union troops in Washington. In the course of the sequence we glimpse bits of the whole terrain of conflict, and have flashlights on famous figures on both sides; we pass through battlefields, naval engagements, camps, prisons, cities, countrysides, and distant villages, in the North and in the South, where war's echoes carry their vibrations of grief or drama.

Hundreds of characters appear in some sudden grip of circumstance, their individual tragedies submerged in the whole great cataclysm. For Evelyn Scott's conception is of the Civil War as a gigantic wave, rising and dashing itself on the shore of time, on which human particles are carried to and fro without individual volition, each appearing for a moment before the observer's eyes, then disappearing without trace. She seeks to register the effects of war on human beings, not by objective presentation, but through the stream-of-consciousness: that endeavor of the novelist to enter into the individual human mind and seize and convey the unuttered emotions, the conflicting sensations, of the inaccessible ego. These intimate experiences, glimpsed in fleeting succession, are set forth with intense emotional subjectivity in the thoughts, the sensory responses, of the human beings undergoing them; they are also invested with tense and vivid realism of detail in the rendering of objects and environment. Original and powerful as experimental literary art, *The Wave* fails of success as a novel: too unwieldy in content, too disintegrated in method, sustained interest wanes and monotony supervenes; it remains a panorama, not a unified creation. The stream-of-consciousness surging swiftly through so many different minds leaves the reader benumbed; these figures borne so suddenly to the surface of our attention disappear as suddenly and are forgotten in the swift succession of others.

Two other unusual methods of treatment are of recent development: one, application of a fictional coating to work of specialized research; the other, simulation of a personal record by an actual historical figure. Philip Van Doren Stern, in *The Man Who Killed Lincoln*, presents an elaborate study of Lincoln's assassination and its pivotal figure, John Wilkes Booth, based on research in government archives and on zealous personal investigations and conveyed as a vivid episodic narrative centering on dramatic character interpretation; with an "afterword" that records sources used and tells how much of the text is strictly factual. Closely related to this—concerned with the imputation that Lincoln's secretary of state was a chief conspirator in the assassination plot—is *"Mr. Secretary,"* in which Ben Ames Williams, Jr., has devised an autobiography of Edwin M. Stanton, assumed to be written in the summer of 1869, which reveals his career as one of sinister machination inspired by egocentric passion for power. Both these novels link directly with the historical work of Otto Eisenschiml (*Why Was Lincoln Murdered?*), who by inference and circumstantial evidence seeks to establish Stanton's complicity in the assassination. Each carries to a hardly defensible extreme the use of ingenious invention and imaginative character interpretation to command acceptance of a "fixed idea" unproven by history's record. Both receive illumination as to fact and enrichment of "atmosphere" from Margaret Leech's later brilliant historical study, *Reveille in Washington, 1860–1865.*

This survey has touched only a few broad groups in the immense, expanding body of American historical fiction that more than any other influence is bringing the American past to contemporary realization. It may, however, indicate the wealth of historical material drawn upon, make clear some of the intentions and methods that shape the novelist's fashioning of that material, and by inviting attention to characteristics and qualities of a few individual novels enlarge appreciation of values that exist in many others also. It has, however, been limited to a single country, and it has opened only a short, restricted vista in the world perspectives of history in fiction.

In its full range the historical novel makes every country and every age its tributary. Masters of English and European fiction have laid its foundations and molded its development. The work of even minor present-day writers, constantly improving in historical veracity and flexibility of technique, has freshness and energy in bringing to light obscure materials and emphasizing aspects of the past that take on special significance for our own time. What this fiction can do in strengthening and vitalizing individual background knowledge of history is not sufficiently realized. For almost every country native novelists have used their art to weave from the fibers of their country's past a tapestry of national experience that imbues with life, color, and immediacy historic traditions, events, crises, famous figures, the conditions of living of men and women through earlier generations. Nearly every age and epoch finds representation and interpretation in this form of fiction. The ancient world—Crete, Egypt, Asia, Greece, Rome in power and decay—has been evoked in brilliant, pictorial realism by a remarkable group of modern novelists: Gudmundsson, Couperus, Mann, Mitchison, Graves, Feuchtwanger, and many others. The medieval world, the world of the Renaissance, the far-expanding horizons of the Western Hemisphere, the opening vistas of our own age, receive similar, more widely radiating illumination. The great panorama of history in fiction sweeps down through more than 3,000 years of man's recorded progress through time.

VII. VISTAS IN EUROPEAN FICTION

*. . . life showing now its natural, now its cultural
face, past turning to present, present pointing back to
past, both preluding future and with her dim foreshadowings already full.*—THOMAS MANN: *The Beloved
Returns*

TIDEWAYS of English and American fiction run their course
in the great sea of world literature. Their channels have been
widened by inflowing currents from all the countries of Europe.
For the art of the novel is a universal art, and the influences that
have helped to shape its contemporary development are impregnated
in the cultural backgrounds of our civilization. Every intelligent
modern reader should have not only some sense of familiarity with
great works of European fiction that, like *Les Misérables, Crime and
Punishment, War and Peace,* have long been part of the common
heritage, but also some realization of the vistas of human experience
and national transition that are opened in contemporary novels by
foreign writers. During the last three decades such novels in ever-
increasing numbers and diversity have been brought to the American reading public in good English translations. Many have taken
their place on our best-seller lists, evidence of the steady improvement in reading taste, the growing awareness of world relationships,
in process in the United States. All have their values as materials of
information and stimulus to thought. They visualize the panorama
of the world's life, deepen familiarity with history and with national, social, and political backgrounds, enlarge narrow horizons of
experience, instill wider sympathy and clearer understanding for
the fateful struggle of free nations against subjection that has locked
the world in conflict. They reduce provincialism and develop ap-

preciation of literary art. They are inseparable from all that is best in the literature of our day.

In its separate national development since the first World War world fiction has followed curiously parallel lines. Influences that have been already traced as shaping the growth of present-day English and American fiction have left similar, often more powerful, impress on the work of continental novelists. There are the same phases of emotional or intellectual or philosophic response to the weakening of religious certitudes, to the changing status of woman, to the dominance of science, to social unrest, to industrialism, to the clash of political doctrines and the recrudescence of world conflict. The wave of postwar disillusion and despair, rising to pacifist intensities, finding expression in revolt against the established order and in contempt for traditional loyalties, that swept alike through the literature of Europe, of England, and of America in the twenties and thirties, manifests the universality of the experience that fiction mirrors. There are the same broad type groups: the family novel, the saga, the biographic novel enlist the art of European as of English novelists; regional, proletarian, and historical fiction flourishes in every national literature. Through foreign fiction run ideas that are seeds of tomorrow, forces that later rise to contort or enlarge or crush the common life. Underlying the similarities of form or theme or response to the time spirit are inexhaustible diversities established by nationality, by environment, by history, by the individual life orbit of a people.

The cycle of world catastrophe sweeping on its course since 1940 gives deeper, more poignant, significance to this foreign fiction. Most of the countries of Europe lie crushed or shackled, their literature suspended, their true national life mirrored only in their earlier fiction, before German aggression had demolished independent contours and choked at its springs the pristine flow of expression. In the European novels of the last twenty years these older vistas of living still hold color and reality. Against unchanging natural backgrounds of infinite variety, depicted with intimate knowledge and loving art, their perspectives shift from the historic past to the emerging present. Here is European civilization, in its age-old race roots, its pervading nationalism and rising internationalism, its individual struggles and stabilities, entering into one of those revolutionary periods in the history of the race when forces long accumulating intensify to the explosion point. Conflict, disintegration, the agonies and visions of foredoomed humanity are portents here of things to come. No comprehensive survey or appraisal of this European fiction can be attempted in these pages. But in a short reconnaissance flight it may be possible to note for different countries a few of the contemporary novels of distinctive quality that in their substance record and interpret ways of life now shaken from their foundations, and in their spirit and method chart the intellectual climate of the modern world. From its starting point over the Netherlands, this flight ranges south and west, then circles eastward and northward and west again.

Holland's solid Old World structure of family life, cemented in patriarchal tradition, and its conventional, self-limiting upper middle-class society, have been given enduring record and analysis in Louis Couperus's sequence-novels of the Hague, *The Book of the Small Souls*. Like Mann's *Buddenbrooks* and Galsworthy's *Forsyte Saga*, this is one of the memorable family chronicles that set their pattern in modern fiction at the opening of the twentieth century. Where Galsworthy studies character and temperament on a larger scale and in more varied range, Couperus is primarily the psychological analyst, probing with keen, delicate precision into conflicting strains of heredity, nerve centers of temperament, and abnormalities latent in the inner self. The four *Small Souls* novels picture social life in Holland before the first World War, within the confines of a little bureaucratic society, where gossip, convention, and social precedence seem to be the only things people live by. Through the successive volumes move four generations of the Van Lowe family, clustered about ancient Mama van Lowe, widow of a former governor-general of Java, who lives alone in her mansion at the Hague and draws her family about her in reunion every Sunday night. A large family, with many connections in official circles, its chronicle, unfolding through the years, reveals sinister forces of heredity and attrition that sap the vitality of the stock and induce decay. Mainsprings of action are laid bare, causes that underlie effects are disclosed. These middle-aged people, apparently alien to romance or melodrama, are ordinary enough at first sight; but the novelist's art transmits the tumults that seethe within each breast: hopes, fears, despairs, anxieties, secret passions, all concealed under the conventional everyday exterior. Dutch life and society are shown here, not historically, in movement and dramatic incident, but statically, as of a nation retired from business, living intent on its own comfort, offering little outlet for originative genius, governed by habit, routine, and mechanical precision. Melting into this interpretation is the background of Dutch landscape, with its rain, mist, cloud, flatness, fitful sunshine, gleams of spring, and mild benignities of summer, yielding again to cloud and rain.

Others of Couperus's many novels have similar setting, and his fame among English readers rests on these psychological and emotional studies of modern life and character. But his art sent its radiations far beyond his own time and country. For his two ruling passions were love of the sun and love of the classics; and the bulk of his work is in a symbolical, historical, or mythological vein, glowing in color and imagery, and reflecting the culture of the ancient world. Of his twenty-odd novels that represent this phase, only three have been translated into English: *The Tour*, lightly ironic, translucent study of Egypt in its later years of decay under Roman rule; *The Comedians*, a fuller bodied, more richly hued tale of decadent Rome in the days of Martial, Juvenal, Tacitus, and the short and savage reign of Domitian; and *Arrogance, the Conquests of Xerxes*, brilliant, pictorial narrative that dramatizes on heroic scale with opulent color and poetic ardor the Greek victory over Persia's world-mastering power, conveys the struggle of two cultures, the European and the oriental, for survival and supremacy, and is infused with the spirit and detail of Æschylus's drama, "The Persians."

Of Mme Jo van Ammers-Küller's novels, some half dozen have

appeared in English translation. Widely popular in Holland for many years, their subject range is varied, running from phases of Dutch history (*The House of Tavelinck*) to modern problems of social change. Her interest turns strongly to problems of youth, especially as they affect women, and to the life of the theater. Her work is competent, solid, practical, rather than creative: a faithful, vigorous stereotype rendering of character and experience. *The Rebel Generation* has distinctive value, in its historical recording of the change in woman's status during the last century and in the authenticity of its background of old-established Dutch life. Here the emancipation of women is traced in the history of a single family through five generations, from 1840 to 1923. The scene is almost unbrokenly in Leyden; and that ancient city takes on palpable actuality, with its narrow streets, its tall, somber houses, its atmosphere of solidity, respectability, and rigor. From the patriarchal household of the Cornevelts—four daughters and four sons, ruled by a tyrannical father in rigid autocracy and puritanical religious domination —issue the several life stories that carry through the years their succession of individual experiences, each linked to the one before it. The theme is closely held throughout, and the novel with its contrasts of old and new in graphic sequence, is valid presentment of social history.

More complex and subtle are the social problems posed in Willy Corsari's novel, *Man without Uniform*. Thoughtful in philosophic quality, psychologically cogent in character portrayal, moving as it conveys intensities of the battle of modern science against cancer, this is the story, from childhood to death, of a man whose life is dedicated to the problem of fighting cancer and who sacrifices to his research all normal human relationships. Linked to this central theme is that of the physician's personal philosophy, rooted in refusal to become a "man in uniform" and accept the regimentation of orthodox religious belief and established ethical codes; his own inner conviction is that to put an end to life in cases of incurable suffering should be, logically, compassionately, a part of the physician's duty. Inability honestly to live up to this conviction shadows his conscience through many years of fine professional service, and the shadow yields only to a deepened realization that life, however painful, is better than death. Childhood in a small Dutch village, later life in Amsterdam and Leyden, the inescapable drama of a doctor's daily experience, hopes and joys and tragedies of many different human beings, philosophic and religious discussions, and the slow but undefeatable advance of medical science toward control of disease—such is the essential substance of a novel that should hold continuing value.

In these novels backgrounds are chiefly of city life among upper middle-class people, with a few fleeting glimpses of the countryside. Rustic village and peasant living in southern Holland—a region once part of the ancient Duchy of Brabant, strongly Catholic, more akin to Belgian Flanders than to the Protestant north—is mirrored in the novel *Dutch Vet*, by Anton Roothaert, that centers on the life and work of a veterinarian, honest, simple, deeply humane, holding to the best standards of his calling amid ignorance, bigotry, superstition, and petty malice. Solid reality, robust earthiness, unfaltering detail of veterinary practice in all its clinical aspects are here, perhaps, too unglossed for the squeamish; but in the story of Dr. John Vlimmen's patient integrity under unjust accusations, in the portrayal of peasant character, with its many variations, from religious fanaticism to noisy mirth, from cruelty to kindness, from double dealing to simple-mindedness, there is dramatic appeal and a full-flavored authenticity of place and people.

In France the very long analytical chronicle of lives and times, seeded from the family saga novel, dominates contemporary fiction. Romain Rolland gave the impetus with *Jean Christophe*, which appeared in successive volumes from 1904 to 1912: life history of a musician of genius, through which flows the rich culture of art and letters and the idealism of purpose to break down mutual French and German antagonism, in hope of the brotherhood of man. Here, said Rolland,

I have written the tragedy of a generation which is nearing its end. I have sought to conceal neither its vices nor its virtues, its profound sadness, its chaotic pride, its heroic efforts, its despondency beneath the overwhelming burden of a superhuman task—the reconstruction of the world's morality, its aesthetic principles, its faith, the forging of a new humanity.

From this lead, through the later postwar years, French novelists developed the enormous flexible cycle-sequences—the *romans fleuves*, or "river novels," flowing on through time from volume to volume—that in Proust's monumental *Remembrance of Things Past* explored the human elements of a decadent, self-consuming society and brought the art of the novel into a realm of new horizons and different dimensions; that in Romains's *Men of Good Will* dissects the whole social, economic, political, material, and spiritual structure of contemporary France from 1908. The immense chronicles of Roger Martin du Gard and Georges Duhamel are of this nature. In them fiction remains the medium for human history that Balzac perfected, but it becomes more expansive and more absorbent as it assimilates and analyzes the complex elements of the whole social organism in an endeavor to discover whether any pattern, any abiding order, underlies the apparent chaos.

Men of Good Will, in English translation, ran to its ninth volume (eighteenth in the French edition) in 1941, and is still uncompleted, the longest novel in modern literature. It has been defined as an encyclopedic attempt at a psychological biography of twentieth-century France: a characterization that epitomizes its material content, but gives no indication of the creative genius that has breathed upon the myriad lives woven into its complex fabric, of the sustained narrative ability that impels continuous motion and maintains unflagging interest, nor of the intellectual poise that is an integrating force throughout. No other work of imaginative literature has effected such a "breakdown" (in the statistical sense) of the life of a people and an epoch into its components of trade, commerce, labor, politics, professions, talents, its inherent forces of self-interest, vice, idealism, intellectual temper, self-delusion, self-sacrifice, greed, apathy, and violence. From the opening, on the morning of October 6, 1908, to the postarmistice days ten years later, these volumes trace the multiplicities and diversities of individual experience that constitute the collective life of a great city. They not only recreate Paris as the core of a France shadowed by the presage and staggering under the beleaguerment of war but also disclose the social and political world of prewar Europe, seamed with old battle scars, channeled by rising creative and destructive forces, inexorably moving toward catastrophe.

Neither Georges Duhamel nor Roger Martin du Gard approach in scope the work of Romains. Their immense novel-cycles, shorter and much less encyclopedic than *Men of Good Will*, are concentrated on a single family history, although that history is seen as part of the time-flow of its own era, which is the era of the first World War. Duhamel's "Pasquier" cycle has, perhaps, the closest kinship to Romains. In English translation, the first three novels of the sequence were published separately (*Papa Pasquier, The Fortunes of the Pasquiers*) then, in 1938, these, with the two consecutive novels were included in a single massive volume under the collective title *The Pasquier Chronicles*. Two years later a similar volume, *Cecile Pasquier*, brought together the three succeeding volumes, thus carrying the work in English through the eighth volume of the French edition. The Pasquiers are a bourgeois family of peasant origin. They represent the Old World concept of the family as a limited hierarchy, commanding united allegiance, that has long dominated French life; and it is the struggle to maintain that concept against realities of individual behavior, pretensions, ambitions, and dissensions that runs in tragi-comedy through the earlier sections of this saga of family fortunes. The characters are vivid and alive, each individual personality tinged in some degree with the family temperament. Papa Pasquier, a Gallic Micawber of fantastic business schemes, illicit liaisons, and inexhaustible exuberance, is at first the central figure. Then interest shifts to the younger generation: Laurent, earnest biologist; Joseph, unscrupulous financier; Cecile, great pianist; Suzanne, actress; and the fluent, dramatic narrative that carries their experiences to July, 1914, conveys also thoughtful, critical presentment of forces of disillusion and disintegration in operation in twentieth-century France.

Roger Martin du Gard, in *The World of the Thibaults*, combines family saga with a far-reaching study of international influences culminating in the first World War; extending beyond the Pasquier cycle, it carries to the close of the war. Tolstoy's *War and Peace* was its inspiration; twenty years were given to its writing, and its eleven volumes appeared at intervals in France from 1922 to 1940. In English translation the collective title links the two massive volumes (*The Thibaults, Summer 1914*) that, closely integrated as they are in substance of family history, yet have an essential separateness in subject and treatment. The Thibaults are an upper-middle-class family, ruled in rigid, somber Catholicism by a father, powerful, wealthy, militant in faith, possessed by blind, inexhaustible egotism. The older son is a doctor, the younger a schoolboy, and it is a school friendship that brings the Thibault family into complex life relationship with the tolerant and kindly household of the Protestant Fontanins. Contrasting personalities unfold in absorbing reality during the years of adolescence, youth, and maturity that carry the two brothers into their own paths of destiny and plumb the depths of emotional experience. The recurrent note of escape and revolt that runs through much of the experience recorded conveys the underlying theme of the whole work. *Summer 1914* carries this theme to ultimate expression. Here the family is of minor importance; the coming of the war is the advancing tragedy, sweeping both brothers into its cataclysm: the younger, Jacques, passionate international socialist, staking his life in a last desperate gesture for peace; the elder, Antoine, physician and rationalist, accepting death in his country's cause.

Humanitarian reaction to war, internationalist pacifism, and social revolutionary ardor are dominant points of view in these novels, as in much of the European fiction of the years between the two world wars. This fiction is essentially literature of peace, instilling so deep a sense of the horror and futility of war, emphasizing so strongly the failures and corruption of the society in which humanity is entangled, that in sincere idealism it has fostered confusion and defeatism of spirit, unaware of or unable to check the advancing avalanche of world conquest. The war years from 1914 to 1918, lived through in a little Belgian village of the Meuse valley, are reflected with simple realism in the autobiographical chronicle, *Jean Clarambaux*, by the Belgian novelist, Jean Tousseul (Oliver Degie), whose symbolic nom de plume conveys the brooding sentimentalism that tinges this long life story. Aspects of stark horror are thrust upon us by Maxence van der Meersch in his novel *Invasion*, which pictures the years of German occupation in his native region in French Flanders. Drawn from childhood experience and firsthand knowledge, there is here a curious objectivity, ironic and rationalizing, in studying the effects of repression, hunger, hate, greed, fear, and jealousy on human beings in the iron grip of war. In the novels of André Malraux there are no French backgrounds, but the spirit of social revolution that runs in deepening current through the present world struggle finds memorable expression. *Man's Hope* is the epic of the Loyalist cause in the Spanish civil war, written on the scene of action, describing real persons, and recording actual events. The underlying theme is indicated in the title: in revolutions the power that moves to endurance, to courage, to ever-renewing effort, is "man's hope" for fulfillment of his vision of freedom and fuller brotherhood of living; "men who have joined together in a common cause, have, like men whom love unites, access to regions they could never reach of themselves." *Man's Fate*, four years earlier, visualized terrorist activities of the Chinese revolution, as they focused on the Shanghai insurrection of 1927, in bloodshed, sadism, betrayal, agony, and stoic self-dedication; and *Days of Wrath* compressed to utmost intensity the danger and terrors encountered in "underground" communist activities against Nazi rule in Germany.

Varied vistas of home life open in many family novels not of the saga type. The ancient fabric of French middle-class rural life, deep-rooted in tradition, held close to the soil, furrowed by old folkways, has been recreated in François Mauriac's readings of human nature in the clutch of consuming or frustrate passions or tragic involutions of relationship. *The Family* brings together two remarkable short novels, one (originally, *The Kiss of the Leper*) of an "arranged" marriage, in which instinctive physical repulsion is sublimated by religious faith to compassionate devotion; the other (*Genetrix*) of dominating jealous mother love, age-old fetish of son worship, standing between husband and wife in blighting possessiveness. *Vipers' Tangle* plumbs fierce intensities of family selfishness and hatred, allayed only by the solvent of religious faith. A different mother love, which is at once passionate devotion, ever-watchful protective diplomacy, and delight in sharing the imaginings and joys of child-hood, is the central theme of Simonne Ratel's *The House in the Hills*, with its Burgundian background of gorse-covered heath, pine woods, and rye fields, and its involved problem of keeping from collapse a marriage built on dangerous foundations and undermined by jealous egotism. Later, in *The Green Grape*, the Durras family are carried from the Burgundian uplands to Paris, through adolescence and young maturity, in a skillful, penetrating novel that telescopes the experience and psychology of that war generation of French youth. Roger Vercel, in *Tides of Mont St.-Michel*, touches with perceptive character depiction the disintegration of a marriage under stress of "depression" conditions; but the continuing value of his novel has little relation to this minor human drama: its significance lies in its presentment of France's precious monument of the Middle Ages. Essentially it is a study of Mont St.-Michel, its setting, its architecture, its beauty, the little community about it, and the life of those within its walls. In loving detail and clear perspective it brings to immediate reality the great structure that in spiritual and historical tradition goes back through Christian ages to Roman rule and earlier prehistoric worship, transmits the spell it holds for those who come under its influence, evokes the sea, the day-by-day cycle of life about it, and reveals the compensation offered those who serve it, in the merging of the personal into eternal beauty.

Lights and shadows of everyday life in a little provincial town and on an impoverished farm are reflected in Geneviève Fauconnier's *Claude*. Undoubtedly in large measure autobiographical, there is psychological subtlety and iridescent transmission of scene and character in this delicate, lucent chronicle, conveyed as memories of the past drawn from old memorandum books, running from idyllic prewar years of childhood, through war and postwar years of muted endurance and unending labor, of loyalty and devotion to husband and children in a marriage where love finds no kindling spark and poverty casts a lengthening shadow. Closely linked in period is *Born of Woman*, Raymonde Vincent's pellucid record of rural life in her beloved province of Berry. This is one of those regional pastorals in which French literary art excels: fragrant with the breath of earth, clear in outline, gravely yet delicately reflective of common experience, and infused with a spiritual sensibility that manages to escape becoming either pietistic or sentimental. George Sand's simple tales, Louis Hémon's *Maria Chapdelaine*, witness to the perfection this genre can attain. The remote region portrayed is a slow-moving world of its own, shut away from turmoil and tension of the world without, held in unbroken Catholic tradition, and giving little evidence that the fifteenth century has ended, except that there are no peasants, only farmers, farmworkers, and villagers, who are descendants of peasants, keeping to the ancestral patterns of living.

There is similar remoteness in the setting of *The Wanderer*, Alain Fournier's many-faceted evocation of youth and its yearnings, first published in France in 1913, which has taken a permanent place in continental literature. On the surface this is a simple story of rural schoolboy life, strongly autobiographical, holding the scenes and stamp of Fournier's own childhood in the lonely region of the Sologne, country of marshes and woods, of scattered hamlets and scanty population, where the life of Old France lingers, untinged by hues of modernity. But in its inner nature the book is not realistic; it is essentially an allegory of the pursuit of happiness and a symbolizing of the traits and qualities of adolescence, its substance of reality penetrated by the mystical and the imaginative. Intensities of Catholic mysticism infuse *The Diary of a Country Priest*, in which Georges Bernanos records the ignorance, pettiness, and apathy of a little country parish in northern France; the strivings, sufferings, and victory in defeat of a young priest who seeks to put his religious ideals into practice there. A pantheistic mysticism of earth worship permeates the lush, sensuous naturalism of Jean Giono in his prose epics of exuberant nature and elemental man in the mountain plateaus, forests, and river-scarred valleys of the Basses-Alpes country. *The Song of the World, Harvest, The Joy of Man's Desiring,* all are outpourings of sensory experience, of primitive emotions, of tragedies, melodramas, and idyls in which the elements, the earth, the animals and man are common participants. More sensitive is the semi-symbolism tinged with legendry of *The Last Hunt*, in which Maurice Genevoix evokes a great French forest, relic of the primitive forest world, where stags and man, the hunted and the hunters, carry on their primitive drama of flight and pursuit; different in underlying theme, more subtle in artistry, there is here fundamental relationship to Felix Salten's forest idyl, *Bambi*.

Spain's panorama as it unfolds in the novels of Vicente Blasco Ibáñez has become in part familiar to American readers. At least ten of his novels of national background have been translated into English, and no other contemporary Spanish novelist has made so great a reputation abroad. In his own country, however, his work is less highly regarded; he is looked upon as an inferior artist, essentially a sensationalist and propagandist, whose transatlantic fame does not reflect his actual rank in Spanish literature. In a measure this is true. Blasco Ibáñez's art is that of the mural painter, covering a prepared surface with sweeping, strongly pigmented brush strokes; applying glowing colors to broadly conceived, powerful designs, impressive in variety and scope. Primarily he was a national painter, although his most famous novel, *The Four Horsemen of the Apocalypse*, has no Spanish setting and won its world-wide popularity as the most vivid early picture of the devastation, horror, and suffering of the first World War, seen from the French front. Most of his novels— certainly all those of the highest merit—are set against a background of Spain and infused with the purpose to reveal evils that he saw sapping Spanish vitality and national development. Their range is from the violent clash and color of the days of Hannibal, when Iberia was a Roman and Carthaginian colony, to city, village, and country life of war and prewar years. Of his many novels, the finest belong to his earlier work: *The Shadow of the Cathedral, Blood and Sand, Sonnica,* and *The Cabin*—all part of the panorama of Spain's national life. His masterpiece, *The Cabin,* shows the curse of ignorance and feud resting on rural Spain. Stark and relentless, classic in brevity and simplicity, it centers on peasant hatred rooted in the impulse of vengeance, striking down the innocent, unmoved and pitiless. *The Shadow of the Cathedral* conveys its theme in its title: the shadow of a fettering ecclesiasticism that stifles thought and arrests development. Here the great cathedral of Toledo is described in elaborate detail, all the inmates sheltered in its nooks and eaves, all its ritual and ceremonial, its servants, parasites, and hangers-on, a community living in the heart of the Middle Ages as the nineteenth century closes. In *Sonnica* garish barbaric scenes visualize the struggle of Carthaginian and Roman for the ancient city of Saguntum. *The Dead Command* reflects in softer tints the Balearic Islands; *The Mayflower* gives vivid rendering of the toils, loves, and dangers of the Valencia fisher folk; and *The Mob* pictures the flotsam of the Madrid slums. Through nearly all his work runs the revolutionary crusading spirit of opposition to monarchical rule and clerical domination, groundswell of the forces that later converged to free Spain from the stronghold of the past and that after brief triumph and high promise were swept in long death struggle to ruthless suppression.

Of Pio Baroja y Nessi's novels, the three-volume sequence (*The Quest, Weeds, Red Dawn*), published under the collective title *The Struggle for Life,* chronicles with steel-cut ironic realism the lawless, poverty-stricken life of those submerged in the great cities in the prewar industrial age. A thread of plot follows the fortunes of Manuel Alcazar, child of Madrid slums, through vagabondage, privation, vice, and harsh vicissitudes to relative assurance of respectable livelihood in a world where anarchy is the only logical forecast for the future. Tragedy, irony, and a strain of sardonic humor run through the half-dozen novels that have brought to American readers Baroja's detached, disillusioned, unsparing presentment of life among outcasts and adventurers, of social and political debasement, of the seamy side of medical education and medical practice, set against metropolitan and provincial backgrounds.

Tiger Juan is a novel of many-faceted brilliancy, by Ramón Perez de Ayala, poet, novelist, and philosopher, a foremost figure in the "new world" of republican Spain that perished in the kindling flames of world conflict. Originally published in two separate volumes, which were merged in the English translation, it is set in the imaginary town of Pilares, scene of most of Ayala's novels—an ancient provincial community, ringed by the mountain slopes and valleys of the Asturias region in northern Spain and dominated by its great cathedral. From the motley community that centers in its marketplace, and especially from the grotesque figure of "Tiger Juan" in his stall, sheltered by three umbrellas, carrying on his trade as letter-writer, blood-letter and money-lender, is developed a universal picture of Spanish society and an illuminating study of Spanish character, in its traditional compulsions, its absorption in philosophic and moral abstractions, its violences and simplicities. At once realistic, idealistic, panoramic, and symbolic, the novel is also remarkable in craftsmanship, for it is modeled upon the principles of a musical composition, broken not into chapters but into divisions according to tempo (adagio, presto, presto, adagio, coda), and it moves in the changing rhythms of its harmonic structure.

In the shadows of human misery and subtle social decay that rest upon these novels; in their spirit of intellectual revolt, crystallized into irony and pessimism in Baroja, into idealism of tolerance and liberty in Ayala, are portents of Spain's tragedy. Ramón Sender's *Seven Red Sundays* has significance as more direct prevision of that tragedy. The story is set in republican Spain before the fascist uprising, and pictures a revolutionary outbreak in Madrid, directed against government tolerance, launched as a general strike by anarchist, syndicalist, and communist workers, running through a week of violence, and closing with defeat of the revolutionaries, but with continuing bitterness and distrust. Sender (an exile since the fascist victory) is one of the most recent Spanish novelists to be translated into English. His novel *A Man's Place*, brought out in 1940 in a translation by Oliver La Farge, is a prewar tale set in a Spanish village in old Aragon, concerned with a peasant tragedy of judicial injustice and its effect on many lives; graphic in background, with sardonic social and philosophic implications underlying its dramatic course.

Italian life in traditional pattern is reflected in Antonio Fogazzaro's novels with a sincerity unobscured after half a century. His famous sequence-novels of the Maironi family (*The Patriot, The Sinner, The Saint, Leila*) opening in the 1840's, illuminate Italy's historic struggle for political liberty and national unity and give expression to the ideals of religious purity and freedom through which Fogazzaro sought to broaden and exalt the Catholic Church. Built on solid substance of everyday living, they depict different elements of Italian society—country people, small tradesmen, gentry, ecclesiastical and professional circles—with simplicity, humor and understanding, and always with a deep feeling for truth and justice. Although most of Fogazzaro's novels were written in the late nineteenth century, they still have social and religious significance and warm human appeal. Beside Fogazzaro, as one of the old masters in Italian fiction, stands the Sicilian, Giovanni Verga. His *Mastro-Don Gesualdo*, originally published in 1888 and brought out in English translation by D. H. Lawrence in 1923, is a chronicle of a peasant rising by his own powerful abilities to great wealth and importance and of the bitterness and hollowness of his seeming triumph. Set in Verga's southern Sicily, almost certainly in his own childhood village, it opens about 1820 and deals with the generation before his own. Its people are living creations from memories and associations that were part of his life. The title gives the theme; for "Mastro" is the address used to a workman or man of lower class, "Don" is the address used for a gentleman. Gesualdo, the hardworking farmer and land toiler, is Mastro; when he acquires wealth, when he becomes allied to the nobility by his daughter's marriage, he becomes Don. But he is always Mastro-Don, of neither one caste nor the other; an anomaly, to be envied and made use of by his old humble associates, to be equally made use of and despised by his pretentious, scornful son-in-law and all his connections. The novel has depth, power, enduring human emotions, and a rich peasant humor; there is much that is tragic, but it is part of the inevitability of life. More rounded, more complete, for all its narrow setting, than Fogazzaro's varied canvas, it offers a delineation of Italian life and character that will remain unfading through time.

Sophistication and originality combine to win for *The Confessions of Zeno* distinction as the most brilliant modern Italian novel. Italo Svevo (Ettore Schmitz) wrote it under the influence of James Joyce, and from his friend Svevo, Joyce drew some of the strains fused in the personality of Leopold Bloom. Supremely ironical, witty, and thoroughly human is this presentation of the neurasthenic, absurd, and eccentric Zeno. Zeno, in fact, portrays himself, for the book is his own elaborate, introspective account of his life, written at the request and for the information of his psychoanalyst. He is an accomplished hypochondriac, a master of indecision, continuously introspective, weighing and balancing every inner impulse and outward action; but he is a lovable creature, for all his absurdity. He captures our sympathy, and while we laugh, the laughter is as much at ourselves as at Zeno, for he is, in essence, the distillation of elements that exist in every individual ego. Zeno chronicles his autobiography in six divisions, setting forth his experiences, objective and subjective; he rationalizes all his emotions, tracing so far as he can root impulses and eddying aftereffects. Such a record might well prove tiresome, but it is so witty, so full of worldly wisdom, and so essentially true to human nature that it holds continuous fascination and amusement.

Italy during the first World War and postwar years, fallow to the seeds of fascism, is background of *Rubè*, Guiseppe Antonio Borgese's somber analytical study of Italian youth in progressive character disintegration and instability. The story of Filippo Rubè, the young lawyer who shortly before the war descends upon Rome from the provinces to make his fortune, who plunges vaingloriously into war, only to recoil, irresolute and self-tormenting, in fear of death, whose vacillation and egotism carry him ever deeper into frantic futilities, is an epitome of war neurosis and a presage of the rise of dictatorship from defeatism, poverty, and unemployment. Borgese, self-exiled from Italy since Mussolini's rise to power, enlarged the theme that underlies the novel in his powerful interpretative study, *Goliath: the March of Fascism.*

If *Rubè* holds presage of fascism, Ignazio Silone's two novels, *Fontemara* and *Bread and Wine*, turn presage into reality. Here is Italy under fascist regimentation and collectivization. *Fontemara* is a burning, bitter chronicle of a little hill village of farmers in northern Italy, taxed, regimented, cheated, oppressed, and crushed into extermination by the combination of government repression, money-lenders' extortion, and the greed, guile, and ruthlessness of rich promoters and exploiters. It is a harsh book, burning with an intense inner fire of rage, unmitigated in tragedy, with fierce and terrible episodes; savagely partisan, but itself of the substance of the soil, akin to the primitive, stark, peasant life it pictures. Silone (like Borgese, long an exile) sees fascism like a miasmic fog enveloping the whole land, but thickest and most deadly over the poor and the small farmers, who are really day laborers. *Bread and Wine*, published three years later, is less passionate and more philosophical in its nature, deeper and more far-reaching in its implications—a powerful and noble novel of a people helpless in the grip of a mechanical bureaucracy, for whom release can come only through a revolution inspired by dedication and self-sacrifice. Silone's concern is still primarily with the peasants, in their age-old bondage to superstition and ignorance, their unchanging toil and unending poverty. His novel centers on the experiences of a young socialist who after fifteen years of exile returns secretly to his own land on the eve of Italy's war upon Ethiopia. Disguised in the habit of a priest, he wanders about the country to observe conditions and to work "underground" for revolution; only to find his efforts futile, his mission ending in a desperate, tragic escape. Beside him is the companion figure of the wise and kindly liberal priest, his old teacher and friend, who has seen the students he loved become tools or victims of the regime or hunted rebels against it, who seeks in tolerance and kindness to appease the evils of the old order and the new. In the title is conveyed the underlying theme: that a people to live must have the bread of subsistence and the wine of freedom.

German fiction no longer flows freely from Germany to the outside world. Since the mid-1930's the modern writers who made Germany's rich national culture have, in desperate exodus, their books prohibited, destroyed, or confiscated, become exiles or refugees from their homeland. Some have perished, victims to Hitler rule; others are scattered in the Americas and countries still undominated by Germany. Most of them have found their way to the United States; and in the United States, chiefly, their books are written, translated into English, and published. This is the exodus of an entire literary generation, the uprooting and transplanting of a national literature. What the effect of this extirpation of creative genius must be upon the country of its origin, how deep an enrichment it will bring to the new soil in which it must take root, only time's perspectives can disclose. But the extent and implications of this exodus are evident in even a partial summary of German novelists in exile, whose work, in some measure, is known to American readers through English translations. Among them are Thomas Mann, his son Klaus, his daughter Erika, and his brother Heinrich. Here are Erich Maria Remarque and Arnold Zweig, whose great novels of the first World War penetrated beyond the tragedy of man in war to the human values of modern civilization; Bruno Frank (*The Persians Are Coming, Days of the King*), brilliant weaver of history in fiction; Leonhard Frank (*Carl and Anna, Brother and Sister*), thoughtful recorder of emotional psychology; Franz Werfel (*Class Reunion, Embezzled Heaven*), sensitive anatomist of life and individuality; Hermann Broch (*The Sleepwalkers*), philosophic analyst of German character and experience in the thirty years from 1888 to 1918; Lion

Feuchtwanger (*Power, Success, Paris Gazette*), brilliant, exhaustive social historian of past and present; Oskar Maria Graf (*The Life of My Mother*); Fritz von Unruh (*Way of Sacrifice*); Alfred Neumann (*The Devil*); Hermann Kesten (*The Children of Guernica*); Walter Schoenstedt (*In Praise of Life*); Franz Hoellering (*The Defenders*); Arthur Koestler (*The Gladiators, Darkness at Noon*); Hans Habe (*Sixteen Days*). Not all these writers are of German nationality, but all are representative of the contemporary German fiction that had perfected subtle, powerful forms of expression and had developed extraordinary sensitivity to the advancing European tragedy.

No commentary is practicable here upon these and other German novels that hold sociological and historical values and poignant human significance for American readers, as they build up the background and register the time-flow of today's world conflict. But the novels of Thomas Mann must have brief consideration. They have the universality that is the stamp of world literature; the vistas they open are of the forces, social, intellectual, and spiritual that play upon humanity. *Buddenbrooks*, first published in Berlin in 1901 and brought out in English in 1924, was the novel that set Thomas Mann at twenty-six in the forefront of German writers. More consistently realistic, less philosophical, than his later work, it is an epical study of the degeneration of a North German merchant family through four generations. The Buddenbrooks family of Lübeck is first seen at the height of its prosperity in 1835, under the unfaltering rule of old Johann Buddenbrooks, highminded, inflexible patrician. Then through his son, his grandson, and his great-grandson the process of disintegration is traced, with its sequence of unsound financial operations, loss of confidence, individualism and self-indulgence, weakened physique and intensified emotions, and the final passing of the name Buddenbrooks into oblivion. Almost wholly objective, straightforward in character portrayal, and full of the flavor of the world it pictures, this is the *Forsyte Saga* of nineteenth-century Germany.

The Magic Mountain, twenty-three years later, moves onward in time, deeply inward in spirit. Set in the famous Alpine sanitarium resort of Davos Platz, it is both a study of pathological and psychological relationship of mind and body and a vast intellectual drama of European civilization on the edge of the abyss. Symbolism is fused into its structure, for in this mountain community of diseased bodies, mixed races, baffled ideals, conflicting passions, and intensities of emotion and conviction, there is reflected the diseased political society of prewar Europe, its repressed passions and fevered infections, that at last burst forth in the blood and fire of world war. There is no definite plot: conditions of human life, the kaleidoscope of human nature, make a drama that does not unfold, but rather assumes a protean shape as we gaze upon its different aspects. A work of consummate art and imaginative genius, it overflows with disquisition upon European civilization past and present, upon the influences that formed and dominate the present social system; and it passes from pathological study of the development and effect of tuberculosis to analysis of the psychological impulses that both cause and manifest disease, and thence to metaphysical ponderings upon tangible and intangible elements that make man's universe.

More brilliant in color, more compelling in its pervasive sympathy and understanding, opulent in beauty, and absorbing in dramatic movement is the "Joseph" cycle (*Joseph and His Brothers, Young Joseph, Joseph in Egypt*), still uncompleted, that in revitalization of the Biblical story becomes a timeless epic of humanity, establishing in myth, in legend, and in tradition the structure of man's worship as the manifestation of man's quest for truth. Here the magnificent backgrounds, the outward life and inner nature of Egyptian civilization are an immediate revelation; here, from "the backward and abysm of time," human history emerges in infinite recurrence of primal patterns; here is an integration of man and his universe, serene and confident, where on *The Magic Mountain* were found disintegration, turbulence, and misgiving. The touch of genius rests on all Mann's novels in an impress that has deepened with time. In *The Beloved Returns* there is a many-sided perfection: the recreation of an older Germany, Goethe's Weimar of 1816, in what seems formal fidelity, yet is luminous with humor, subtle in implications we recognize today; the evocation of Goethe in his effect on the lives that touched his, in himself as a human being, in his nature as a genius—a composite living creation infused with irony, tenderness, and wisdom that is at the same time "an allegory of all that genius is and means in all times and all places." Even in the short tale *The Transposed Heads* the fantastic Hindu legend becomes a universal distillation, humorous, sardonic, philosophic, compassionate, of the conflict between mind and body, flesh and spirit.

Poland and Czechoslovakia, crucified and voiceless today, have sent strong currents into the world-stream of fiction. Nationalism was never more brilliantly enshrined for any country than for Poland by Henryk Sienkiewicz in the magnificent trilogy that in the Walter Scott tradition chronicled the nation's historic past in its most picturesque and stirring era. *With Fire and Sword*, first in the sequence, depicts the Russian conflicts of 1648 to 1651, chiefly of the Cossacks against the Polish commonwealth; *The Deluge* follows, with the Swedish invasion of 1655; *Pan Michael* carries through the Turkish invasion of 1672, and the heroic resistance that broke the sweep of oriental conquest. An immense canvas, rich in color, surging with violent adventure, full of vitality and resilience in character depiction, after half a century it lives as one of the great panoramas of national history. In direct succession to Sienkiewicz is Stefan Zeromski, whose torrential epic, *Ashes*, chronicles Poland's part in the Napoleonic wars. Here life in rural Poland under Austrian rule is graphically presented, in the serfdom of the peasants, the domination of the masters, the excitements of hunting, dancing, and feasting, and romantic fervor is focused on a passionate, tragic love story. Then the field enlarges, and in unflagging movement, in word pictures of beauty and horror, are poured out the experiences of two Polish youths who, with the dream of a free Poland inspiring them, fight with Napoleon's armies in Spain and Austria. Beside these epics of Poland's history must stand *The Peasants*, Ladislaw Reymont's epic of Poland's life of the soil. Its four volumes, *Autumn, Winter,*

Spring, Summer, follow the seasons of a single year through a small peasant community in a chronicle of folk life imbued with dramatic ardor and poetic beauty, massive and primitive. Built about the drama of a particular family, it reveals psychology, customs, religion, and superstitions that are the peasant heritage; the hopes, ambitions, and terrors of life itself against the harshness and the tenderness of nature.

Karel Čapek's fiction evokes neither historical nor natural backgrounds of Czechoslovakia. In fiction and in drama the electric current of his imagination plays upon a universal social theme: the dangers that the modern machine-world holds for human life and the human soul. It was his play *R. U. R.* that first gave the word "robot" to the world. *War with the Newts,* his brilliant fantasy-novel, invests with terrifying reality a dispassionate pseudo-factual narrative that records the discovery of a strange variety of newts in Malaysian seas; their breeding into working creatures for man; their increase in numbers and in power, until at last their teeming millions, undermining the continents, involve man in desperate war for his own survival—an absorbing, provocative parable. The human quality of Čapek's art finds expression, and there is a reflection of the Czech countryside in *The First Rescue Party,* in which the experiences of volunteers sent into a mine wrecked by an explosion are reported step by step, in simple, moving precision, by a youth who with his companions shares a task seen, not as heroism, but as common, matter-of-fact "duty."

Contemporary Russia receives revealing illumination from the Russian fiction that opens vistas of a past and a present irrevocably split apart, yet remaining indivisible. A quarter-century has seen the transition from the ancient traditional life of imperial Russia through cataclysmic upheaval and seething welter of revolution to the new-built structure of the socialist soviet state, which has abolished private capitalism and established the principles of communism. Few historians are likely to transmit more vivid realization of the seismic convulsion that submerged the nation's life in chaos and then cast it violently forth in strange new contours than is conveyed by Russian novels that mirror the earlier and the present day.

Tolstoy's *War and Peace* holds the unfading image of the older Russia in the dawning nineteenth century: its massive social structure, its great estates, the life of the soil and of the cities, the premature influence of the French Revolution, and the first fermenting of Russian intellect and idealism into the wine of revolution. Russian fiction through the nineteenth century carries on the panorama of contemporary history in memorable panels of social and racial portrayal. Turgenev expresses and interprets the potencies and impotencies of the Russian temperament and with intuitive perception observes shadowy portents of revolution. Special significance attaches to *A Sportsman's Sketches*, his short character studies of life on the estate of a great landowner, with its many serfs, its feudal authority, its cruelties and indifferences born of absolute power; for this was the delicate, keen instrument that severed the bonds of serfdom for the Russian peasant. Ivan Goncharov's novel, *Oblomov*, with lightness of touch and play of humor as well as penetrative power, renders the inertia that corroded the Russian's mental gifts and potential energies and surrendered control to the efficient, indefatigable German. The picture of childhood on the great Oblomov estate, where masters and dependents alike spend their years "falling asleep in a half dream," has a pervading reality of time and place; and the novel, written in the mid-nineteenth century, takes on later significance as predictive commentary on the collapse of Russia's cultured, intellectual, and leisured classes before the driving force of revolution. Linked to *Oblomov* in evocation of backgrounds of imperial Russia is Ivan Bunin's autobiographical novel, *The Well of Days*, work of one of the famous Russian writers of prewar years, in exile since the revolution, who in 1933 received the Nobel prize. Here again we view the indolent, easygoing existence of a great family estate in the old regime that drifted serenely toward ruin; the impoverished estate itself, ill-kept, half-decaying, is seen through that sad, poetical atmosphere that permeates so much of the older Russian fiction; lovely glimpses of the countryside, delicate etchings of provincial types, from nobles to servants and peasants, mingle with wistful meditation, as age looks back upon the past. Religious backgrounds of the older Russia are reflected in Nikolai Lyeskov's simple, graphic, warmly human novel *Cathedral Folk*, picturing the Orthodox Church, with its patriarchal domestic and communal relationships, its mixture of peasant kindliness, petty officialism, and superstition.

The shadow of coming events lies upon *The Possessed*, Dostoyevsky's enigmatic novel of evil incarnate, in which the genius that from the terrors and agonies of the human mind drew a gospel of patience, endurance, and Christlike forgiveness, envisions a time when "Russia will be overwhelmed with darkness and the earth will weep for its old gods." Here a band of anarchist revolutionaries, who spread terror and crime through a countryside, are seen as beings possessed of devils, like the Gadarene swine, rushing toward destruction of themselves and others. Most of the elements of conspiracy, revolutionary psychology, and violence that fused in the flame of the Russian revolution are incandescent in the narrative, which was written in 1871 and is imbued with Dostoyevsky's revulsionary horror of nihilism; it is not strange that during later years this novel has come to be regarded by many as a work of semi-mystical presage, in which Dostoyevsky, as René Fulop-Miller has said, speaks as "the inspired prophet of the present era."

In 1917 Russia's historic past died; her self-created future struggled to birth. By that violent and dramatic change the body of Russian literary expression was destroyed, new elements were mingled with its remnants, and the resulting substance was molded and remolded according to crude and rigorous patterns. At first, in 1918–1919, literary production was virtually extinguished; all reviews stopped publication; the old newspapers ceased to exist; printing presses became government property. In 1920 the year's book production fell to 2,000, as against 34,000 in 1913. To create a proletarian literature young proletarians were subsidized by the government, and everything they wrote was published; the older generation of writers was eliminated by censorship or interdiction, and there was soon a medley of conflicting groups supporting different theories of the kind of writing best adapted to uphold communist principles; from these came some of the most original and powerful early Soviet fiction. Later a "five-year plan" for literature was launched, and writers were required to center on "contemporary themes," to expound industrialization, to celebrate the class struggle; thus a stereotype pattern of the so-called "production novel" was established. In 1932 this literary dictatorship was dissolved and replaced by a general "Union of Soviet Writers," taking for granted loyalty to communism and tolerant of individual factions and variant methods. Rigorous preventive politico-economic censorship continues, but more freedom is given to imaginative literature than to any other form of writing. Soviet novels that have been translated into English reveal, in its pristine violence, the scope and intensity of a revolution that established a new cycle in human history, plucking an old world up by the roots and planting a new world in a strange social framework, to propagate a civilization of different pattern. Here are glimpses into whirling, lurid phantasmagoria: men and women, ragged and filthy, crowding in factories and public works in intense group competition; warfare of primitive ferocity; clash and conflict of human relations, cruel, heroic, tragic; peasant simplicity and political shrewdness; brutal realism in details that shock and disgust, and episodes touched with tenderness, romance, and poetry; sordid venality, and passionate idealism for a communist Utopia. And all, in its bewildering multiplicity and variety of scene and incident, is stamped with sameness; for all is proletarian.

Maxim Gorky may be regarded as the father of Soviet literature. His tale *Mother* was a kindling spark to the revolution; his massive novel-sequence, *The Life of Clim Samghin*, is a reconstruction of Russia's history from the assassination of Czar Alexander II, in 1881, to the great cataclysm of October, 1917: the "forty years" of the Russian subtitle. Of its four volumes, the first, *Bystander*, covers fifteen years, embracing the reign of Alexander III, and ending in 1896, soon after the coronation of Nicholas II; *The Magnet* carries through the next eleven years, to the uprising of 1905, which in the succeeding volume, *Other Fires*, is followed to its suppression in 1906; *The Specter*, fourth and final volume (left uncompleted by Gorky's death), is concerned with the following ten years and the emergence of the Soviet state. These 2,700 pages form a continuous biographical narrative of the life of Clim Samghin, of a middle-class, semi-intelligentsia family, from childhood to middle age, which is essentially a study of the dissolution of a bourgeois society in the underflow of revolutionary currents. Clim is throughout a "by-stander," a reticent, skeptical observer; his personal experience has no individual dramatic development or depth of character portrayal. Rather, it is simply the frame within which is set a panorama of Russia during these years, particularly a panorama of conditions, activities, ideals, and confusions of the middle class. Scenic backgrounds change; characters, endless in number and type, also change through the years; interminable conversations rise and fall and intermit and resume on every imaginable abstract subject; in neither events nor action is there sustained dramatic impulsion. Prodigious variety and detail are here in setting and figures, but the total effect is dulled and diffused by disintegration of the parts: no dominating structure is built, no central pulsing current of life flows through the whole. With entire honesty, with an ever-recurrent pondering upon the mysteries, cruelties, inconsistencies, and contrasts of life, Gorky portrays a Russia, chaotic, primitive, bound in fetters of ignorance and medievalism, and with unmeasured potentialities of achievement.

Overlapping Gorky's chronicle and carrying onward the seething sweep of the revolution, Alexei Tolstoy's novel, *Darkness and Dawn*, holds higher values for American readers, in compression and sustained dramatic power. The six years from 1914 to 1919 are covered in this vivid, crowded canvas, with effective transmission of the chaos and terror of the time, and from a historical rather than a partisan point of view; it is a work based on deep personal experience, for Alexei Tolstoy, who as anti-Bolshevist escaped from Russia in 1919, later returned, reconciled to the Soviet regime, and is accepted as one of its leading novelists. The same period is reflected from the personal experience of a writer exiled in 1922 from the Soviet state, in *Quiet Street*, Michael Ossorgin's poignant yet balanced story of a secluded street in Moscow and the changes brought by revolution into the lives of those who lived there. The foremost Soviet novelist of today is Mikhail Sholokhov, whose colossal epic of revolution and civil war has enlarged the great tradition of Russian fiction. *The Silent Don* is the collective title under which *The Don Flows Home to the Sea* is set beside its earlier companion novel, *And Quiet Flows the Don*. These two massive volumes unfold a magnificent barbaric panorama of Cossack farms and villages on the banks of the Don, from the prewar years of peace, through the World War and the revolution of 1917, to the close, in 1921, of the fratricidal civil wars that spread their fiercest destruction in the Don region, where Red Cossacks, in victorious minority, were fought tooth and nail by White Cossacks, in guerrilla warfare, in local uprisings, in deadly foot-by-foot resistance. The struggle ceases not in absolute victory or defeat, but in time's solvent of exhaustion, of satiety, bringing acceptance of Soviet power and an awakening sense of the futility of unending bloodshed. Sholokhov is a communist, but his "proletarian realism" is devoid of partisanship; he has understanding and insight for Reds and Whites alike. This is primitive drama, epic narrative, romantic and brutal, glowing with vivid, beautiful backgrounds—the river, the vast steppes, the forest, the great horse farms—alive in its human characterization. It holds terrible, savage, and tragic scenes, for it is an evocation of war, revolution and counter-revolution, of death, famine, and pestilence, and it echoes to the tread of those four horsemen. But it holds also beauty, humor, the sap of living, and the tang of earth.

In Soviet novels brought out in English translation since the early 1920's many aspects of Russian life after the whirlwind are vividly illuminated. Only a few of these may be noted here. Alexander Neverov's novel, *City of Bread*, is the agonized epic of the Russian famine of 1921. As portrayal of mass starvation, it is true for many dark vistas in world history, past and present. Drawn from the abyss of personal experience, this is the chronicle of two children who make the journey from famine-stricken Samara to distant Tashkent, in Turkestan, "city of plenty, city of bread," to bring home bread for their families and good seed to sow for grain. Twelve-year-old Mishka is the leader, the pitiful, unconquerable hero; he goes with his friend, eleven-year-old Seroshka, and successive unforgettable scenes follow their experiences in the frenzied hunt for a morsel of bread among hordes of hunger-driven men and women. Libedinsky's short novel, *A Week*, pictures the early communist regime among the peasants, and the week of sullen, stubborn revolt when the peasants refused to obey the Soviet order to send their grain to the Soviet storehouse, to be held and distributed by the state. Linked to this is Sholokhov's novel of agrarian collectivization, *Seeds of Tomorrow*, related to but separate from his "Don" epic, which is a realistic, closely factual study of the conversion, in 1930, of a Cossack village of kulaks and poor peasants into a collective farming unit.

Soviet education is unforgettably depicted, in its earlier phases, in Ognyov's *Diary of a Communist Schoolboy*, which has been truly called a window opened on the new generation of the new Russia. This ingenuous, vivid narrative gives a fifteen-year-old boy's record of the full school year (twelve months) of 1923–24, and reveals the point of view, background, ideals, and everyday living of the boys and girls of the Soviet schools. Written from the personal experience of a Soviet teacher, it is "alive," authentic for its period, and provocative. *The Diary of a Communist Undergraduate* (which in the original is the second part of the complete novel) continues the narrative, carrying the former provincial schoolboy to the university in Moscow and depicting with the same animation and reality, intensities of youth striving toward a higher education, itself newly patterned, chaotic, and dogmatic. A later phase of Soviet student life is shown by Benjamin Kaverin, in his novel *The Larger View*, which pictures young men and women of the great professional schools of Leningrad and reflects their feverish ardor to share in the building of the state. The social reversal stamped on new Russia's design for living is epitomized in Panteleimon Romanov's novel, *Three Pairs of Silk Stockings*, which in English translation bears the subtitle: "the life of the educated class under the Soviet." Here is a dramatic, subtly significant picture of a communal dwelling (once a luxurious apartment house) in the Moscow of 1930, and of the existence of those once wealthy, cultured and respected, now furtive or hypocritical hangers-on, ostracized or penalized in a hostile or indifferent world. "Production novels," centering on the communist reconstruction of Russia's ravaged economic life, on the "proletarian enthusiasm" and "labor heroism" of group competition in pushing great industrial enterprises to completion, are exemplified in Gladkov's *Cement*—a tense, brutal, ardent recital of mass mobilization and "shock brigade" rivalry in the building of a great power station; in *Time, Forward!* Valentine Kataev's dynamic five-year-plan tale of a twenty-four hour speed-up competition in a concrete construction plant in the Urals; and in Ilya Ehrenbourg's *Out of Chaos*. These novels, it should be added, reflect earlier, more chaotic phases of Soviet life; later years have modified many of the conditions there depicted.

Novels from the countries of northern Europe differ markedly in their characteristics from the French, Spanish, and Italian novels that represent what may be called Latin qualities of literary art. In the Latin group there is, as a rule, a more highly sophisticated art, a strong note of social irony, or a somewhat cynical contemplation of human passions and emotions. Slav and Scandinavian fiction is at once more simple, more deeply rooted in primitive instincts, with a more powerful creative genius, and with more imagination and less irony in psychological interpretation. In the Scandinavian group, where Iceland and Finland naturally take their places, there prevail a deep sense of the tragic course of human destiny, a fundamental concern with the struggle between material and spiritual forces in the inner life, and a constant mingling of the physical with the introspective. Vigor, independence, and self-sufficiency are strong elements of the life reflected in this fiction.

Icelandic backgrounds, historical and modern, are mirrored in the novels of Gunnar Gunnarsson, one of the few Icelandic writers

whose work has appeared in English translation. Set almost entirely
in Iceland, concerned with simple, sturdy peasants or middle-class
householders and business or professional people, his novels have a
tragic, epic quality, a shadowed reserve and dignity, that is romantic
rather than realistic. *Seven Days' Darkness* is his most powerful and
original achievement, in its mingling of the factual and the symbolic.
The scene is Reykjavik, Iceland's capital, during the peak of the
great influenza epidemic that raged at the end of the first World
War, and the grim narrative, in reverse perspective, depicts the battle against death waged for seven days in a city plunged in darkness
by a volcanic eruption, and a parallel psychological battle waged
between religious faith and materialist rationalism. Here, in essence,
the sudden impact of overpowering calamity intensifies all psychological values, the nightmare of actual physical experience becomes a
spiritual experience also. Kristmann Gudmundsson's two novels,
The Bridal Gown and *The Morning of Life*, are evocations of more
primitive isolated living that diffuse the boldness, the elemental
moods, and the fierce pride of a people who cherish a thousand years'
unbroken tradition of independence.

In historic vistas, as in their attitude toward life, there is close
kinship in these northern novels. Icelandic, Danish, and Norwegian
fiction alike hold echoes of the Viking sagas and trace the heritage
of the Northmen as it lives in the Norse fisher folk of today. The
Danish novelist Johannes Jensen, in his epic cycle, *The Long Journey*, turns back to human beginnings on the planet, and in three
linked volumes chronicles the journey of mankind from its first
wanderings in the tropic world of the age of fire, through the terrors of the ice age, down through the development of the Norse
peoples into seafarers and race builders, to the voyage of Columbus
and the discovery of America. The Icelander, Gudmundur Kamban,
welds from ancient saga accounts of the Viking expeditions to Vin-
land the saga novel *I Saw a Wondrous Land*, which records the adventures of Eric the Red and Lief the Lucky across the seas and
conveys the daring, heroism, passion, blood-lust and blood-feud of
that barbaric Norse world. Medieval faith and life are made as actual

and moving as the most absorbing drama of men and women of our own generation in Sigrid Undset's magnificent parallel novel-sequences, *Kristin Lavransdatter* and *The Master of Hestviken*. Trilogy and tetralogy, they complement and supplement each other, weaving for fourteenth-century Norway a deep-hued texture of history that is also a texture of universal experience, drawing its threads from individual passions, conflicting natures, the many-stranded soul-stuff of human life. These are among the great historical novels of world literature; like Naomi Mitchison's *The Corn King and the Spring Queen*, they are works of scholarship and historical authority, but they are also transfiguration of the dry bones of history into flesh and blood of humanity, under the focus of the creative imagination.

Norway, indeed, is especially rich in novels that fuse the materials of the past into the substance of the present and penetrate to primitive and traditional bases of experience and character. Trygve Gulbranssen combines saga, pastoral, and idyl in his two linked novels, *Beyond Sing the Woods* and *The Wind from the Mountains*, chronicling three generations of the Bjorndal family, powerful, rugged landowners, who in their remote domain of mountain, forest, village, and fishing station, have held feudal rule through a century, shut off from the world and independent of it. There is beauty and deep insight into human nature in this simple unfolding of experiences that are the sum of human drama—tragedy, hate, joy, inner growth—and that convey without somberness or moralizing the picturesque, ample life of the old Norwegian patriarchal homestead, the magnificence of mountains, forests, river, the magic of changing seasons, the closeness of wild nature, with its dangers and its powers over man. Northern Norway is the scene of Olav Duun's six-volume saga of peasant life, *The People of Juvik*, which follows through seven generations during a century and a quarter the history of a Norwegian peasant family. Himself of peasant stock, farmers and fisher folk, his work distills the nature of his own people; he has been called the spokesman for the peasant mind. The setting throughout is in his native valley of the Namdahl, north of Trondhjem, where beside the fiord lies the ancient farm of the Juviks, a sturdy clan whose successive generations transmit alternating hereditary currents of daring and irresolution, of strength and weakness. Upon the earth itself, as base and seedbed of human living, Knut Hamsun built his masterpiece, *The Growth of the Soil:* epic of man's labor transforming the wilderness, as the peasant Isak raises his turf hut on the Norwegian mountainside and sets in motion life processes that are to bring a community into being. The power and meaning of primitive human life that is part of nature, independent of the inventions and creations of civilization, is made manifest here in Biblical simplicity and dignity, with a sharp-cut detail, a strength of elemental emotion, and a brooding tenderness that make us see these toiling, ignorant, harsh, uncouth men and women, lacking all graces of mind and expression, as children of earth, dumbly feeling the beauty of nature, sharing in love and pain and hope and, though inarticulate, expressing in their lives patience, duty, and self-sacrifice.

Regional vistas are opened all through Scandinavian fiction. Norway's dauntless fishermen, who before the age of motor power sailed their open boats hundreds of miles to the Lofoten islands, are commemorated by Bojer in *The Last of the Vikings.* Gösta af Geijerstam invests farm life on an island in a Norwegian fiord with charm and serenity in the family pastoral *Northern Summer* and its companion chronicle, *Storevik.* From Selma Lagerlöf a generation of American readers have come to know Sweden's farmlands and forests, the folklife of the people, and varied aspects of living, always touched with a breath of the mystical, the supernatural, sometimes as peasant superstition, sometimes as lofty religious idealism. More complex is the modern reading of Swedish life that Vilhelm Moberg gives in his trilogy, *The Earth Is Ours,* published separately at intervals in Sweden and brought out in English translation, in a single massive volume, in 1941. Solidly wrought, slowly cumulative, tinged with the socio-philosophic spirit of our day, this is the working out of a man's life problem through years of youth and maturity, from 1900 to 1938. It is akin to the work of Hamsun and Duun in the deep identification of the life of man with the life of the soil, the materialism and medievalism of peasant existence, earthbound, heavy, and harsh, with its love of possessions, its severity of toil, its mingling of matter-of-fact sensuality with a religious moralism that is part superstition, part spiritual fervor. But here also is traced the beginning break-up of the old-time peasant way of life under an inflowing of youth, bringing freed intelligence and new ideas of man's power to control his destiny. The theme is the conflict between the life of the soil and the life of the city, as it shapes one man's life story. He is a peasant youth, sensitive, intellectual, self-centered, starved for things of the mind, oppressed by the harsh narrowness of his native village, the tyrannical restrictions and hopeless toil of his farm home. He escapes to the city, shapes his life to the longed-for pattern, but finds only frustration and unrest until, painfully and slowly he resolves his problem by returning to his native place, and through slow process of adjustment accepts his task as helping toward a better community life. As he watches the world plunge toward war and sees freedom on earth crushed under primal force, this task still holds: "My good dream is to strive for something better than the life now lived on this earth. For this dream I live, and in this dream I find something worth dying for."

Social and philosophic currents are strong in these novels. To the rising labor movement in the new twentieth century Martin Andersen Nexö's great novel-sequence *Pelle the Conqueror*, with its backgrounds of industrial Copenhagen and of Danish farm labor, gave an impetus carrying far beyond national boundaries. Its companion sequence, *Ditte*, has the same power of factual realism, the same transfiguring human understanding, and deeper tragedy in its life chronicle of a girl born, as Pelle was, to poverty and toil, but helpless against harshnesses of social struggle which he, with man's immunity, could conquer. The quest for spiritual reassurance that has been the internal struggle of our age is studied in J. Anker-Larsen's sensitive, profound novel *The Philosopher's Stone*, which with varied character portrayal and scenic vividness reflects many phases of Danish town and country life.

Finland reveals its historic backgrounds and common living in

novels brought in translation to American readers only within recent
years. Strongest present-day interest, perhaps, attaches to *Sun and
Storm*, Unto Seppänen's memorable chronicle of Finland's struggle
for freedom from Russia, set forth in the story of Markku, Finnish
farmer, and his children, from the 1870's to Finland's attainment of
independence in 1920. Built on solid structure of fact, authentic in
detail and in sequence of events, this is human substance of national
history, its underlying force the hatred of Russia that goes back
to the days of serfdom, its dominant characteristic the elemental
mingling of beauty and violence in nature and in man. The primitive is strong in the panoramic scope of this novel, which embraces
the life of the soil in its rank earthiness, the social and economic interests of family and community, the natural surroundings of forest,
moors, and interlinking lakes, and the personal dramas, turbulences,
and vicissitudes of people under whose sturdy vigor volcanic passions burn close to the surface.

There are similar backgrounds in the two novels of Franz Emil
Sillanpaa, Nobel prize winner in 1938. *Meek Heritage* is peasant
tragedy: the sixty-year lifespan of Juha Toivola, born to direst poverty, who, from a childhood in the famine years of the "hungry sixties," passes through life helpless, simple-minded, exploited, knowing only toil and privation, to extinction as an unregarded victim of
civil war. In *The Maid Silja* there is quiet simplicity, direct but gentle realism. Its theme is familiar: the "last flourishing of an old family
tree," conveyed in a young girl's short life story. It opens vistas of
rural Finland: scattered hamlets, remote farms, peaceful country
churches, coarse primitive living, the long, dark discomfort of winter, the sudden joy and promise of summer. Silja herself makes the
book; her experience saturates its backgrounds, her personality suf-
fuses its events. Yet she is almost negative, so far as speech, action,
expressed emotion, are concerned; it is her integrity, her silent
courage, her deep, cherished inner memories and dreams that make
her a real person, moving and beautiful, portrayed with a delicate
spiritual perceptiveness, an enveloping unexpressed compassion, that
linger subtly in remembrance. Humble life in the Åland Islands,

midway between Sweden and Finland, is pictured in two novels by Sally Salminen, *Katrina* and *Mariana*, that center on woman's toil and devotion. Both are warm and vital recreations of common experience, of everyday events, of the joys and tragedies of home, marriage, and children, and the long struggle for livelihood from the soil or from the sea.

These are a few scattered glimpses of world vistas that open from contemporary European novels. Even this fragmentary, inadequate survey should deepen realization that we have today no deeper, broader, more revealing medium for the record of human experience and the interpretation of human nature than the medium of modern fiction.

VIII. FICTION FROM LATIN AMERICA

*There must come a conception of life which, without
denying the fundamental union between man and the
earth would lift him past the barriers that had held
him back until then to lead him to the more complete
forms of existence.*—CIRO ALEGRÍA: *Broad and Alien Is
the World*

TO THE vast majority of readers in the United States, Latin
American fiction is more remote, more exotic, than any of the
fiction of Europe. The two Americas share a hemisphere; they have
never shared a common understanding. Underlying their deep separation are fundamental differences in folk roots, in historical development, in religion, in social and cultural conditions that set up
barriers to mutual sympathetic response and that are not resolved
by friendly trade relations or political agreements. With the rise
of world conflict "hemispheric solidarity" has become not simply
a pious phrase of political aspiration but a profound and urgent
necessity. There is deepening realization in both continents of the
need of closer social and cultural ties—of reciprocal relations in education, and of a much more extensive exchange of literature between
the Latin American countries and the United States—if any real
bond of understanding is to be established between them.

Many cultured Latin Americans read English and are familiar
with the work of North American writers, many of whose books
also have been translated into Spanish; English is required in the
schools of ten of the Latin American countries, and its study is
steadily increasing in all. But Latin American literature is virtually
unknown to the general reading public of the United States. That
the most widely known novel (*The Thatched Hut*) of the Ecua-
dorian novelist José Icaza should have been translated into six lan-

guages, one of them Chinese, but not into English, shows this limitation of our literary horizon. Yet the mind of a people reveals itself in that people's literature, and through the books of Latin American writers it is possible to gain a knowledge and understanding that otherwise can come only from personal experience.

Since the early 1920's there has been a sporadic endeavor to acquaint cultivated readers in the United States with the variety and vitality of contemporary Latin American fiction. Isaac Goldberg, Waldo Frank, Anita Brenner, Carleton Beals have been among the leaders in this endeavor; and about thirty novels by Mexican and South American writers were published in English translation in this country during this period. They reached only a limited audience; commercially, they must have registered loss rather than profit. But their publication marked a step toward fuller representation in our current book production of this young American literature, that, like our own, is an expression of American culture, and that, also like our own, holds portent of American development and American destiny. A further step was taken in 1940, when a prize contest for the best book, preferably a novel, by a Latin American author was initiated by the New York publishing firm of Farrar & Rinehart, with the aid of the Division of Intellectual Coöperation of the Pan-American Union and of literary groups in the different Latin American countries. Ciro Alegría, exiled Peruvian novelist, was awarded the prize in March, 1941, for his novel *Broad and Alien Is the World;* and three other novelists received honorable mention: Enrique Gil Gilbert, of Ecuador, for *Our Daily Bread;* Cecilio J. Carneiro, of Brazil, for *The Bonfire;* Miguel Angel Menéndez, of Mexico, for *Nayar.* Other similar contests are to follow, to include fiction, non-fiction (biographic, sociological, or philosophic), and a book for children. To make this fresh-flowing stream of Latin American fiction—so varied, so significant—more available in English translation, to strengthen and stimulate appreciation of its interest and potential values should be a more effective means of realizing aims and ideals of intracontinental relationship than chamber of commerce excursions, scholastic dissertations, or political oratory.

Much Latin American fiction undoubtedly carries an impact of shock to many North American readers. The shock is less than it would have been a few years ago, before so many of our own novelists had turned to harsh transcription of brutal experience in their recording of social and economic evils; but its immediate effect may be painful or benumbing. The exotic pictorial vividness of these novels seems crude or garish; their violence of action, their mingling of primitive barbarism with sophisticated European culture, gives a sense of unreality; in structure and development they may lack coherence and climax; often they reek of human suffering and are veined with cruelty, as they picture oppression and exploitation, political corruption, and revolutionary conflict. All this, however, represents the creation of a self-sufficient, individual literary culture. Latin American novelists have broken the traditional bond with nineteenth-century Spanish letters. They have drawn their substance from their native soil, and their qualities of expression, in exuberance, in abruptness, in disorder and intensity, are the manifestations of the life they delineate. Their preoccupation with social problems, their dominant tendency to the tragic, their absorption in natural settings of savage beauty, impart an inner unity to what is essentially a literature of national and social transmutation. Russian fiction nearly a century ago extended the boundaries and enlarged the horizons of the novel in its exploration of the human spirit; today Latin American fiction opens for exploration the processes of social evolution in the New World that is part of, but completely different from, our own.

Mexican fiction has had very little representation in the influx of books about Mexico that came into being about 1928, under the influence of D. H. Lawrence, Anita Brenner, Stuart Chase, Carleton Beals, and Waldo Frank, and that still continues, though in lessened volume. But the few Mexican novels that are available in English translation illuminate significant backgrounds of the contemporary scene and give color and reality to the folk life of the people.

The Under Dogs, Mariano Azuela's novel of the revolution of 1911–17, is the most famous modern Mexican novel. First published when its author was in exile in El Paso, it went unheeded for ten years; but by 1927 its fame had spread throughout the Spanish-speaking literary world, and it will long remain a vital evocation of the break-up of a country under the sudden flare of civil war, assassination, hate, the uprising of the "under dogs" from centuries of servitude into a savage freedom of fighting, comradeship, and brutal pillage. Azuela, by profession a physician, went himself as military doctor with the guerrilla band that was transformed into a Villa army which swarmed like locusts, burning, killing, looting, and carousing through the states of Zacatecas and Jalisco. From this experience he drew the material for his novel; its last scene, we are told, was written in a cave overlooking the annihilation of the band, and the rest was composed later, in exile. The book is short: direct, dramatic, vivid. Its central figure is the guerrilla leader, driven from his patch of land, his hut and cows and wife and child, drawing about him followers like himself; half-naked *pelados*, swept into the whirlpool of revolution, hardly knowing how or why; victims and perpetrators alike of ruthless violence and brutal crime. One savage, picturesque scene follows another in extraordinary flesh-and-blood reality; and through all the tragedy, futility, coarseness, high exploits, and abysmal cruelties there is conveyed a sense of pity for the poor and ignorant, to whom Villa was the reincarnation of the old legend: "Villa as Providence, the bandit, that passes through the world with the blazing torch of an ideal: to rob the rich and give to the poor."

Beside Azuela's novel must stand the narrative of Martín Luis Guzmán, *The Eagle and the Serpent*,[1] often regarded as fiction, though it is in fact personal reminiscence in dramatic dialogue form, which gives a first-hand record of the revolution during the years of Villa's power. Personal experience, adventure, vigorous character etching, quickly moving drama, mingle in this absorbing, authentic narrative. It is detailed, following no single plot-thread, with the flavor of mixed good humor, sardonic indifference and devil-may-care casual-

[1] Martín Luis Guzmán, *The Eagle and the Serpent* [El aguila y la serpiente]; trans. by Harriet de Onis, New York, Knopf, 1930.

ness which is characteristic of the Mexican temperament, even in grim danger or tragic circumstance. There is no artificiality, no writing for effect; even the most monstrous scenes of ruthless cruelty are invested with a direct simplicity. Guzmán, like Azuela, wrote from his own experience. He was a follower and champion of Villa, never deserted him, and sees him always with admiring eyes—even his cruelty, ruthlessness, irresponsibility, infantile pomposity, crass sentimentalities. Both books have continuing value as historical material.

Azuela has written many other novels; his work as a whole forms a broad fictional canvas of the social-revolutionary struggle, from the last days of the Diaz regime, with the dominance of the rich landowners, through the rise and fall of Madero, the devastating conflicts of rival parties, and the disillusion, corruption, and persecutions of later years. Always he deals with the exploited classes: the Indian peon, the tenant farmer, the middle class, helpless under political rascality; all under dogs in a complex social struggle. Of these novels only one has appeared in English translation: *Marcela*— a passionate love story of Indian peons on a feudal estate ruled by a cruel and dissolute owner, its folk life curiously mingling subtlety and fierceness, its pervading superstition blending ancient Indian lore and Catholic ritual; its feuds and lusts and cruelties pervaded by the exotic beauty of its natural setting.

More limited but of deep significance is the aspect of Mexican life portrayed in *El Indio*, the novel by Gregorio López y Fuentes, that won Mexico's first National Prize of Literature, in 1935. This is a study of the Mexican Indian in his own tribal life and in his traditional fear and distrust of white or mestizo civilization. It deals with a remote Indian village, high in the Mexican mountains; its people, proud, quiet, wary of strangers, speak Aztec, not Spanish. None of them are named, for they are not only individuals but also, as López y Fuentes sees them, symbols of a conquest that has continued for more than four hundred years; yet they have individuality, and their everyday living takes on a warm and moving reality. Their story runs through a period of years. It opens with the arrival of white prospectors, greedy and treacherous, bringing terror and violence and leaving suffering in their wake; it closes with requisitions of food and conscription of labor imposed by officials of the towns in the valley below—the exactions of a government that regards these people only as materials for exploitation. Dramatic and moving episodes are woven into the texture of this primitive living. There is dignity, integrity, courage and devotion in individual experiences; and the communal folkways, with their witch-doctor miracles, their council meetings that give judgment in controversies, their fiesta that opens with solemn ritual and closes with machetes flashing in drunken fight, their ancient sports that have come unchanged from the Aztec past, all compose a fascinating and impressive pattern. There is a quality of classic beauty in the calm simplicity, the stoic dignity, with which the tale is told.

Although they are very different, a certain similarity exists between *El Indio* and *Nayar*, the novel by Miguel Angel Menéndez that received honorable mention in the Latin American prize novel contest. Both books are a manifestation of the deepening Indian— as opposed to Spanish—influence in contemporary Latin American literature, which accepts the elemental pattern of tribal Indian life and the qualities and powers of the race as potential sources of a rich indigenous national culture, and seeks to expose exploitation and oppression exercised under the civil, military, and religious domination rooted in Spanish conquest. The scene is a remote province (Nayarit) on the west coast of Mexico, a region of mountains, forest jungles, salt marshes, and obscure villages, where the remnants of two primitive Indian tribes lead a harassed existence, victimized by both whites and mestizos, held in bonds of poverty, ignorance, superstition, and magic, and in a sudden flaring of civil and religious conflict ultimately crushed between opposed forces of government and revolutionaries. *Nayar*, however, has an emotional exuberance, an intensity of color and action, far removed from the restraint of *El Indio;* the work of a poet (later, Mexican minister to China), it weaves a complex social problem into a vivid, uneven web of tragedy.

Even a partial gleaning from the South American fiction that is available in English translation will reveal its rich variety of content and its historical and social significance. For such a gleaning we have books by representative novelists from seven of the South American countries. These, following a rough topographical order from north to south, are: Venezuela, Colombia, Peru, Brazil, Chile, Argentina, and Uruguay. Countries from which no fiction is represented are Ecuador, Bolivia, and Paraguay. Of course, in these a native literature exists; in Ecuador, especially, novelists of talent are exploring their country's composite human elements; but it must be remembered that very little of the whole body of South American fiction has been translated into English; and in the translations that have been made, the work of Argentinian, Brazilian, Colombian, and Venezuelan writers predominates.

Perhaps a word should be said first concerning the whole field of South American fiction. The Latin Americans have always been a literary people; they have as heritage the traditions and the culture of the Roman Catholic Church, and that heritage found expression through the four centuries of their history in a continuous, changing flow of literary productions. Prose narratives and heroic poems of conquest and discovery mirror the early colonial period. Dramas, poems, and devotional writings were strongest in the static years of undisturbed Spanish rule. The opening of the nineteenth century and the rise of the Napoleonic era saw the advent of the revolutionary years and the birth of an entirely different literature of national aspiration and passionate purpose, as the struggle for independence from the mother country plunged the Spanish colonies into ruthless war. Yet throughout most of the nineteenth century the colonial spirit and manner of life persisted. Not until the last quarter of that century did the rising wave of reform and innovation wash away traditional literary conventions and disclose a new creative spirit. No general literacy yet exists in South America; until the turn of the century public education bore the stamp of medieval Europe rather than that of the modern world. Literature has been the field of an intellectual élite, which cultivated it as the means and the sign of culture. Authorship in the past did not mean earning a living; even today few of the leading South American authors depend on their books for their full income—they are usually also journalists, teachers, lawyers, doctors; most of the older men can look back on a common life experience of revolution, prison, political vicissitudes; nearly all were pamphleteers, poets, and dramatists before they became novelists. This has meant that the literature they produce is generally of high literary quality: their books are written, not for commercial reasons, but to express convictions, ideals, or the inner urge of the spirit.

Within the twentieth century the audience for South American writers has greatly increased, and since 1930 a native book production has come into existence that has broken down former literary border lines between the different countries and virtually eliminated the "literary colonialism" that depended on Spain for its book supply. The publishing house of Ercilla, established in Santiago de Chile in 1932, has become a center for publication and distribution throughout South America. Whereas formerly Argentine books were little known in Ecuador, and Venezuelan writers found fewer readers in Chile, the Ercilla firm now handles books by all Latin American authors and makes them available to all Latin American readers. During the first five years of its existence (to January, 1937) it published 1,120 books by many hundreds of authors, including not only the work of writers from every Latin American country but also books of leading French, Italian, German, Russian, English, and North American authors, issued in Spanish translation.[2] Influences for growth and strength have flowed into Latin American literature from Spain's tragedy. The extinction of the Spanish Republic under fascist victory and the resulting extirpation of Spain's modern thought and culture by destruction and interdiction of books, restriction of education, and exile of writers and scientists, have brought deepening and widening intellectual life to Spanish America. In Mexico publishing, printing, educational, scientific, and

[2] Willis Knapp Jones, "Editorial Ercilla, Dominant Factor in Latin American Literature," *Books Abroad*, XI (No. 2, 1937), 173.

literary activities have been centered, under sponsorship of the Spanish Government in Exile, in Mexico City. Exiled Spanish writers, scholars, and artists in many fields are also at work in other Latin American countries; and the dissemination of modern continental and English literature in Spanish translation steadily increases.

This expanding audience, this birth of a continental spirit, finds its manifestation in the rise of fiction. Poetry has always been the leading form in Latin American literature, the mark of culture and idealism. But within a generation, while poetry holds its place, there has been widespread development of novels and short stories, by writers who have disregarded the older aristocratic limitations, who are going for their material to life itself, reflecting and interpreting the common experience of the world and the people amid which they live. Of this contemporary fiction Waldo Frank says:

There are novelists like the Mexican, Mariano Azuela, who are depicting the life of the Mexican Indian, soldier, mestizo, in the passionate years of revolution. There are novelists like the Colombian, José Eustacio Rivera, who bring the cruel and deep suffering of mankind in the jungles into their pages. Argentinians, like Ricardo Güiraldes, Leopold Lugones, Horacio Quiroga, tell the tales of the gaucho, of the small country village lost on the pampa, of the northern forests where gigantic snakes still dispute the land with the pioneers. Venezuelan novelists, like Rufino Blanco-Fombona, reveal the political and social fabric of their complex world; and like Teresa de la Parra the struggle of women to be free of the medieval trammels of the church. In Chile, there is a whole school of admirable novelists devoted to the pastoral life of the villages beneath the Andes.[3]

In summarizing the books of the novelists chosen, the most effective course seems to be to follow the map, opening with the most northern country, moving southward, then westward, then south again; and attempting to trace in these novels the backgrounds, historical and social, of the countries whose life they reflect.

For Venezuela we have Rufino Blanco-Fombona, one of the older leading figures in contemporary Latin American literature, whose

[3] Waldo Frank, "Contemporary Spanish American Literature," *Publishers' Weekly*, CXVIII (1930), 1841-43.

life is part of his country's annals of revolution; and the younger novelist, Rómulo Gallegos, most widely popular of present-day Venezuelan writers.

Blanco-Fombona, born in Caracas, in 1874, of old Spanish aristocratic stock, represents the mingling of the aristocratic and insurrecto strain as it was exemplified in Simón Bolívar, "The Liberator," —also born in Caracas nearly a century earlier—and in the young creole aristocrats who died by thousands for the cause of independence. In a volume of critical and biographical essays (*La Lámpara de Aladino*, 1915) he has written his own epitaph:

This man, like one beloved of the gods, died young. He knew how to love and to hate with all his heart. He loved fields, rivers, fountains; he loved good wine, he loved marble, steel, gold; he loved nubile women and beautiful verses. He despised the timorous, the presumptuous, and the mediocre. He hated traitors, hypocrites, calumniators, venal spirits. . . . In the midst of his injustice he was just. . . . He attacked only the strong. He had ideals and struggled and made sacrifices for them. . . . Only one thing did he ever refrain from giving: advice. . . . It is not known whether he was moral or immoral or amoral; but he placed beauty and truth—his truth—above all. He enjoyed and suffered much, spiritually and physically. . . . His life was illogical. His thought was contradictory. His one unchanging attribute was his sincerity, both in feeling and thought. . . . He preached liberty by example; he was free. He was a soul of the sixteenth century and a man of the twentieth. He rests in peace for the first time. May the earth, which he loved, be propitious to him.[4]

Very evident here is the quality of oratory, the flow of rhythmic eloquence, that is so strong an element in Latin American politics and literature and that finds intensified emotional expression in fiction.

His stormy political and public career, his varied literary work, in poetry, criticism, sociology, politics, and fiction, make Blanco-Fombona an important contemporary figure. From the age of eighteen, when he was a volunteer in the revolution against Presi-

[4] Translated by Isaac Goldberg in his *Studies in Spanish-American Literature* (Brentano's, 1920), pp. 307-9; Chapter VI is a comprehensive survey and appreciation of Blanco-Fombona's life and work.

dent Andueza, he participated in his country's many political struggles, held consular and governmental positions, twice visited the
United States (where he contracted a violent dislike for the country and its people), suffered imprisonment, fought duels, escaped
assassination; traveled widely in South America as well as in Europe; and lived in Paris and Madrid.

As a novelist, his reputation has long been established. *The Man
of Gold*, translated into English by Isaac Goldberg in 1929, is a companion novel to his previous book, *The Man of Iron*, considered
his most important work, which was written when he was in prison
in 1907 and has not, so far as I know, appeared in English translation. These two novels, as Goldberg points out, form an ideological
unity—the second the natural outgrowth from the first. Both titles
are ironic: *The Man of Iron* is an honest, simple, creature of passive
nature, easily molded, the victim of his virtues; *The Man of Gold*
is a creature of alloy, a repulsive miser and usurer, whose single passion is gain and whose story is an ironic composition on the theme
of the triumph of evil over good. Both novels are placed in the romantic, languorous setting of Caracas, and both apply stinging
satire and bitter irony to social and political conditions in Venezuela
under the Castro regime. *The Man of Gold* strikes most vigorously
at the machinations and greed of politicians, undoubtedly veiling in
caricature some recognizable figures in the political annals of Caracas. Its central figure is the miser and moneylender, withered and
hideous, who lives in filthy penury with his crippled, miserable old
housekeeper and who is brought into business relationship with
three well-born spinisters and their beautiful young niece, Olga,
the single object of their devotion. Olga, selfish and ruthless, conceives the idea that the youngest of her aunts should marry the
miser: she will undoubtedly outlive him and inherit his wealth, and
Olga will be her heiress. On this purpose the plot is woven, carrying
the miser to growing political importance as his wealth brings about
him sycophants and corrupt officials. There is a play of satirical
humor throughout; cruel, sometimes vulgar, realism and harsh physical details are curiously combined with limpid charm; and the vivid

portrayal of many different types conveys a sense of varied, distinctive life.

Very different is *Doña Barbara*, the slight but vivid and fascinating novel by Rómulo Gallegos which mirrors ranch life on the Venezuelan plains. It mingles realism and romanticism, and it unrolls a memorable panorama of magnificent natural backgrounds, of wild and vigorous life amid wide streams and vast savannahs, with the far-ranging herds, the lighthearted swaggering plainsmen, and the primitive isolated ranches set down in illimitable expanses. Especially interesting are the contrasts and similarities of this exotic frontier with our own early western cattle country, and the differences of temperament and tradition between the Latin American plainsman and his Nordic counterpart. The story centers on the fortunes of an old Venezuelan family, decimated by an ancient feud, still keeping its great homestead on the plains, though it has fallen into ruin and is being gradually absorbed through the chicaneries of the nearest ranch owner, the powerful, notorious Doña Barbara, a woman of half-Indian blood and lawless background who has made herself despot of the region. The only son and survivor of the ancient family has been educated in Caracas and admitted to the law, but the heritage of his plains ancestry still lives in him. He returns to the half-abandoned ranch to consider selling the property; and then his childhood memories, his inborn nature of the plainsman, reassert themselves. He remains, to regain and restore the family domain and to inaugurate, so far as possible, an era of justice and fair dealing. But he is confronted by the power, greed, and passions of Doña Barbara and by the rascalities of the North American hunter and trader ("the foreigner"), who has established himself in squatter sovereignty on Doña Barbara's land. The courts are corrupt, and the very law that young Santos-Luzardo seeks to invoke has been enacted through the influence of his enemies. His anger is roused, and he determines to fight them in their own fashion; but his natural high principles hold him to honest dealing, and in the end he wins victory through finer means. A love story that is both dramatic and appealing is woven into the plot. The charm and dramatic interest of the novel lie in the portrayal of the plainsman's life: the herding and branding of the cattle, the breaking of the horses, the details of ranch management, the personalities of the plainsmen themselves, their superstitions and customs; and the impressive, beautiful panoramic background of the plains under all the changes of the seasons.

Gallegos is regarded as the most important present-day literary figure in Venezuela. He displays high dramatic ability and a romantic spirit, yet he writes objectively, without expressing personal intensities of feeling, as does Blanco-Fómbona. He understands the psychology, landscape, and language of his country, and in some half-dozen novels he has given brilliant portrayal of different turbulent or formative periods in Venezuelan history.

We pass now to Colombia—that country of which most North Americans know very little, set in the northwest corner of South America, adjoining the isthmus of Panama. Bogotá, the capital, center of the country's literature as of its social and political life, is one of the most remote and inaccessible of cities, far in the interior, behind great mountain ranges and mighty rivers, raised up on its high tableland to an elevation of 8,500 feet. To reach Bogotá required in the old days a journey of at least three weeks; today there is a modern air service, but those who do not fly must give nearly a week to the transit. On account of this isolation the people have kept many of the ancient native and Spanish characteristics, and life has changed comparatively little from its earlier pattern. The intellectual class has held to aristocratic traditions; in literature, poetry has been predominant, and it is only within recent years that liberal forces have begun to find expression among the younger writers. Fiction of the older type is represented in Colombia by the most widely read novel written by any South American: the famous romance *María*, by Jorge Isaacs, published in 1867, still one of the standard school "classics," familiar in Europe and the United States. This is an idyl of young love cut short by death, picturing benign and patriarchal home life on a great estate in the valley of the Cauca; traditional in its lachrymal sensibility, it is simple and charming in its details of family relationship, picturesque in its vivid incidents of hunting and its depiction of native customs.

More representative of modern literary art is *Pax*, by Lorenzo Marroquín, who died in 1918: a novel that deserves to rank with the serious and powerful anti-war fiction of the present day. *Pax* is a long novel, elaborate, somewhat overweighted with detail, but colorful and moving in its presentation of love, intrigue, religion, politics, and revolution. It is infused with a passionate sincerity of desire to portray evils that consume a beloved country. Lorenzo Marroquín knew his people and their customs, the landscape, the social and historical backgrounds, the vanishing nobility and its ideals, the rising lower classes and their purpose. His sympathies were with aristocratic ideals, with religious faith, and with patriotic self-sacrifice for both; but his deepest feeling was of the waste and horror and futility of war. It is the same feeling that underlies *The Four Horsemen of the Apocalypse* and the later war novels, from Remarque to Hemingway; and it is expressed in his title, which symbolizes "a war-sick world crying 'Peace! Peace!' through the silenced voice of sacrificed youth." The tale opens in peace time and shows a cross-section of Colombian life—in the city and in the country, at home, at the opera, at the race track, in business offices, in political departments, at banquets, weddings, and funerals, in church, and in literary assemblies. Then comes outbreak of civil war, bursting forth from political strife over a national industrial project (what we should probably call a battle of rival interests over public utilities), and destruction and death are let loose over the country. Youth is drawn into the vortex, revolutionary forces meet in conflict, there are burning cities, ravaged fields, fleeing refugees, congested hospitals, and battlefields strewn with dead and dying. The novel moves to a somber tragic climax in its vision of war, its passionate appeal for peace; but it holds sustained human interest in the fortunes of the many characters, the lights and shadows of experience, the romance and caricature and satire that are part of its fabric. It is a book that will repay careful reading; for it imparts social, historical, and human understanding of a country and a people.

The Vortex, the single novel of José Eustacio Rivera, is probably the most remarkable production of Latin American fiction. It was born of personal experience in the rubber forests of the Rio Negro, where the author, distinguished poet and diplomat, served on the commission that traced the definite boundary between Colombia and Venezuela. His book was conceived in the heart of the jungle, where, like the hero of his novel, he trudged "through leech-infested swamps, bare-footed, half-starved, crazed by mosquitos and fevers," writing, not on paper, but in his mind, and reciting in the evening what he had "written" during the day; his death, in 1928, was caused by a mysterious malady contracted at that time. This is the fevered, brilliant narrative of a youthful poet and lover, who has fled with his sweetheart from Bogotá to escape pursuit of the law, invoked by the girl's parents. The two find haven first in the grasslands, on a great cattle ranch, in a wild, primitive existence of feuds, round-ups, drinking, cockfights, gambling, and promiscuous lovemaking. Then violence and betrayal separate them; the youth, again a fugitive, plunges deeper into the wilderness and is caught, with other miserable human beings, in the vortex of the rubber jungles, to be held in a slavery of hopeless labor, starved, tortured by ants, leeches, and poisonous insects, cheated by sadistic traders, surrounded by appalling cruelties, experiencing love, lust, exaltation, horror, and despair. The monstrous conditions of the rubber traffic, as exposed in the famous Casement report on the Putomayo jungles in Brazil, live again in this extraordinary narrative, which combines introspection and objectivity, romantic lyric emotionalism and starkly brutal realism.

Peru has a long tradition of literary art, flowering in poetry and in essays, fruitful in serious works of research, but with little representation of fiction, except in the form of the *cuento*, or short story. The only contemporary Peruvian novel that has been brought in translation to American readers is *Broad and Alien Is the World*, by Ciro de Alegría, prize winner in the Latin American novel competition of 1940. Alegría, as a member of the Apra revolutionary political party, which was defeated in 1932 and later outlawed, went into exile after a term of imprisonment and makes his home in Chile. His novel may be considered an expression of the "Aprismo movement" in Peruvian literature, dedicated to the social-political struggle and the championship of the native Indian race against oppression and exploitation. There is a close relationship between this novel and *El Indio*, although the Mexican Indian folk life depicted by López y Fuentes is less civilized and more isolated than is that of the Peruvian Indian community, which, unchanging through centuries, still carries traces of the communal socialist pattern that shaped the ancient Inca civilization of Peru. Here in colorful panoramic narrative, with intricate variation of scene and incident yet with complete unity of the whole, unfolds the tragedy of the small Indian village of Rumi, high up in the Peruvian Andes. For generations it has maintained a happy and industrious communal agrarian existence, primitive and toilsome, but giving independence and livelihood to its people. There is poverty, ignorance, and superstition, but there is also tolerance, communal loyalty, sturdy self-respect, and dimly sensed abilities for self-development. Government is in the hands of a mayor and four councillors, elected to their office; and the mayor, Rosendo Maqui, whose life is followed from youth to death, is the central figure: rugged, wise, shrewd, the father of his people, their fellow worker and leader, dying in prison, still their defender. The fate of Rumi is portended when Don Alvaro Amenabar, rich and predatory landowner of the town in the valley, institutes suit against the community, charging that the land it had occupied for generations rightfully belonged to him. The land itself has no value; but he owns silver mines in the region beyond, and cheap labor for them may be gained by dispossession of the Indians. Upon Rosendo Maqui falls the responsibility to fight Don Alvaro in the courts and try to save his people, panic-stricken and helpless.

This life-and-death struggle against hopeless odds is the substance of the novel. We see the Indian community cheated by tricky lawyers and corrupt officials, uprooted and bewildered, moving silently up the mountainside to more barren lands to begin again to establish their community, to meet privation, difficulties, despair; again to be attacked by military force as a center of revolt, machine guns sweeping the cliffs where only the sick, women, and children remain, in a final triumph of tragic repression. We follow individual victims into strange servitudes in a broad and alien world: to the long-drawn-out miseries of the malarial coca plantations; to the terrible purgatory of the rubber swamps and jungles; to the hopeless lot of the Indian soldier, herded to fight in strange causes of which he knows nothing. Some, the bolder and stronger, become bandits; the countryside, once peaceful, is torn by violence, menaced by danger. Powerful, deeply moving, picturesque and vital in characterization, there is a strong poetic quality in Alegría's novel; tragic and compassionate, it is also challenging in its portrayal of Indian dignity and integrity and of native abilities that need only education and opportunity to fulfill themselves. The leader who in the second community succeeds Rosendo Maqui strives for such fulfillment. He carries out draining of the land by dynamiting a channel from an "enchanted lake," haunt of a Chaco, or evil spirit. That would bring more crops, the village would thrive, a school would be established: "once they had a school, then in ten or twenty years nobody would believe in enchanted lakes or Chacos." He, too, perishes under machine guns and Mauser bullets. The pitiful, unequal conflict, in its essence and its implications is the conflict that grips the world today —freedom against despotism.

Brazil, bordering Venezuela, Colombia, and Peru, stretching far southward beside Bolivia and Argentina, is a world in itself: a mighty empire—Portuguese, not Spanish, in its European origin and language—a union of states greater in area than our own, underpopulated, undeveloped in relation to its size and resources, but holding unpredictable power in the future of the Americas. To the literature of Brazil, Isaac Goldberg devoted a substantial close-packed volume; but very little has appeared in translation for English readers. Four Brazilian novels, however, that have been made available in English represent a varied literary art and illuminate Brazilian life in past and present aspects. Oldest and most famous of these is *Canaan*, by the scholar and diplomat Graça Aranha, among whose numerous works this is considered by many the masterpiece of Brazilian literature. It is, indeed, a philosophic-realistic-symbolic epic of human brotherhood rather than a novel; its theme, the quest in the New World of a simpler, more humane, more moral, freer and happier society than European civilization can ever attain to. The quest is futile: the German immigrant who seeks in Brazil this promised land, finds there only a continuing re-enactment of the eternal tragedy of man's hatreds, selfishness, brutalities, hypocrisies, egotism, and injustice. Long, elaborate, ranging from abstract philosophical disquisition to ruthless scenes of horror, with backgrounds that shift from city to wilderness, the book has remarkable qualities: rich and powerful imagery, vivid descriptive rendering of tropical beauty, distinctive characterizations, and an ingrained spiritual fervor.

Irony and realism dominate Aluizio Azevedo's tale of the making of a Brazilian millionaire, *A Brazilian Tenement*. Set in the late nineteenth century, it is a picturesque, episodic chronicle of ruthless greed and of mounting power over the lives of others: the building of a fortune by way of petty, obscure rascalities, exploitation of workers, ownership of a teeming tenement, speculation in real estate, to the emergence of a great capitalist with far-reaching "interests."

Brazilian history is reflected in *Domitila*, by Paulo Setúbal, one of the writers most loved in his native country. Setubal had originally intended to be a lawyer, but he began writing poetry and gave up a legal career to devote himself to historical romances that should make the history of Brazil their theme. *Domitila* is a rapid, dynamic novel, rendering one of the dramatic incidents of the reign of Dom Pedro I, first emperor of Brazil. Brazil, it must be remembered, discovered by the Portuguese in 1500, became a Portuguese colony and is today the only country in the western world that speaks the Portuguese language. It was ruled by an imperial governor until 1808, when the King of Portugal fled before Napoleon's invasion, and taking his court of 1,200 persons transferred his seat of government to Brazil. This changed Brazil from a colony to the governing capital of the Portuguese world. For twelve years this continued; then, in 1820, after Napoleon's downfall, the king returned to Portugal, leaving his son, Dom Pedro, to govern Brazil. In 1822 the young prince yielded to the growing Brazilian movement for independence, proclaimed Brazil independent of Portugal, and became Dom Pedro I, founder of a new empire in a new world. He ruled until 1831, when he abdicated and returned to Portugal and was succeeded by his son, the famous emperor Dom Pedro II, who ruled for the next half century and abdicated in 1889, when the Brazilian revolution was accomplished and Brazil became the present republic of federated states, the United States of Brazil. Setúbal's novel deals with the reign of Dom Pedro I, from the proclamation of Brazilian independence, in 1822, until 1829. It centers in the rise to power, the triumph, and the downfall of the beautiful Domitila, mistress of the emperor, who for ten years held the strings of political power and who came within a hair's breadth of achieving her passionate ambition of being crowned as empress after the death of Dom Pedro's wife. Historical fact is closely followed; most of the characters are actual persons, politicians, courtiers, officials of the days of the first empire. Costumes and customs, letters and documents quoted and referred to, dramatic incidents, and the whole sequence of events are part of historic record. It is a brilliant, picturesque evocation: a mingling of Old World magnificence and the tropical luxuriance of the semi-barbaric New World. Character portrayal, psychological values, and realistic detail are negligible; the tale is essentially a vivid, pictorial unfolding of passion and intrigue, of a woman's consuming ambition, and of the absolutism and selfish pleasure-seeking of a young ruler, swayed only by his emotions. While the novel has romantic and dramatic interest, its significance is as a reflection of the brilliance, luxury, and tense political conflict of this chapter of Brazil's history.

On the novel by Ferreira de Castro rests the enormous shadow of the jungle. Here the high-keyed intensity of Rivera's phantasmagoria of the Colombian rubber forests is transposed and stabilized into a tempered, thorough, sympathetic, and deeply interesting presentation of life on a rubber plantation in the Rio Madeira jungle of southwestern Brazil. *Jungle: a Tale of the Amazon Rubber-Tappers* has continuing values of firsthand knowledge and of bringing to simple, clear reality the remote, savage little colonies whose existence centered in the struggle to obtain rubber. Undercurrents of exploitation, of suffering and cruelty, are here; there is psychological insight and distinctive character portrayal; and the mysterious, terrifying atmosphere of the jungle is infused into this story of a young university student, a political exile from his native Portugal, who is suddenly thrust into the barbarous, almost hopeless life of a rubber tapper, but who rises from the slavery of "the avenues" and at last returns to freedom.

Chile's most famous novelist is Alberto Blest Gana, whose ambition was to be the American Balzac. His life spanned nearly a century (he was born in 1830 and died in 1922), and in its two periods of literary activity, separated by thirty years of diplomatic service in Europe, he produced more than a dozen novels concerned with Chilean history and with critical, penetrating study of contemporary society. *Martin Rivas*, published in 1862, is his masterpiece. It is a long, elaborate novel, old-fashioned in manner, but a mirror of the life and character of its day and place. It is set in Santiago, about 1850. Martin Rivas (truly a hero of the Victorian stamp of nobility and rectitude!) is a young man from the country who makes his home with the family of a wealthy financier, who had built up his riches by fraudulently gaining from Martin's father the silver mine that was the source of his fortune. In this household Martin becomes indispensable; while carrying on his own studies at the law, he is also secretary and adviser to the father, friend and helper to the silly, foppish son, and cherishes a deep, hidden devotion for the beautiful and willful daughter, Leonor. The mother is lazy and luxury loving, devoted to her lapdog; and there is an attractive young cousin, whose unfortunate love affair educes the dramatic and tragic elements of the plot. This family of wealth and pretensions, ambitious for social advancement, is set in contrast with a lower-class family (mother, two daughters, and worthless, scheming son) in a very interesting portrayal of caste lines and differences in customs and manners of living. There are intricate love involvements, resulting feud and complexities, and Martin's participation in the revolutionary uprising of 1851. He is arrested and condemned to death; his danger brings Leonor to realization of her love, and she manages to enlist influences that enable him to escape, so that a "happy ending" is successfully accomplished. In spite of its length and its Victorian qualities, the variety of scenes and the complex interest of events make the story move rapidly and hold its interest to the end. Reality and vitality are established: the reader steps into a living world, into social and home life, into politics, into the festivities and cross currents that made the everyday existence of Chileans of that particular period, all conveying the historic and human reality which is the achievement of fine fiction.

Argentine fiction is more generously represented in English translation than is that of any other Latin American country. In these novels we may find the historical aspect, reflecting the fierce civil wars of the second quarter of the nineteenth century; the aspect of modern social problems and changing economic conditions; the romantic and dramatic rendering of regional and local backgrounds. Argentina made its first definite impact upon English readers early in the present century, when belated recognition came to W. H. Hudson's novel, *The Purple Land*, with its exotic, pictorial backgrounds, its powerful portrayal of the violent years of struggle against the tyrant-dictator Rosas. Those years, in fact, brought an uprush of passionate expression from Argentine writers, for the whole country was torn and convulsed under the conflict. To understand this, it should be said that after the separation from Spain, Argentina was organized as a centralized or "unitarian" republic, with the capital in Buenos Aires. The provinces, however—the vast plains, with their great ranchos and the half-Spanish, half-Indian gauchos who made up most of the population—refused to accept the rule of the city, rose in rebellion, and demanded a federal republic with a large measure of local autonomy. There were years of civil war; the unitarian party was beaten by the federalists under the leadership of Juan Manuel Rosas, who for twenty-three years, until his downfall in 1852, exerted absolute power and carried on merciless extermination of his enemies. Not until nearly fifty years later was the political conflict finally resolved, when Buenos Aires was made a federal district and capital of the republic. Rosas represented the gauchos of the interior, what would probably today be called the proletariat; his policy of extermination was directed against the intellectual and aristocratic elements, so that the struggle against him was inspired and maintained by the educated classes, the journalists, poets and writers. Many fled to Chile, where they brought a freshening vigor to Chilean literature and infused in it their own vehement protest against despotism.

Foremost among the Argentine writers of this period is José Mármol (1817–71), whose novel *Amalia* lives as a passionate exposition of the tyranny and degradation of the Rosas dictatorship. Mármol at the age of twenty was imprisoned as a conspirator, scribbling on the walls of his cell a quatrain denouncing the tyrant. This denunciation he continued through years of danger and of exile, in long poems, in quatrains, and in his memorable novel. *Amalia* conveys the incandescent intensity of his hatred and gives also a remarkable social study of this period in Argentine history, by one who was himself an actor in the events he portrays and who experienced the feelings he describes. It is a long, elaborate historical novel, patterned on Sir Walter Scott, which centers on the tyranny and ferocity of Rosas and the social degradation existing in Buenos Aires under his rule. Its chief actor is a young man, Daniel Bello, enlisted in the struggle against the dictator, but protected in his operations because he is the son of one of Rosas's supporters, and so working skillfully and subterraneously with those who are plotting Rosas's overthrow. The love story, which is a central thread, is woven about Amalia, Daniel's cousin, and a young rebel who is wounded and left for dead in an attack by police and hidden in her house, where she nurses him back to health. The youth is tracked down by Rosas's agents; danger and intrigue menace the lovers and bring the tale to a tragic climax. The novel has unity, power, and sustained interest; a depth of personal feeling and a vividness of description and characterization that give it value as an evocation of time and place and personal experience.

Manuel Gálvez, in *Nacha Regules,* represents the Argentine novelist of modern development, studying the problems and mores of the life he knows. This was the first important postwar novel of Argentina, and for it the city of Buenos Aires awarded Gálvez the prize for letters for the year 1920. One of the leading authors of his own country, his work has been widely translated into other languages, and his name has been put forward for the Nobel prize for literature. Nacha Regules is a girl of the streets, who by chance wakens the pity and interest of a Buenos Aires lawyer, a thinker and an idealist. The story tells of his efforts to save her from degradation and suffering and to bring home to society a realization of evils for which it is ultimately responsible. A Tolstoyan touch of idealistic and humanitarian philosophy is evident throughout, but there is Latin emotionalism in the contest of mutual self-sacrifice that is carried on between Nacha and Dr. Monsalvat. The conclusion is one of defeat and disillusion on the surface; but with love and idealism unextinguished and spiritually triumphant. *Holy Wednesday,* Gálvez's second novel to be translated into English, is slighter, simpler, and has a similar undercurrent of idealism. In it we hear the sins of a great city through the grating of a confessional box as we follow one day in the life of Father Solanas, the most popular confessor in Buenos Aires.

The romantic, the dramatic, and the pictorial prevail in the work of Gustavo Martínez Zuviría ("Hugo Wast"), most popular and prolific Argentine novelist, several of whose books have been translated into English. Of these, *The Stone Desert* should have interest and fascination for any reader; it is the author's own favorite—the novel, he says, which he "most desired to write." Its title comes from the name of a tract of land at the upper end of a great ranch near the top of a remote mountain zone of central Argentina. The old and childless owner of the ranch has received in his home a nephew, whose daughter of twenty is left to maintain and carry on the management. Her struggle and the dangers she encounters are woven into a dramatic, exciting plot, accompanied by strange, impressive natural backgrounds, glimpses of primitive, picturesque ways of life, and arresting characterizations. *Black Valley* is the Zuviría novel that received a prize from the Royal Spanish Academy. It, too, has strong romantic and dramatic, often melodramatic, flavor, and it strikes a deeper note of tragedy than *The Stone Desert*. It is set in the same remote, mountainous locale—which is the author's native region—a lonely, haunting valley, a place of storms and silence; it weaves a complex plot of inherited feuds, family enmities, and deep-channeled passions, and it closes on a note, not of romantic fulfillment, but of renunciation. *The Strength of Lovers* is a re-telling of one of the famous tragedies of the Discovery era: the story of Captain Sebastian Hurtado and his beautiful, valiant wife, Lucia Miranda, who were members of the Sebastian Cabot expedition that sailed from Spain for the new world in 1526 and who met death together at the hands of the Indians of the Paraná River region. English readers may remember that in Charles Kingsley's *Westward Ho!* this story is related by Don Guzman, the Spaniard captured by Amyas Leigh and held for ransom in Devon, as an example of the devotion and courage of his countrymen.

For the traditional life of the Argentine pampas, Ricardo Güiraldes's novel *Don Segundo Sombra* will long remain a modern classic. It has been called the South American Huckleberry Finn; and in its portrayal of boyhood and youth in the cattle country it has, for all its exotic background and Latin spirit, qualities that justify the comparison. Don Segundo is the philosophical old gaucho under whom the boy who has fled from his home to escape restrictions and monotony serves his apprenticeship as herdsman and for whom he has unwavering reverence and affection. A story thread is entwined in the vivid, rough-cast chronicle of the hard work on the pampas, the casual loves, the friends and associates and adventures of the wandering young herdsman, who comes at last to his own family rights and assured well-being. Unusual in warmth and rich human vitality, charm and delicacy are here, in spite of brutality and harshness and rough realism of speech. This is one of the South American novels that linger in memory as do the books of W. H. Hudson.

Don Segundo Sombra is linked in such illuminating relationship with *Martin Fierro*, the famous folk ballad of the gaucho, by José Hernández, that a word should be said of that national epic of the Argentine. Hernández's poem, of which the first part was published in 1872 and the second part seven years later, both immortalizes and symbolizes the gaucho, in the figure of Martin Fierro, who, as Walter Owen says, stepped out of its pages "to become the embodiment of his hardships and rugged virtues, the champion of his wrongs, the spokesman of his class for social justice." It is a verse narrative of gaucho life, mingling the epic and the lyric, redolent of the pampas, of the rank, pristine living of plain and outpost, of round-up, and cattle brand, and Indian raid. A series of vivid, authentic pictures of a life and a time now past, it challenges the government practice of forced recruiting, the official corruption and injustice of which the plainsmen were victims. Translated by Walter Owen into English verse that is designed to keep the chanting, ballad form of the original, it was published in a limited English edition in 1935 and in facsimile American issue a year later,[5] and it should be known and enjoyed by many English readers.

Varied aspects of Argentina's literary art, as of its life and backgrounds, are revealed in Waldo Frank's volume *Tales from the Argentine*. Here are gathered seven stories by writers who were masters in their fields, reflecting conditions and scenes that are now part of the country's past. These tales open vistas of the tangled jungles, of the primitive villages of the pampas, of the secret wild creatures of the great rivers and the forest wilderness; they depict different human types, the gaucho, the vagabond, the dwellers in country towns; and they convey the color and fever of life in Buenos Aires during the stormy days of the past. Most original and fascinating is the story that closes the volume: "The Return of

[5] José Hernández, *The Gaucho, Martin Fierro;* adapted from the Spanish and rendered into English verse by Walter Owen, with drawings by Alberto Güiraldes, New York, Farrar & Rinehart, 1936.

Anaconda," by Horacio Quiroga, native Uruguayan, who is the leading Argentine short story writer of today. This is a little masterpiece of fantastic, imaginative conception: the tale of the strong and beautiful young serpent, Anaconda, who leads a rebellion of the jungle against man, the intruder, sweeping down through her vast hunting grounds on the turbulent flood waters of the mighty river, swollen and irresistible after the deluge of rain; only to meet disaster through the overpowering force on which she had planned her triumph.

Last in this gleaning is Uruguay, represented by a selection of Quiroga's remarkable short stories and by one novel in English translation. This, *Castanets*, is the work of Carlos Reyles, leading novelist of the Rio de La Plata region; but it is Spanish, not South American, in theme and setting: a swift, passionate tale of prewar Seville, exhaling the traditional atmosphere of bullfight and dance. Of Reyles's various novels that reflect life and character in his native Uruguay, none have as yet appeared in English translation.

Latin American Fiction in English Translation
(*Selective list*)

ARGENTINA

Frank, Waldo, *ed.* Tales from the Argentine; trans. by Anita Brenner. New York, Farrar, 1930.

Gálvez, Manuel. Holy Wednesday [Miércoles Santo]; trans. by W. B. Welles. New York, Appleton-Century, 1934.

—— Nacha Regules; trans. by Leo Ongley. New York, Dutton, 1922.

Güiraldes, Ricardo. Don Segundo Sombra: Shadows on the Pampas; trans. by Harriet de Onis. New York, Farrar, 1935.

Mármol, José. Amalia; trans. by M. J. Serrano. New York, Translation Pub. Co., 1919.

Martínez Zuviría, Gustavo A. ("Hugo Wast"). Black Valley [Valle negro]; trans. by Herman and Miriam Hespelt. New York, Longmans, 1928.

—— Peach Blossom [Flor de durazno]; trans. by Herman and Miriam Hespelt. New York, Longmans, 1929.

—— The Stone Desert [El desierto de piedra]; trans. by Louis Imbert and Jacques LeClerq. New York, Longmans, 1928.

Martínez Zuviría, Gustavo A. The Strength of Lovers [Lucia Miranda]; trans. by Louis Imbert and Jacques LeClerq. New York, Longmans, 1930.

BRAZIL

Azevedo, Aluizio de. A Brazilian Tenement [O cortiço]; trans. by Harry W. Brown. New York, McBride, 1926.

Ferreira de Castro. Jungle: a Tale of the Amazon Rubber-Tappers [A selva]; trans. by Charles Duff. New York, Viking, 1935.

Goldberg, Isaac, ed. *and trans.* Brazilian Tales. Boston, Four Seas, 1921.

Graça Aranha, José Pereira da. Canaan; trans. by Mariano Joaquín Lorente. Boston, Four Seas, 1920.

Setúbal, Paulo. Domitila: the Romance of an Emperor's Mistress; trans. by Margaret Richardson. New York, Coward-McCann, 1930.

CHILE

Blest Gana, Alberto. Martin Rivas. New York, Knopf, 1918; also, Boston, Heath, 1936.

Prieto, Jenaro. Partner [El socio]; trans. by Bianca de Roig and Guy Dowler. London, Butterworth, 1931.

COLOMBIA

Isaacs, Jorge. María; trans. by Rollo Ogden. New York, Harper, 1890, 1925.

Marroquín, Lorenzo. Pax; trans. by Isaac Goldberg and W. V. Schier-brand. New York, Brentano's, 1920.

Rivera, José Eustacio. The Vortex [La vorágine]; trans. by Earle K. James. New York, Putnam, 1935.

MEXICO

Azuela, Mariano. Marcela: a Mexican Love Story [Mala yerba]; trans. by Anita Brenner. New York, Farrar, 1932.

—— The Under Dogs [Los de abajo]; trans. by E. Munguía; il. by J. C. Orozco. New York, Brentano's, 1929.

López y Fuentes, Gregorio. El indio; trans. by Anita Brenner; il. by Diego Rivera, New York, Bobbs-Merrill, 1937.

Menéndez, Miguel Angel. Nayar; trans. by Angel Flores. New York, Farrar, 1941.

PERU

Alegría, Ciro. Broad and Alien Is the World [El mundo es ancho y ajeno]; trans. by Harriet de Onis. New York, Farrar, 1941.

URUGUAY

Quiroga, Horacio. South American Jungle Tales [Cuentos de la selva]; trans. by Arthur Livingstone. New York, Duffield, 1922.

Reyles, Carlos. Castanets [El embrujo de Sevilla]; trans. by Jacques LeClerq. New York, Longmans, 1929.

VENEZUELA

Blanco-Fombona, Rufino. The Man of Gold [El hombre de oro]; trans. by Isaac Goldberg. New York, Brentano's, 1920.

Gallegos, Rómulo. Doña Barbara; trans. by Robert Malloy. New York, Cape & Smith, 1931.

IX. SPELLS, SIGNS, AND SYMBOLS

*Man knows his littleness; his own mountains remind
him; but the dreams of man make up for our faults
and failings; for the brevity of our lives, for the narrowness of our scope; they leap over boundaries and
are away and away.*—LORD DUNSANY: *Don Rodriguez*

FANTASY, satire, allegory, symbolism, and extravaganza are
forms of Romance as it survives in fiction today, in contrast to
Reality, which is the province of the novel. This fiction of romance
has a far range and many different manifestations. It carries heritage
from a long succession of precursors: from fable and parable, from
epic hero-chronicles, from allegorical narratives of spiritual or philosophic edification, from the elaborate romances of chivalry and
fabulous adventure, from the "Gothic tale" of terror and the supernatural. Though it may merge with the novel in substance and
method, it remains interveined with imagination, touched with
poetry, freed from fetters of fact. Fantasy and symbolism tinge the
ambience of Hawthorne's New England; allegory and mysticism
transform Melville's *Moby Dick* from the history of a whaling cruise
into an epic of material and spiritual conflict. Hudson's *Green Man-
sions*, filtering poetic allegory through the lights and shades of
tropical forest adventure; De la Mare's *Memoirs of a Midget*, with
its underlying compassionate, philosophic parable; Dunsany and
James Stephens, turning fairy lore and ancient magic to humor,
irony, tenderness, and beauty of imagination; Arthur Machen's
transmutation of the material world into strange spiritual substance
of mystery and terror; Aldous Huxley's ruthless fantasies of mechanized, decadent humanity—these are a few siftings of the richness,
variety, and significance to be found in this field of fiction.

Values here are neither factual nor informational. For fantasy is a medium that reflects reality through unreality, that interprets life through illusion and plays with shimmering implications and urgencies over human experience and human character, pricking out follies, tragedies, absurdities, frustrations, telescoping time, generating its own light rays for past, present, and future. It deals in prophecy; through satire, burlesque, and make-believe it assays human qualities; through poetic mirage it penetrates to the realities of the heart. In structure and method it is often also a medium for experimentation in expression, for invention in word usage, for novel mechanics of narration or visualization. Its values are the values of imagination: as a means of conveying emotional or intellectual perception of truths not openly presented; as detonator of the high explosive of ideas; as a weapon of mockery for attack or defense; as stimulus to the sense of beauty and the sense of humor; and as release of the spirit of wonder and frolic that belongs to the eternal child within us. Thus, imaginative response is necessary for the enjoyment of fantasy; and as there are more literal-minded people than imaginative ones, this fiction in its purer manifestations has comparatively little appeal to the great body of readers who find satisfaction in the novel that pictures life and interprets character in terms of their familiar backgrounds, their everyday experience. The spirit of fantasy, however, as it fuses into the realism of modern fiction, imparts the transforming touch of glamor that is the secret of the story-teller's art.

For all its wide range and the free leeway it seems to offer the writer, fiction of fantasy makes more rigorous demands upon intention and craftsmanship than does the novel of every-day realism. Essentially an exercise of the creative imagination, creation must "come off," imagination must reveal itself: Dr. Jekyll and Mr. Hyde must be convincing human personalities as well as symbols of man's double nature; the pitiful plight of Wells's invisible man must be an obvious, credible circumstance of incredible experience. Even a flight of fancy, whether through Wonderland or to the Brave New World, must have a starting-point, follow a course, and arrive somewhere. The symbolic motive, however elusive and enigmatic to pursuit, must yield itself to intuitive perception. Idea must be integrated with dramatic substance; subtlety of insight must be balanced with strong pictorial power; and both must be deftly controlled to focus on the writer's conscious purpose. The fact that in the world of fantasy irrationalities, impossibilities, dreamlike intensities of poetic vision or haunting nightmare receive calm and matter-of-fact acceptance, demands that consistent credibility within the frame of incredibility be maintained by the writer and acceded to by the reader.

Great as is the diversity of fantasy fiction, it includes certain patterns that constantly repeat themselves, in structural adaptation, extension, or embellishment, or in changing modes of expression. Within these patterns are established different types that in their variations and their relationships indicate the range and the values of a body of fiction which is to the novel of realism what poetry is to prose. Among them I would note the fantasy-chronicle, the fantasy-idyl, and the fantasy-novel. The fantasy-chronicle is the most elaborate, sometimes taking on saga dimensions: complex in structure, often intricate in detail, luxuriant in phrase and imagery, veined with symbolism or infused with allegory, this is a medium for social satire, for philosophic or aesthetic idealism, for irony or despair or mockery or hope concerning man's nature, man's experience, and man's aspirations. The fantasy-idyl is on a smaller scale, simpler, more concentrated, fragile yet intense; poetic, meditative, ironic, sentimental, or gay; sometimes tinged with transcendental, sometimes with religious ardor. In the fantasy-novel there is a stronger element of realism; tipped or underlaid with symbolism or allegory, it has a sustained current of dramatic excitement, and usually some play of adventure, some unexpected glamorous or ironic climax. An ancient and prolific type is that of the Utopias, evangels of the perfectibility of man's future, revisions of the world as it is, previsions of the world as it will be. From this type stems the more modern exploration and comparison of past, present, and future through travels-in-time, in which fantasy seizes on marvels of modern science, concepts of the new physics, and theories of past and future coexistent in a timeless universe and turns them into vehicles of social, political, and ethical prophecy. Interplanetary voyages are excursions as familiar as travels-in-time, and there are many other subsidiary types: scientific fantasy, adventurous, satirical, or monitory; doctrinaire fantasy, bizarre excursions in wishful thinking; psychic fantasy, pursuing adventures of the interior self; esoteric fantasy, drawing from the arcana of occult lore. Literature, history, biography, are also caught in fantasy's net, to be teased with nipping humor or enmeshed in satiric interpretation. Primitive fable, myth, fairy tale, and ghost story, in modern incarnation, all have their types in this fiction of make-believe, mingling humor and terror with wisdom, folly, ribaldry, and tenderness.

Two fantasy-chronicles, one American, one English, command first attention in any survey of this present-day fiction of romance. James Branch Cabell's chronicles of Poictesme, through some ten years, from 1917, established a new province on the map of make-believe; Eric R. Eddison's realm of Zimviamvia, unknown to the mapmakers until 1935, has been charted since then by virtue of the chronicles that trace its boundaries. Both are sequences of saga amplitude, immense mosaics of arabesque design, worked out with exuberance of invention and high literary art from rich materials of erudition. Each also conveys its own philosophy of life, one ironic, the other aesthetic; and while neither is likely to appeal to readers at large, each has its lure for sophisticates or virtuosos.

The rise of James Branch Cabell stands as an example of the rapid creation of a literary cult through the peremptory enthusiasm of fellow writers and the stimulus of official censorship. The imaginary land of Poictesme—perhaps a province of medieval France—which Mr. Cabell has invented and populated with brilliantly colored figures, in part legendary, in part evoked from curious Middle Age chronicles, is the background, present or implied, for the whole sequence of elaborately interrelated tales, which Cabellian devotees have called a greater fictional epic than Balzac's "Human Comedy." Thus, in the earlier novels of modern Virginia, known as the Lichfield group, Poictesme is still a dream country of refuge or an ancient, hereditary motherland of desire and disillusion, while the elaborate "Lineage of Lichfield," historic-genealogical accompaniment to the complete sequence, traces a continuous line of descent for all the characters of the eighteen volumes, who are conceived as figures representing the extended lives of the two germ characters, Dom Manuel and Jurgen, of Poictesme. For Poictesme is the soil in which Cabell has planted and cultivated the twin themes, of romance and of woman, that dominate his literary art. His theme of romance is of romance as illusion. Illusion controls and shapes man's conception of life, giving him the only conception that makes life endurable. In reality (if there is reality), life is meaningless and unprofitable, the floating moment of experience of futile creatures who know nothing, achieve nothing, and are themselves frustrate or contemptible. But through illusion they create unrealities, so-called ideals—religion, virtue, heroism—which they regard as beautiful or noble or inspiring.

His theme of woman centers on sex. He sees her as invested with a power of mystery, exemplified in the traditions of witches and sorceresses, and as the object of man's dreams and yearnings. She must have eternal youth and beauty, she must be always both the unfaltering temptress and the eluding object of man's quest, which finds its culmination in sensuous ecstacies. This "woman worship" ("domnei," in the old French term) runs through the chronicles in a richly tapestried pseudo-medieval imagery and symbolism that veil and for many conceal the erotic meaning. Insistent repetition of these two themes, however ornamented by exotic inlays and flourishes of ingenious raillery, gives sterility and monotony to Cabell's art. His spirit, rooted in despair, puts forth its buds of irony to wither and die in unchanging succession. *Jurgen* came with a shock of novelty, as a fresh, witty, insolent challenge to puritanism and provincialism; suppression of the book by the New York censor, and the long and celebrated trial that finally revoked the suppression, helped carry it to popular success. But even Jurgen proved tiresome to many readers, and his precursors, successors, and associates— Dom Manuel, Duke Florian, Count Emmerich, Perion, Horvendile, and their glittering and dubious queens, dames, and damsels—

resolve themselves into an array of brilliantly colored puppets, re-
peating over and over again in artificial advance, retreat, and gesture,
the motions of a phallic dance.

Jurgen, at once the germ, the crux, the pattern, of all the Poictesme chronicles, is a work of great literary ingenuity. The depth
and breadth and width of its symbolism are fortunately undeter-
minable by most readers. Very few realize what lore of the erotic
has been drawn from the whole fabric of literature, from primitive
fable and classic legend, and molded into this elaborate composition
of sex adventure, in which "double meaning" in the French sense
has been brought to consummate expression. The journeyings of
Jurgen, the little paunchy pawnbroker of Poictesme, through realms
of legend, fantasy, and ancient fable, have enlisted all Cabell's mordant wit, his medievalized fancy, his sardonic imagination, and his
gift of sensuous imagery and word embroidery. Jurgen has adven-
tured in search of his wife, sharp-tongued and unlovely, who has
been spirited away by Koschei (one of the Cabellian similitudes
of God); also he seeks to discover the system of justice on which
the universe is governed. His tour carries him to the garden of men's
illusions, to Hell, to a chat with Grandfather Death, to an interview
with God, and amid a glittering, ever-moving array of hamadryads,
nymphs, witches, heroines of legend and epic: Guenevere, Helen
of Troy, temptresses and beauties of all the ancient lore of the
world. His illusions and ideals are scattered and lost, he finds all
the heroines of his dreams essentially the same, desire loses itself
in satiety, he learns that in life there is no justice, no order, no essential meaning; and he returns to his commonplace wife, who has
been restored to him, and to his pawnbroking. While *Jurgen* was
one of the earliest Poictesme chronicles and remains the most widely
known, it is integrated among the later narratives within the framework of "The Biography," which is the collective conception of
the work: the life story of Dom Manuel of Poictesme, recorded
as that life was lived by him in varying fields, and as it has been
perpetuated in the descendants of Dom Manuel down to the present
day. *Domnei, Figures of Earth, The High Place, The Silver Stallion*

in Poictesme chronology precede *Jurgen;* but their design and texture is essentially the design and texture of *Jurgen.*

Cabell's fantasy-chronicle stands as an important contribution to American fiction. It first developed in the American reading public a continental attitude toward erotic literary art; its injection of a philosophic salacity, a Rabelaisian humor, into the evocation of sex experience, broke down the inhibitions of a century of American prudery. It opened to American writers a form of expression that has flourished in all world literature, but that had been suppressed and clamped down under the lid of nineteenth-century moralism in American literature until *Jurgen* triumphed over the censor.

Eric R. Eddison's epical conceptions shape themselves in a prose saturated with poetic glamor and romantic exuberance. The prelude to his chronicle-sequence is *The Worm Ouroboros,* published in 1926, a surging, glittering fantasy of warfare waged between two great kingdoms of the planet Mercury. In flowing, antiquated English it pours out battle passages that have the magnificence of Viking sagas and visualizes strange and beautiful material surfaces with an intensity that infuses them with immediate reality. There is no conscious artificiality: this is a flight of the creative imagination toward illimitable horizons of timeless conflict between beauty and evil. Sign and symbol hint of themes that underlie more strongly the later chronicles: joy of life as joy of conflict heroically waged; love as service and protection of beauty, beauty as ultimate power, evil as continually overcome and reborn, and personality as multiple and inextinguishable, existing simultaneously in different dimensions of time, eternally renewed: "the end ever at the beginning and the beginning at the end for ever more." Nine years later came the main chronicle of the sequence, *Mistress of Mistresses,* a vast, unique, and beautiful arabesque of fantasy and phrase, set in the land of Zimviamvia, which is apparently also a region of the planet Mercury and, like Poictesme, has its carefully traced geography, cartography, and chronology, its dynasties, principalities, and powers. Zimviamvia, "sacred to the lordly races of the dead," is the land, Mr. Eddison says, "of which the philosophers tell us that no mortal foot may tread it, but the blessed souls do inhabit it of the dead that were great upon earth and did great deeds, that scorned not earth and the delights and glories thereof, and who here forever again live, love, do battle, and even for a space die again."

Over an intricate substructure of poetry, philosophy, and love, against changing backgrounds of extraordinary vividness, flows a narrative of romantic adventure in eternity, where time is counted, though it is really timeless, and love in many successive experiences is really one experience. It eddies around that Lessingham who played the part of observer in *Ouroboros:* English descendant of the Vikings, personification of knightliness, ardor, and learning, master of fabulous wealth and power, and worshipper of the glorious Aphrodite, "mistress of mistresses," who in many incarnations shares and inspires his destiny. The prologue tells of Lessingham's death in his Norse castle, which he commands shall be burned as his funeral pyre. Then, entered into Zimviamvia, he lives the first day of his transfiguration amid dream-plots and counterplots, battle, love, danger, guile, and triumph; but in Zimviamvia, as in Valhalla and Paradise, one day is a lifetime. There is throughout a sweeping, changing luxuriance of language, sometimes of Swinburnian rhythm, sometimes vigorous Elizabethan, lordly or plebeian, sometimes Romanesque, sometimes echoing the cadences of Greece; and an atmosphere of magical enchantment, like a shining, iridescent bubble, is beautifully sustained.

A Fish Dinner in Memison carried the chronicle to fuller development in 1941. More complex in treatment, equally massive in bulk, there is here stronger emphasis on the philosophic themes of ultimate reality as subsisting in a masculine-feminine dualism; and of individual personality as divisible and inexhaustible, continuing timeless coexistence on different planes of being. Thus, we have a "daylight" narrative, love story of Lessingham and his Mary, covering twenty-five years of English life (from 1908); and a Zimviamvia narrative that, running contemporaneously, covers a single month in the dream drama of sensuous beauty, of love, hatred, villainy, and valor played by the dwellers beyond earth horizons. Both narratives interweave; transition from one to the other is indicated only by shift of scene and action and change in phrasing from stately, sensitive English to the more archaic vigor, glowing color, and idiomatic variety of Zimviamvian discourse. Both groups of personages are living at the one moment in several dimensions of time; the six lovers, mundane and supermundane, are divined as ultimately but one pair: two persons, not six, each at three several stages in the eternity of being. In Lessingham, conscious of transition to the realm beyond earth life, is a refraction of the personalities of Zimviamvia's king and his son Barganax; in Lady Mary Lessingham, conscious of transition as reunion, glint the personalities of Amalie, Duchess of Memison, the king's mistress, and of Fiorinda, beloved of Barganax; and in Fiorinda-Amalie-Mary is manifest the divine Aphrodite, hymned by Sappho: ultimate, undying beauty, power of desire and the desired. *A Fish Dinner*, in Zimviamvian chronology, precedes *Mistress of Mistresses*, but its slower pace and more involved structure make it appeal most strongly to the reader already familiar with this fabulous world; for here the materials and the organization of the whole chronicle may be discerned, and the intimations of infinity that radiate through it come to a focus in that marvelous birthday feast (true symposium) given by the Duchess of Memison—"A fish dinner: sea-fare, in Her praise that is bred of the sea foam."

Chiefly in the idyllic pattern are Robert Nathan's delicate fantasies, with their charm of humor and grace, their philosophic overtones, and ironic penetration. Their range is wide. Sometimes they link in miniature chronicles (as in *The Fiddler of Barly* and *The Woodcutter's House*), now and then they turn to the realism of the novel, tipped with make-believe (as in *One More Spring* and *They Went On Together*); their themes, whether fable or legend, reading of life, or romance of youth and love, deal simply with elemental emotions; and always they touch a melodic note peculiarly their own —a note as of an aeolian harp, rather than of any more sonorous or ordinary instrument. It is keyed below the common pitch, delicate and clear: a crystal tinkle, moved by a current of gentle, ironic, compassionate meditation on life. Mr. Nathan observes this planetary scene somewhat as Ariel might look upon it, and he points his commentary with a keen honesty that pierces accepted surfaces yet is so demurely muffled in fancy that not many realize how much that lies below has been revealed. All his books mingle imaginative conceits and shrewd characterization, humor and everydayness, romantic tenderness and what Unamuno calls the tragic sense of life, spontaneous delight in children, in animals, and in nature.

Fable and fancy are strongest elements in the two chronicles of Barly, set in the sylvan world around Hemlock Mountain, where forest and meadow and brookside are peopled with philosophical and loquacious dogs and beetles, mice, wasps, and horses, participants and advisers in a rustic idyl. Lucent satire, deft and penetrating in its implications, plays in *The Bishop's Wife* over the historic difficulty of serving God and Mammon and also over equally historic difficulties of love and marriage. The bishop, harassed and efficient under worldly burdens, needs a new assistant and remarks that only an archangel could fill the job. Then, surprisingly supplied, appears the new assistant, Dr. Michael, who is, in fact, the well-known archangel of that name; and then, as the bishop's charming young wife encounters the beautiful young archangel, come the waking of new emotions in the bishop's wife, inevitable under the circumstances, and a solution of the problem that is of age-old simplicity and verity. *There Is Another Heaven* waves the Ariel wand over Heaven: Heaven as the vision, the creation, of individual hopes, beliefs, and desires. Its theme is that if the heaven that delights someone else is unsatisfying to you, don't despair: there is another heaven that holds fulfillment of your nature, your individual heart's desire. Every man and woman craves happiness and creates for himself a heaven where happiness may be found. This implication lies in the experiences of a group of newcomers to Heaven: a lonely boy, an equally lonely professor of archaeology, a Jew who has left his ancient faith for this Christian community where he is superfluous and alien. To each comes the realization that "there is another heaven" which they must seek for their own happiness.

There are deeper tones and richer variations in other Nathan volumes. Legend and allegory mingle in *Jonah*, one of the earliest and still one of the most perfect. Here are the prophets of ancient Israel, dwelling in caves and rude huts in the desert beyond the Jordan. The young prophet, Jonah, from his desert resting place, where he holds theological converse with his friend the little fox, makes his way to Bethel, to carry to King Jeroboam the message of an angel. His utterance inspires Israel to victory, and Jonah is hailed as the new great prophet of his people. Yielding to the incense of deference and honor, he still cherishes his dream of love and simple human happiness; then, wakened from that dream in bitterness and despair, he flees vainly from his ordained service as prophet and is brought to final surrender by the ministrations of the kindly, argumentative whale, and the lesson of the withered vine—all as the record has come down through the ages. This, however, is not a paraphrase of the scriptural legend, but an imaginative apologue, ironic, meditative, and charming. Its characters are distinctive and firmly etched: Deborah, the mother of Jonah, to whom her prophet son, for all her adoring pride, is but a child to be soothed, and encouraged, and comforted; Aaron, his brother, the young herdsman, who considers this living in the desert rather a nonsensical thing to do and the life of a prophet no calling for a young man; Amaziah, high priest of Israel, who finds Jonah too idealistic for the ministry —"We churchmen are obliged to be practical; the important thing is that there should be uniformity"—all are flitting figures in the eternal human comedy, unchanging through time.

Nathan's finest work, *Road of Ages*, came in 1935, as a many-faceted, moving, and strangely prescient envisioning of one of the crucial world-themes of our day: a study of the destiny of the Jewish people, driven on unending roads of exile, bound together by common faith and common tragedy, but split asunder among themselves by differences of character, of aims, of circumstances, of opportunity. It is worked out in the future. The Jews have been expelled from virtually every country on earth, including Palestine; but the Mongols have been kind enough to offer them the Gobi desert as a last refuge. So, in interminable, straggling columns they wind their way across the Hungarian plains, through Yugoslavia and Rumania, across Russia, and on into Siberia: all the hosts of Israel, toiling on by ox cart and push cart, by motorcycle and bicycle, by battered old automobiles and beautiful, costly limousines. All sorts and conditions of mankind are here: liberal rabbis, strict rabbis; bankers, French, German, American; captains of industry from every world metropolis; shabby small shopkeepers, peddlers, actors from Hollywood, gamblers from the stock exchange, communists, socialists, great scientists, poets, physicians, British nobility —men and women, fathers, mothers, children, lovers, friends, and enemies. All have their hopes, their own ambitions, their deep mutual bonds; and all are at odds over how the future is to be planned. All have their partisanship, individual wills, strife, rivalries, passionate convictions, in faith, in love, in ways of living. Clearly but subtly, not a single race, but all mankind is mirrored in this realistic fantasy, which to any thoughtful reader poses the question: Is there really, after all, such a thing as "the Jewish problem"? Jews are like all other human beings: they conform to no average type; they may be capitalists, socialists, communists, orthodox or unorthodox, Frenchmen in France, Englishmen in England, citizens in whatever land their lot has been cast, like all other citizens. Culture and ignorance, self-sacrifice and selfishness, moral strength and depravity, brilliance and stupidity, honesty and deceit, faith and doubt, courage and cowardice—all are to be found among the Jewish race. And everything that is to be found among them is also to be found among the other peoples of the world they live in.

Simpler, stronger in realism is *They Went On Together*, a 1941 reading of the recent past, the immediate present, and the imminent future. Essentially, it is not fantasy, though only two years earlier it would have been so regarded, but reality distilled into imaginative prescience: a chronicle of tenderness and beauty, short, lucent, powerful and poignant, of America in war—just the same kind of war that came to other free and peaceful countries that cherished neutrality, placated or temporized with aggression, and made it their purpose to "keep out of war." There are no identifiable backgrounds; America is never mentioned; but this simple narrative of childhood and kindly living caught and carried to doom in the whirlpool of death and destruction is pure American substance, shaped in the common mold of human experience under German aggression. This is an American refugee pilgrimage: a little family of poor folk, mother and three children, in the vicissitudes and perils of flight, struggling on, they know not where, among crowds of others from peaceful farms, villages, and countrysides, along roads tangled with despairing troops, shadowed by swooping deathplanes, under skies darkened by smoke from burning towns. Warning and portent, rather than fantasy, hover over this moving, homely pilgrims' progress through terror and danger, that is a tragic historic reality of our day.

Radiations of fantasy, playing through myriad patterns, cast upon every aspect of life their beams of illumination, their enigmatic shadows of interpretation, their flashes of realization; for, as "A.E." says, "the human imagination is perpetually recreating the world." There are similarities to Nathan's work in Sylvia Townsend Warner's ironic, symbolic renderings of contemporary social themes: *Lolly Willowes*, delicately suggesting that the only escape for the spinster doomed to English conventional social restrictions is, quite literally, to go to the Devil; *The Return of Don Juan*, fusing the ancient legend with the tragic antinomies of modern Spain, in a fantasy novel of mingled realism and magic; *Mr. Fortune's Maggot*, doing with magnetic humor, feminine intuitiveness, and ironic skill what Sinclair Lewis did with bludgeon, hammer, and tongs in *Elmer Gantry*. This, one of her earliest books, is still fresh and timeless: the tale of the Reverend Timothy Fortune, warmhearted, middle-aged missionary, who spends three years on a South Sea island, seeking to convert the engaging, childlike, but logical-minded natives; who makes and loses just one convert; and who discovers for himself, in tragi-comic disillusion, that theological dogmas count for little beside the simple, universal facts of human nature. More power, more bizarre originality, and more latent poetic intensity are in David Garnett's short narratives (*Lady into Fox, A Man in the Zoo*), which interweave realism and allegory with a Defoe-like veracity that transforms a preposterous imagining into a carefully accredited fact. Richard Hughes, in *The Innocent Voyage* (*A High Wind in Jamaica*) fused fantasy and realism, absurdity and grim horror, to produce a unique, unforgettable psychological penetration of the strange self-contained secret world of childhood; Christopher Morley's *Thunder on the Left*, gay and poignant mingling of allegory and everyday actuality, plays over the intangible, insurmountable barrier that separates childhood from maturity; and realism and childhood mingle in the fantasy-tipped pattern of Enid Bagnold's novel *National Velvet*.

James Hilton's *Lost Horizon* is a fantasy novel, investing realistic dramatic adventure with a mirage-lure of unreality. Original and charming in its mingling of the factual and the imaginative, in character portrayal and wistful philosophic undertones, it carries the reader from the world's tumult to a secret ancient monastery in the remote heights of Tibet, and unfolds a way of life centered on beauty, tranquillity, and the pursuit of wisdom. More limited in popular appeal, finer in creative quality is *The Far-Away Bride*, Stella Benson's miniature fantasy novel, unique in its prismatic radiation of humor, imagination, and vivid realism. This delightful tale is concerned with a family of Russian refugees living in one of the Korean villages of Manchuria: the father, an old, grumbling, tearful, sentimental intellectual; his wife, disheveled, kindhearted, violent in temper and action; and their nineteen-year-old son, an emotional, purposeful youth, eager to exchange stagnation for adventure. The youth's journey to the Korean city of Seoul to collect 200 yen due to his father becomes the chronicle of "the far-away bride," the Russian girl, reputed to possess the evil eye, whom he encounters, marries, and with whom he returns to his parents, having recovered the money and been shepherded through many vicissitudes by an eloquent, virtuous, Oxford-bred Chinese companion. Brilliant in depiction of exotic scenes, in portrayal of a medley of Chinese, Korean, and Russian characters, a constant play of demure humor turns the dramatic or tragic into the absurd, and a lively concern and tenderness for the animal creation is matched by a quizzical indifference toward human woes or perplexities. Fantasy hovers lightly over the progress of Seryosha, his dog, his bride, and his protecting companion—which is natural enough, for this tale is, in fact, a paraphrase of the Story of Tobit, in the Apocrypha, worked out with whimsical exactitude and alluring parallelism. Very different is Aldous Huxley's fantasy novel, *After Many a Summer Dies the Swan*, distilling its essence of pessimism and scorn of the human race in a bitter, burlesquing satire that is like the savage humor of Swift. Southern California, in glittering ruthless caricature, furnishes setting for a fantastic plot through which is pursued the theme of escape into an orientalized philosophy of nonpersonality and peace from the futility, fear, animalism, and greed of common life today. One of the dominating elements of the tale is obscenity: not the material obscenity that is part of mortal living, but the obscenity of intellectual absorption in, pervading consciousness of, corruption and vice.

There is a gentle art of parody that springs from fantasy: an art that seeks, as Thomas Mann says, to "destroy without hatred, to abandon with a smile; imitation yet a jesting mockery. To reproduce the admired, the beloved, old and sacred pattern, on a plane and with a content that sets the stamp of parody." Such a reproduction is *The Trojan Horse*, Christopher Morley's brilliant transference to modernity of the ancient legend that Chaucer retold as the first great poem in English. This time projection of *Troylus and Cryseyde* into the thought, environment, and tempo of America's radio age is at once satirical, poetic, fantastic, and philosophic; holding with exactitude to the details of the Chaucer tale and transmitting the full measure of its spirit, its gentleness and courtesy and wit, its gaiety that touches compassion. The butterfly net of fantasy is rarely thrown so lovingly and skillfully over a great creation of literature.

John Erskine, more widely known than Morley in this art of parody, has woven about age-old legends an ingenious mesh of allegory or extravaganza that, half in mockery, half in preachment, is charged with social satire. *The Private Life of Helen of Troy*, his first book in this vein, won instant acclaim; it still remains his best, having an element of beauty, a freshness and sparkle that he has never recaptured. Essentially it is a series of discussions on life, love, birth, death, destiny, and beauty; and the investiture of its classic heroic figures (though the tale of Troy has ended) with modern speech and modern psychology is deft and amusing. But in all the later tracings of the Erskine key pattern—the arid, ironical rationalizations of Galahad, Penelope, Tristan—there is a cheapening and monotony in what has become an automatic process. Between Cabell and Erskine a certain kinship may be discerned; but whereas Cabell reduces all man's efforts and ideals to illusion and desire, Erskine comments and argues and reasons on the incompatibility of human conduct with the moral principles on which human relationships are presumably maintained.

Utopia is Nowhere-land. That name, invented by Sir Thomas More for the imaginary island of his famous speculative political treatise, has for more than four hundred years fathered innumerable expositions in imaginative social prophecy. As an exercise of the imagination, the Utopia pattern is fantasy, but it is also one of the most familiar mediums for serious social-philosophic doctrine or ruthless social criticism, and its many present-day variations give popular currency to possibilities of modern science and to new theories of the mathematics of time. Edward Bellamy's *Looking Backward* is the most famous American Utopia novel, not for its literary quality, which is nil, but for its continuing influence on social thought. First published in 1888, it still keeps its hold on the popular imagination as portrayal of a socialist millenium flourishing in Boston in the year 2000; in 1897 its sequel, *Equality*, appeared, to carry on the exposition of how crude socialist ideals of the nineteenth century were realized in future perfection: disappearance of the profit system, acceptance of a common religion (a sort of

Christian humanism), abolition of war, and abolition of poverty. In both books are many curious and fascinating anticipations of inventions and material developments that were unknown when they were written. Poetic charm and ethical idealism pervade the Utopia novel of W. H. Hudson, *A Crystal Age*, based on the persuasive idea that there can be no millenium, no rest, no permanence of peace until sexual passion has been eliminated from living. In this crystal universe truth and peace prevail and terrestrial visitors meet baffling, ironic vicissitudes. For nothing here remains of the world we know but a quintessence of freedom in which all live for art and beauty and love one another (without knowledge of sex) with tender passion.

Utopias of Wellsian vision are much more dynamic and various. Always his passionate belief in human perfectibility, his view of human history as a race between education and catastrophe, have given both the impetus and the aim of the amazing outpouring of scientific fantasies, adventures in the future, auguries and forewarnings of human destiny, that have made H. G. Wells a major prophet of the modern age. Nearly half a century ago, in his time-projection fantasy, *When the Sleeper Wakes*, he forecast for the year 2100 airplane warfare, television, air conditioning, and other inventions of the present day; but it was in 1923, in *Men Like Gods*, that the full specifications of his Utopia were set forth. This perfect state exists on another planet, unknown, adjacent to earth, but in another dimension of space. Inhabited by human beings, taller, more beautiful, and stronger than earthlings, its life closely parallels earth life but is in advance of it by three thousand years of high intelligence and scientific progress. There is no vocal speech, but communication is by transmission of thought when desired; sounds are used only for poetry, pleasure, moments of emotion, and to call at a distance, or with animals, but not for transmission of ideas. The outline of the development of his Utopia is a brilliant and searching exposition of Wells's own doctrine of social brotherhood, selective human breeding, scientific education, and co-operative effort. "Utopia has no parliament, no politics, no private wealth, no business competition, no police, no prisons, no lunatics, no defectives, no cripples, and it has none of these things because it has schools and teachers who are all schools and teachers can be." Said the Utopians: "Our education is our government."

Ten years later Aldous Huxley's *Brave New World* obliterated Wellsian ideas of amity, well-being, freedom, and intelligence, and set up a future totalitarian world-state, ruled by scientific materialism, dehumanized, industrialized, breeding denatured human beings to fit into rigid classifications. Huxley's despair and contempt for the modern world finds its most powerful expression in this brilliant, cruel satire of Swiftian savagery; it will stand, perhaps, as ultimate utterance of the "lost generation" of the first World War: soul-shocked, embittered intellectuals, whose stamp of disillusion is strong upon the fiction of the 1920's and early 1930's. Then, in 1940, Utopia was reorganized on a neo-Bellamic basis, with the older ideals of brotherhood and communal equality repolished and shining. Granville Hicks achieved this reconstruction in *The First to Awaken*, where, as in *Looking Backward*, a man of the present day is put to sleep for a hundred years. He awakens in March, 2040, to record in his diary sights and experiences encountered in a world based on a co-operative economy, where there is work for everyone in a four-hour workday, where arts and sports and leisure flourish, where housing, food, clothing, transportation, and medical care are free to all. Here there is a thirteen-month year, a duodecimal system of arithmetic, houses are translucent, rooms are lighted by fluorescent paint, automobiles are guided by radio beams, movies replaced by television, and clothing is made of plastic materials. Within the socialist-communist framework of a classless society, uncorrupted by the idea of property, by greed, or competitive struggle for money, is constructed this 1940 model of the perfect state.

Travels-in-time represent, of course, the usual mode of transit to Utopia; but there is much time-travel in other directions—science, adventure, and the plight of the world today impel to multitudinous flights of fantasy. Only a few, typical of themes now dominant, can be noted here. Most original and powerful imaginative projection

into the "mysterious universe" of the physicist-astronomers is that
achieved by Olaf Stapledon. His *Last and First Men*, "a story of
the near and far future," sweeps through some two billion years of
human history on the most colossal time-scale in fiction, records the
rise and fall of civilizations on earth, the development of successive
races of man on Mars, Venus, and Neptune, and carries down to
the eighteenth (and "last") race and the extinction of the solar
system in A.D. 2,000,000,000. In *The Star Maker* he ranges beyond
the solar system into life throughout the universe. Here each planet
experiences internecine wars; when these end, wars between planets
follow; the planets of one star unite in interplanetary peace, only
to engage in war with the planets of another star; star-clusters then
wage war against other clusters; gradually the universe grows too
cold to support life; but this universe will be succeeded and im-
proved upon by another creative effort of the Star Maker. Time-
travel into world catastrophe abounds. In *The Deluge* S. Fowler
Wright gave fascinating credibility to a world-wide earth movement that changed the surface configuration of the planet, swept
civilization to extinction in a second deluge, and struck back to
primitive existence the few survivors spared by chance or circumstance. There is more immediate symbolic portent and warning in
The Hopkins Manuscript, R. H. Sherriff's thrilling, plausible, and
moving narrative of cataclysmic collision of earth and moon, fore-
known, inevitable, to be awaited, prepared for, and endured; of
man's power to repair destruction wrought by nature, only to wreak
more complete destruction upon his fellow men. Mordant, pregnant
political prophecy underlies the imaginative horror of Joseph
O'Neill's *Land under England*, excursion into an underworld of
darkness, of fungi and strange reptiles, inhabited by an automaton
race with "no volition other than that supplied them by the state."

The second World War had many anticipations and reflections
in fantasy fiction. H. G. Wells forecast the growing menace in his
short, haunting allegory *The Croquet Player*; symbolized the origin, parallelism, and conflict of fascism and communism in *The
Brothers*; built a solid, elaborate counterfeit presentment of the

development of a dictator in *The Holy Terror;* and in *All Aboard for Ararat*, partly through witty, ribald extravaganza, partly through eloquent exposition, set forth specifications for a new Ark in which the best of mankind might be rescued from the flood of disaster loosed in 1940: "Let us set ourselves honestly to the only brave thing in life, which is beginning again." Clemence Dane attacked dictatorship in her fantastic allegory, *The Arrogant History of White Ben*, scarecrow with a mandrake heart, brought to life in England of the 1950's, rising to mad, perverted power, and in bloody tyranny exterminating the race of creatures for which he has a pathological hatred. Hendrik van Loon set in 1960 the "personal recollections" of *Invasion*, recording with meticulous verisimilitude a Nazi attack upon the United States, that simulated against an American background the actual course of events in Norway and Holland under German aggression in 1940.

These are a few of the patterns of fantasy in contemporary fiction. There are many others: patterns of dream, vision, and nightmare; of beauty and terror; of fancy, fable, and farce. The legacy of Aesop sparkles in present-day settings: wit and wisdom on human behavior radiate from the gay and sagacious chronicle of Christopher Morley's dog hero, Mr. Gissing, in his search for *Where the Blue Begins;* from G. B. Stern's philosophic excursions into the dog world of *The Dark Gentleman* and *The Ugly Dachshund;* from *My Talks with Dean Spanley*, Lord Dunsany's tantalizing glimpses into the former dog-existence of a dignified cleric; from Robert Nathan's gently quizzical Yorkshire-terrier odyssey, *The Journey of Tapiola*. Fable, legend, nature lore, pungent satire, schoolboy prankishness, and picturesque historic panoply of medieval England are all tossed together in the compound of imagination, humor, and wisdom from which T. H. White shaped his triple Arthurian fantasy-chronicle. *The Sword in the Stone*, first of the cycle, has the imperishable *Alice in Wonderland* quality. It should remain one of those classics of humorous imagination peculiar to the English genius, which play with ageless zest over the child-world of make-believe. In the brilliant harlequin enchantment of Merlin's magic—

the sage who lives backward instead of forward and so knows all that is going to happen next—the education of young Arthur to kingship unfolds through sharing the world wisdom of living creatures and learning by experience the code of honor, courage, and self-mastery. The succeeding volumes vary in character: farce and burlesque dominate *The Witch in the Wood;* psychological drama is conveyed with beauty and insight in *The Ill-Made Knight,* retelling the story of Arthur, Guenevere, and Lancelot. Streamlined to modernity, sparkling with topsy-turviness, the whole sequence is a unique, many-faceted commentary on Arthurian legend and on the deep-rooted, traditional English way of life. To many readers they may seem books for children; but in reality they are full-fledged fantasy at play for old as well as young. So is *The Hobbit, or, There and Back Again,* that adventure into the land of Faerie, where dragons, elves, goblins, dwarves, and creatures of magic still challenge the dominion of men. Written by J. R. R. Tolkien, professor of Anglo-Saxon at Oxford, for his own children, it fuses legend, tradition, and the dim beginnings of history into a robust imaginative creation that mingles homely simplicity, humor, drama, pictorial beauty, and a truly epic quality.

What, then, are the values of fantasy fiction? Imponderable in the scales of fact, intangible in the solid grasp of practical utility, baffling or obscure to the literal mind, they are values that stimulate the mind, refresh the spirit, and illuminate the many-colored web of life. Perhaps "A.E." best epitomizes them: "Imagination is the most powerful thing in human affairs. Intangible itself, it moves bodies. Invisible itself, it changes visible civilizations. The temples of old gods become ruins and desolate when the imagination is withdrawn from them. When imagination withers the world becomes stagnant."

X. THE LURE OF CRIME

*It is my opinion that mistakes will ultimately be
cleared up, justice done, and the true state of affairs
come to light, in spite of the false colours that may
for a time obscure it.*—WILLIAM GODWIN: *Adventures
of Caleb Williams; or, Things as They Are*

TIME does not wither nor custom stale the allure of the fiction
that centers on crime detection and the solution of mystery.
Although its roots go back into the remote past, tracing to ancient
episodes of astute deduction or to primitive folklore of supernatural
theme, as a distinct form of literary art it is barely a hundred years
old. Its growth for three-quarters of a century was sturdy, but mod-
erate, developing variations of type and reaching a steadily enlarging
public. Not until 1918 did its great advance in popularity begin, with
the impulsion of President Wilson's enthusiasm for *The Middle
Temple Murder*, first high light in the seemingly inexhaustible succession of "Fletcher mysteries." Since then its numbers have multiplied, its variations proliferated, it has enlisted alike novices and veterans of the writing craft, and it has become the popular indoor sport
of a predominantly masculine reading public. For men are still in the
majority among "mystery addicts," although the number of women
readers constantly increases and among practitioners of the art
women have won place in the first rank.

The art itself has taken on an immense diversity in type, building
on a basic substructure ingenious modern elaborations, scientific,
psychological, factual, idiomatic; while in its quality as literature, especially in the work of the younger writers entering the field, it
shows high narrative skill and apt delineation of character.

Many times within recent years the prediction has been made by
critics, publishers, and booksellers that the demand for detective and

mystery fiction would wane. But this has not happened; demand and supply alike continue. Each of the three leading American book review periodicals now maintains a special department for the appraisal of novels of this type, and nearly all the general publishing firms carry their own "line" of "mysteries." Knopf, who first brought J. S. Fletcher's detective tales to American readers; Appleton, with Nathalie Sumner Lincoln; Little, Brown, with Oppenheim; Dodd, Mead, with Agatha Christie; Doubleday, with the Crime Club volumes, were early in the field. Their example was soon followed by others; and in the favorable opportunities for publication is an incentive that has undoubtedly influenced many beginning writers to try their hands at this kind of work.

With this rise in public interest there has been a changing point of view concerning the taste for detective fiction. Not so long ago it was looked upon by many reputable readers as a discreditable avocation, an indulgence of lazy messenger boys and idle ne'er-do-wells, or as the abnormal idiosyncrasy of an otherwise respectable adult intelligence. Now that its adherents have become more outspoken as well as more numerous, it is generally accepted as legitimate mental entertainment—if not, as Philip Guedalla has said, "the normal recreation of noble minds." Its greatest popularity is with men of intelligence and achievement; pre-eminently, I think, with brain workers: philosophers, scientists, astronomers, scholars in many fields, lawyers, and many writers. Carl Van Doren, in his *Three Worlds*, mentions that Edwin Arlington Robinson read as many detective stories as he could lay hands on during the winters when he was not writing poetry; and Robinson's long narrative poem, "Avon's Harvest," reveals his own powers of working out a complex criminal mystery plot—he himself called it "a dime novel in verse." Physicians, judges, and statesmen are conspicuous in this brotherhood of readers—as are invalids, aviators, small boys, and motormen. Virtually all our recent Presidents have been numbered among its members. Mary Roberts Rinehart has told of the rebuke she received from Theodore Roosevelt for what he insisted was a false clue in one of her books. President Wilson, during his illness, found distraction in having the Fletcher tales read aloud to him; and his physician, Dr. Cary Grayson, in an article in the *Bookman* (December, 1920), "Books as a Mental Diversion," was one of the first of many medical men to urge the therapeutic value of such reading in giving both interest and refreshment to a keen but tired mind. Herbert Hoover, Franklin D. Roosevelt, Chief Justice Hughes, the late Dwight Morrow, J. Pierpont Morgan, Lloyd George, and Bernard Shaw are a few of the connoisseurs in this special field of contemporary literature.

Reasons for the appeal of the detective novel have been expounded by many experts; most of them are valid; all are defensible. To men of active mind, constantly under high pressure of affairs, such books afford congenial mental diversion and the rest that comes from substitution of one form of mental activity for another. An active mind cannot fall into coma when wearied or saturated with its special interest. The mystery tale distracts, but does not oppress; does not keep the mind to a familiar grindstone of preoccupations or personal problems; does not register too deeply on the mental cylinder. It is one of the tested palliatives in insomnia—always provided the reader does not let it too strongly invade the brain cells—and for invalids or convalescents its complete lack of relationship to immediate realities, its superficial intricacies that prick curiosity, but do not stir emotion, may be either lenitive or tonic.

Primarily, of course, its appeal lies in the universal allure of a mystery. This is evident in the daily press, in casual conversation, in the instinctive tingle that stirs in even a sluggish mind when it comes against some strange or perplexing problem or incident. The detective novel assembles all the elements of suspense: suspicion, menace, reasoning, the marshaling of possibilities. It centers on a fact to be explained; that this fact is a crime, usually murder, tightens the grip on attention. For the fascination of murder—its absorbing interest as a public topic—cannot be disavowed. The literature that deals with it in factual narrative and analysis has long flourished in England, where it has its own fellowship of readers, its line of distinguished specialists, from De Quincey and Borrow to William Roughead and Tennyson Jesse. In America this literature has had no such development; the late Edmund Pearson is our only writer of distinction in the field; and fiction has been our chosen medium for the lore of crime. Perhaps the reason for this is that Americans in general prefer the lighter touch of invention to the somber, sordid annals of reality that demand for their enjoyment a solid traditionalism in point of view or the robust, insensitive humor—such as we find in *The Ingoldsby Legends*—that gives "body" to English literature.

By its nature the detective novel is divorced from reality. It may convey a gooseflesh thrill of peril and portent, provide unsparing details of homicide, possess verisimilitude of setting and authenticity of accessory material; but essentially it remains a closely patterned exercise of ingenuity between the author and the reader. This is one of the compelling reasons for its appeal. It is like a game of solitaire or a crossword puzzle; it puts the reader's mind to work and keeps it busy until the end of the game. In a first-rate detective novel the reader takes quite as much part in the solution of the mystery as does the "investigator" himself. Clues are watched for, compared, and weighed; familiar signals, made according to code, are observed and identified; devious new techniques of first-degree mystery are approved or rejected: and even if the reader solves the problem early in the game there is sustained interest in following through the author's method of working out his pattern. As Willard Huntington Wright said: "In one sense a detective novel does not fall under the head of fiction at all, but really belongs in the category of riddles."

These reasons explain, I think, the great popularity of this type of fiction among intelligent readers. They may not be valid for "addicts" who do no other kind of reading; but the number of these is more limited than is commonly supposed. With most disciples of the detective novel this particular taste is a habit, like smoking, not necessarily a vice. They have other reading interests as well, and they are likely to be followers, in some degree, of Harold Nicolson's advice to read two books at a time—"only they must be different sorts of books; to read two books at the same time which affect the same frontal lobes is to create conditions in which cerebral inflammation may occur, or merely fuzz."

Even a brief survey of contemporary detective fiction demands a backward glance at the history of its development. In furthest perspective is *Adventures of Caleb Williams*, by William Godwin, the first English murder mystery novel, published in 1794, which antedates by nearly fifty years the work of Edgar Allan Poe, founder of the modern school. In *Amenities of Book Collecting* Newton calls it "Godwin's one other book that has escaped the rubbish heap of time" (his *Enquiry Concerning Political Justice* is the first), and says: "It is the best of what might be called 'The Nightmare Series,' which would begin with *The Castle of Otranto*, include his own daughter's *Frankenstein*, and end, for the moment, with Bram Stoker's *Dracula*." *Caleb Williams*, however is a novel of murder, not of the supernatural or abnormal, though it dispenses philosophic and psychological observations and was designed particularly to show, in Godwin's words, "the tyranny and perfidiousness exercised by the powerful members of the community against those who are less privileged than themselves." It centers on the murder of a villainous country squire, for which two men who have cause to hate him are executed; but which was committed by a neighbor of the victim's own class, the proud and benevolent Squire Ferdinando Falkland. By the secret of his crime and its consequences Falkland is plunged into an inner state of torture and misery and becomes a brooding recluse. His guilt is discovered by the insatiable curiosity of his young secretary-librarian, Caleb Williams, who taxes him with it, but promises not to betray him; and from then on the youth is subjected to relentless persecution, tracked from one refuge to another, by the murderer determined to crush his accuser. "To Mr. Falkland disgrace was worse than death. 'Though I be the blackest of villains, I will leave behind me a spotless and illustrious name.' "

Read today, it is hard to realize that this book commanded immense popularity for more than forty years and that as a play, *The Iron Chest*, it was a stock dramatic thriller until the late nineteenth century. An elaborate, grandiose narrative, full of turgid sentiment and preposterous inconsistencies, the secret of its vitality lies in the interest of the central plot and its unraveling, especially the ruthless harrying of the unfortunate Caleb through successive perils and escapes. Probably all that Godwin contributed to the pattern of detective fiction is the requirement of a solid foundational basis for the crime problem and a usage still commonly accepted—that of making the murder victim an obnoxious person whose extinction few can regret.

Factual and deductive processes of crime detection are negligible in Godwin's novel. These fundamental elements of modern detective fiction derive from the *Memoirs* of Vidocq, that almost legendary "great detective" who was head of the Paris detective force from 1812 until his retirement in 1827. The detective novel, indeed, could not have come into being earlier than it did, for until the advent of Vidocq in France and Sir Robert Peel in England, organized and intelligent investigation of crime was nonexistent. "Detectives," says E. M. Wrong, "cannot flourish until the public has an idea of what constitutes proof, and while a common criminal procedure is arrest, torture, confession, and death." Many of its annalists have pointed out that detective fiction is essentially a democratic institution: that its great development in England, France, and the United States reflects the concern of all citizens in maintenance of civil rights, fair play, conclusive evidence of guilt, and discovery and punishment of the actual perpetrators of crime.

Published in Paris in 1829, in four volumes, and issued almost simultaneously in English translation, Vidocq's narrative established in the public mind the enthralling figure of the famous detective, past master of disguises, expert in stratagems, trailing criminals and exposing crime through the sinister haunts of the French underworld. Crudely told, vivid, and sensational, its authenticity has always been questioned; but the more reasonable conclusion is that its material is genuine, though probably including added or exaggerated incidents, and that it was worked over for publication by a Paris journalist, just as many present-day memoirs and autobiographies are put in readable shape by ghost writers. Vidocq was an exconvict, once condemned to the galleys; it was as a police spy that his work with the Paris *Sûreté* began. His early life is presented as a picaresque vagabondage of roguery, imprisonment, and escape; and all through his memoirs he brings out with unforgettable realism and real compassion the horrible conditions of the prisons, the hopelessness, brutality, and despair of the convict's lot. This aspect of his book sent its appeal to Victor Hugo, who drew from Vidocq material that his genius transformed into the immortal story of Jean Valjean in *Les Misérables*. Dickens found in Vidocq suggestions for the convict scenes of *Great Expectations;* Poe, the inspiration for his "Murders in the Rue Morgue"; Conan Doyle, a fascinating repository of method and incident. Vidocq himself remains the progenitor of the multitude of great detectives and master investigators who pass and repass through the fictional world of crime. Long out of print, the memoirs were again made available to English readers in 1935, in a translation by Edwin G. Rich, "edited and abridged to fit the modern tempo." [1]

Edgar Allan Poe is accepted as the actual founder of the modern school of detective and mystery fiction. His three great detection stories furnished specifications for a technique later brought to perfection by Conan Doyle and developed by skillful present-day writers into a code of practice that sets up the rules of the game. Most famous is "The Murders in the Rue Morgue" (published in 1841), which Dorothy Sayers has said, "constitutes in itself almost a complete manual of detective theory and practice." Here, on a basis of comprehensive factual observation, we have the process of keen-witted analysis of evidence, suggestive inferences, rigidly tested deductions, and logical reasoning, all carrying to the correct solution of the problem. "The Purloined Letter," possessing a more subtle fascination, is essentially a statement of principles, centering on psychological deduction and emphasizing the crucial significance of motive and the importance of the apparently unimportant. "The

[1] *Vidocq: the Personal Memoirs of the First Great Detective*, edited and translated by Edwin Gile Rich, Boston, Houghton Mifflin, 1935.

Mystery of Marie Roget," less widely popular, has always had special interest for connoisseurs, for here the principles of detection are all brought together and applied, though with no specific indication of the solution, to the genuine records of an actual murder, unresolved at the time Poe's story was written. In each of these tales there appears the young Frenchman C. Auguste Dupin, first in the line of illustrious private detectives, who, usually accompanied by a more-or-less fatuous assistant, are household names to present-day readers. Dupin, elegant recluse, living in fantastic gloom, absorbed in his books and the exercise of his analytic powers, set the model for the distinctive personality that, in so many variations, characterizes his successors, from the mighty Sherlock to the omniscient Philo Vance and the impeccable Lord Peter Wimsey. The professional detective entered the field with Sergeant Cuff, of *The Moonstone*, in 1868; but though he is industrious, efficient, often an expert, he is of more ordinary fiber than the gifted private practitioner.

The seed sown by Poe was slow in germinating. Its fruitage came twenty-four years later, when Wilkie Collins published *The Moonstone*. Here is mastery of plot, of analysis, of interwoven clues, of skillful unraveling, and logical conclusion. Of it Dorothy Sayers says:

Taking everything into consideration, *The Moonstone* is probably the very finest detective story ever written. By comparison with its wide scope, its dovetailed completeness, and the marvellous variety and soundness of its characterization, modern mystery fiction looks thin and mechanical. Nothing human is perfect, but *The Moonstone* comes about as near perfection as anything of its kind can be.[2]

There was, of course, other notable English fiction dealing with mystery and crime. Most memorable, perhaps, was the work of J. S. Le Fanu, brilliant Irish novelist, whose power of creating and sustaining the atmosphere of mystery and the portent of impending doom still exerts its spell in *Uncle Silas* and *Wylder's Hand*. In these

---

[2] In the Introduction to *The Omnibus of Crime*, edited by Dorothy L. Sayers, New York, Payson & Clarke, 1929. This introduction is the most brilliant, clear, and cogent brief analysis and exposition of the whole subject of mystery fiction that has yet been published.

books, however, melodrama and mystery were stronger elements than crime detection. Even Wilkie Collins's *The Woman in White*, published eight years earlier than *The Moonstone*, and ranked as the first English novel dealing with detection of crime, is primarily a masterpiece of melodrama.

During this period of the sixties and seventies Emile Gaboriau was establishing in France the French school of detective fiction, which had strong formative influence on English writers. Closely restricted in background, it was sharply focused on crime in its more sensational aspects, and it foreshadowed the underworld type so popular in recent years. Multiple murders and bizarre episodes abound; the great detectives usually belong to the police force; and the plot is likely to unfold through elaborate expositions of trial proceedings and transcripts of court evidence. Vidocq's memoirs were obviously its fountainhead. Lecoq, the master mind of Gaboriau's most famous books—*File 113, Widow Lerouge, Monsieur Lecoq*— is a presentment of Vidocq himself, following closely the self-portraiture of the memoirs. The work of Gaboriau stamped a pattern developed by many other French writers, from Fortuny du Boisgobey, in the eighties, to Gaston Leroux (*The Mystery of the Yellow Room*, his *chef d'œuvre*) and Maurice Leblanc (with *Arsène Lupin*) in the early 1900's; its influence is especially evident in the more sensational English detective fiction, such as that of Fergus Hume and Edgar Wallace. This French school continues to flourish, its twentieth-century flowering being most notable in the work of Georges Simenon, whose immense series of "police novels," centering about the figure of Inspector Maigret, of the Paris detective force, were brought in English translation to American readers in 1940. In the United States, Anna Katharine Green's *The Leavenworth Case* (published in 1876) was a pioneer example of one of the most popular early formulas of ingenious plot construction and surprise ending.

With the approach of the present century a new influence appeared, so transforming and compulsive that any historical survey of detective and mystery fiction falls automatically into two periods—

preDoyle and postDoyle. At Christmas, 1887, a tale called *A Study in Scarlet*, by an obscure young English doctor, was published as a lurid paper-back—now one of the rarest of collector's items. The author received twenty-five pounds for the copyright. Continuously reprinted during his lifetime, pirated and reissued in many lands and in many forms, it never brought him another penny. But it did bring a commission to write for *Lippincott's Magazine*. Here, in 1888, appeared the second Sherlock adventure, *The Sign of Four*, and in 1890 there began, in *The Strand* in London and in *Harper's Weekly* in New York the series of detective tales that until 1927 were to follow one another in uneven sequence, establishing in literary immortality "that lean and sinewy figure which was to become a symbol as familiar as the Nelson monument and the Tower of London." [3] No other work in this field has had such varied and continuous perpetuation: on the stage, on the moving-picture screen, over the radio; and few in any field have gathered about them so large and ardent a body of enthusiasts as is represented by the Sherlock Holmes Society in England and the Baker Street Irregulars (as founded and named by Christopher Morley) in the United States.[4]

Conan Doyle was the fresh force that swept the stream of detective and mystery fiction into the floodwaters of today. He gave vitality and charm to the Poe formula, yet maintained its integrity; he brought humor, common sense and simple realism into the working-out of intricate crime problems; following the rules of the game with entire fairness, he could baffle the sharpest-witted reader; he appealed alike to the ingenuous and the intellectual. The Sherlock Holmes volumes are classics in their originality, skill of workmanship, their sustained interest and plausibility. Doyle still remains the master of the field, studied by all later writers, and as a model he

[3] Vincent Starrett, *The Private Life of Sherlock Holmes*, New York, Macmillan, 1933.
[4] This organization appears as sponsor for: *221B: Studies in Sherlock Holmes*; edited by Vincent Starrett. New York, Macmillan, 1940. Here, under a title that conveys the famous Baker Street address, are gathered 16 memoirs and studies, factual, conjectural, biographical, and analytical, by Holmes devotees, exploring with erudition, wit, and gusto problems and hypotheses in the life and work of The Master.

ranks with Poe, Gaboriau, and Collins. His ingenuity of detail remains a perennial delight. Chesterton, in *The Uses of Diversity*, remarks: "One of the best of the Sherlock Holmes stories turns entirely on a trivial point of housekeeping: the provision of curry for the domestic dinner"; and the famous "Examination Paper on the Life and Work of Sherlock Holmes," by E. V. Knox ("EVOE," of *Punch*), will challenge the skill of the most erudite Holmesian.

The advent of Sherlock brought immediate stimulus to the volume and variety of detective fiction, both in the long and the short form. It opened the floodgates ever more widely to an outpouring that so far shows no sign of diminution, but constantly overflows into a bewildering diversity of interlinking channels. All the developments of present-day scientific knowledge, the increasing range of mechanical devices, the whole modern paraphernalia of invention, discovery, and experimentation are drawn upon for crime problems or for lethal instruments; every stratum of human activity, professional, business, social, underworld or upper-crust, sophisticated or barbaric, furnishes background for the perpetration and unmasking of crime. Chemistry, physics, electrodynamics, telephony, radio, photography, psychoanalysis, anthropology, archaeology, are among the subjects to which present-day writers turn for material in the creation and solution of their mysteries. Their work in the mass shows progression in clear presentation, better literary expression, more conformity to probabilities; their treatment, contrasted with earlier mass production, is more compact and impersonal, with settings and incidents more sharply visualized; the florid and emotional qualities once popular have been eliminated; love interest is apt to be admitted only as a minor element.

Today the eminence of the great detectives is diffused among an ever-growing army of experts; but their individual characteristics still persist. It is interesting to note idiosyncrasies and personalities that stand out as the descendants of Dupin and Sherlock Holmes move down the years. Martin Hewitt, the silent, shrewd "investigator" of Arthur Morrison's solidly built problems, was one of the first to follow in Sherlock's footsteps. After him come The Thinking Machine, Jacques Futrelle's irascible, wizened, intellectual wonder; Hanaud, the shrewd, rotund, impassive French detective of A. E. W. Mason's two notable detective novels; Chesterton's Father Brown, silent, bland, innocent, and guileless, with all the wisdom of the ages focused upon the mysterious motives and impulses that are born of men's passions; Craig Kennedy, one of the first modern scientific crime detectors, put through his paces by Arthur Reeve, in experiences that, at first arresting, later become automatic and unconvincing; Hercule Poirot, temperamental little old French detective, who proves his prowess under Agatha Christie's direction; Reginald Fortune, in the H. C. Bailey *Call Mr. Fortune* tales, sleek, impassive, flippant young special adviser to Scotland Yard, always perfectly groomed, leisurely, luxurious, and moving in the highest society as he tracks crime mysteries to solution; Max Carrados, the only blind detective, his physical handicap offset by his intensified intuitive perceptions, whose feats are chronicled by Ernest Bramah, better known for his *Kai Lung* volumes; Charlie Chan, the philosophic, patient Chinese detective, endued by Earl Derr Biggers with continuing vitality; Philo Vance, languid, supercilious connoisseur, diffusing erudition over the intricate involvements of S. S. Van Dine's enigmas; and that Admirable Crichton, Lord Peter Wimsey, wistful, aristocratic, chivalrous, fulfillment of the romantic ideal of the feminine heart, who dominates the masterly work of Dorothy Sayers. Sometimes a writer's later creation succeeds or alternates with the original one—as with H. C. Bailey's Joshua Clunk, the mild, saccharine, hymn-singing little lawyer, who operates quite independently of Mr. Fortune; or the lively Mr. Montague Egg, who adorns several of Dorothy Sayers's non-Wimsey tales. Once born, these experts are slow to die; for a feature that differentiates the detective novel from other types of fiction is its inherent propulsion toward a sequel: the success with which its formula may be applied over and over again to a new scenario, in which recognition of a familiar figure presiding over a familiar but different problem instills a pleasing warmth in the reader's bosom.

Much has been written on the formula by which the detective and mystery novel is compounded; but its chief requirements may be briefly stated. Primarily, it must set, analyze, and solve a single problem according to rules that give fair play alike to the author's ingenuity and the reader's perspicacity. The problem is projected by the criminal and the solution is worked out by the detector, who is, in fact, the protagonist of the affair. In its severest form it is an analytical exercise, rigidly limited in framework, impersonalized in demonstration; but, according to the writer's powers of conception and expression, it may expand into more spacious backgrounds and be invigorated by vitality or sympathy in characterization, by a diffused human interest in the working out of plot relationships. There is much work of excellent literary quality, especially from English writers, who have always taken this kind of fiction more seriously than Americans and have given it of their best abilities. There is a very large middle ground, which represents skillful routine workmanship; and a still larger hinterland of crude, cheap, and garish mass production. However different in quality it may be, in general, conformity to formula prevails. Indeed, some publishing firms provide specifications on which manuscripts accepted for publication must be based; so that the fundamental characteristics of this type of fiction tend to become more accentuated as its popularity increases.

It should be remembered, however, that in spite of this trend toward regimentation there is increasing diversity in pattern and in technique. Mystery does not necessarily center upon murder; other problems, criminal or psychological, may be involved. Sometimes the key to the mystery is given to the reader at the beginning and the process of fitting it to the right lock sets the riddle. Manner of presentation also has infinite variations, from *The Moonstone* method of separate narratives contributed by the participants and the Doyle practice of first-hand reporting by an assistant or observer, to the bizarre device of a "crime file," larded with samples of actual "evidence"—telegrams, a strand of hair, a bit of ribbon, and so on.

A detective novel may be "fair" or "unfair," according to the degree of honesty with which it follows the rules of the game. It is fair when the author lays all his cards on the table; that is, presents (or at least indicates) all the facts, incidents, elements, which form a part of the mystery and its solution. Of course, the author can, and does, stack the cards for his own advantage; but the reader must be aware of that. To say that the cards must be laid on the table means simply that they must be placed there: their relationship or their comparative importance need not be divulged; but they must be there. It is unfair to slip in at the last moment a card—that is, a vital fact or factor—newly dealt and unknown before. All characters in a mystery novel are unknown quantities. Suspicion may attach to any one or to all in turn. As Chesterton says: "it is a story in which even the moral sympathies may be in doubt"; it is "almost the only romance in which the hero may turn out to be the villain, or the villain to be the hero. We are quite sure that Col. Newcome's company has not been conspired against by his son Clive, though possibly by his nephew Barnes. But there is a stage in a story like *The Moonstone*, when we are meant to suspect Franklin Blake, the hero, as he is suspected by Rachel Verinder, the heroine." [5]

All moves in the game should be logical. One step must follow another. At the end the reader should be able to look back and see the sequence clear and consistent, link by link. Godwin says that he invented first the third volume of *Caleb Williams* (bringing apprehensions and calamities to their climax), then the second (providing "a dramatic and impressive situation adequate to account for" what was to follow), and last of all the first ("to account for the fearful events of the third"). Many present-day mystery writers follow this course. Perhaps the most common practice is to write the last chapter first, to work throughout according to a thorough preliminary synopsis of plot and action, and to rigorously check the completed manuscript backward and forward for precision and consistency in detail.

Indications of solution must be consistent. There may be many such indications, all conflicting; but those that prove correct must be consistent and must on rechecking be seen to hold the clue. It is

[5] G. K. Chesterton, in his Introduction to Bernard Capes, *The Skeleton Key*, New York, Doran, 1920.

unfair to introduce some quite unknown, unhinted perpetrator, except where events have indicated this possibility; the detector himself must not commit the crime; nor may supernatural or preternatural agencies be employed. This rule was successfully broken by Agatha Christie in the *The Murder of Roger Ackroyd* by an effectively delusive method that once practiced could not be repeated; but even here there were indications from which a sufficiently percipient reader might have received some instillation of suspicion as to the identity of the criminal.

Besides these main rules, which are generally accepted, there are various specific requirements advanced by the more rigorous exponents of the art. Father Ronald Knox, himself a detective-story writer of ability, prescribes the following:[6] The criminal must be someone mentioned in the early part of the story, but must not be anyone whose thoughts the reader has been allowed to follow; not more than one secret room or passage is allowable; no hitherto undiscovered poisons may be used nor any appliance which will need a long scientific explanation at the end; twin brothers, and doubles generally, must not appear unless we have been duly prepared for them; no accident must ever help the detective, nor must he ever have an unaccountable intuition which proves him to be right.

G. K. Chesterton regarded as outside the pale the mystery fiction that presents vague but immense world plots and centers on colossal diplomatic or business intrigues. The skillful writer, he says, does not introduce into his story

a vast but invisible secret society with branches in every part of the world, with ruffians who can be brought to do anything or underground cellars that can be used to hide anybody. He does not mar the pure and lovely outlines of a classical murder or a burglary by wreathing it round and round with the dirty and dingy red tape of international diplomacy. He does not lower our lofty ideals of crime to the level of foreign politics. He does not trace the crime hurriedly in the last page or two to some totally insignificant character whom we never suspected because we never remembered.

[6] In his Introduction to *The Best English Detective Stories* of 1928, edited by Ronald A. Knox and Henry Harrington, New York, Liveright, 1929.

This, of course, is chiefly an expression of personal taste; it characterizes cheap and sensational products of some highly popular writers, such as Oppenheim, Beeding, and Edgar Wallace; but also impugns such legitimate and skillful work as Buchan's *Thirty-Nine Steps* and Eric Ambler's more recent tales of international intrigue.

Willard Huntington Wright, who, as S. S. Van Dine, established his own rigorously mechanized type of detective fiction, is perhaps the most logical and exacting of these codifiers. His counsel of perfection is embodied in his famous "Twenty Rules for Writing Detective Stories," which is included as an appendix to the last Van Dine novel, published posthumously in 1939.[7] This volume is both a memorial to Wright and an interesting object lesson in his method. His practice was to write each of his mystery novels three times, first in a synopsis of about 10,000 words, completely outlining the plot, then in a second version telling the story in full but omitting the elaboration of character, dialogue, and setting, which were developed in the third and final writing. His last novel, uncompleted when he died, is given here in its second version; and in this compressed form it shows the structural use of what the author himself calls "a thorough-going and self-conscious technical equipment."

Variations of type in this field of fiction are legion. Each has its distinctive characteristics, its individual reading appeal. In the underworld or gangster type, as brought to its highest modern popularity by Dashiell Hammett, there has developed a staccato machine-gun technique of action, an ironic depravity of dialogue, and an insistent chill brutality, that curiously reflect the sadism released by conflicting forces upon the present-day world. Men, far more than women, find interest in this type; as they do in the "straight" mystery—intricate, but worked out with matter-of-fact everyday detail—of which Fletcher's work was an early example and that of Erle Stanley Gardner represents a later model. There is the international-intrigue type; the elite social-scene type; the Robin Hood type ("The Saint" tales, an exemplar); the "screwy" or humorously fantastic type (Elliot Paul's *Hugger-Mugger in the Louvre* set a pattern here); the

[7] S. S. Van Dine, *The Winter Murder Case*, New York, Scribner, 1939.

type that centers on a single avocation or profession; the romantic melodrama type (Daphne Du Maurier's *Rebecca* might claim a place here); the steadily growing array of war, escape, or espionage mysteries (Helen McInnes struck high level here with *Above Suspicion*); a large group concerned with psychological analysis rather than with crime detection (in this, Claude Houghton has many followers); and the larger group that turns to psychic or superpsychic elements and that merges into the famous older fiction of mystery and horror and the supernatural, which is quite separate from modern detective and mystery fiction.

There is some differentiation to be made between the work of men and that of women writers. Men predominate in mastery of the art, in originality of conception and range of interest, and in volume of production. A few women won early recognition, but it is only within recent years that women have given evidence of high productivity, facility, and distinction in this kind of writing. Among the pioneers, Anna Katharine Green was skilled in logical plot construction, otherwise her tales are florid and artificial; Carolyn Wells, with immense productivity, is never more than third rate, her plot-inventiveness smothered under fantastic improbabilities, flippancies, and trivialities; the veteran Mrs. Belloc Lowndes, though her powers have weakened with the years, still stands in the first rank with her earlier novels, which are grim, logical, admirable in construction, and excellent in expression. Today Dorothy Sayers's name leads all the rest. In the fabrication of problems that will tax the ingenuity of the adept, in the subtlety and vigor with which those problems are presented and elucidated, in vitality of character depiction, depth of background, lively humor, and pervading flavor of English literature, no present-day writer in the field surpasses this young woman, who combines the gifts of the novelist with the erudition of the scholar and the acumen of the critic.

The work of most women writers possesses characteristics that carry particular appeal to women readers. Women, apparently, are more temporal and practical in their interests than men; less prone to metaphysical or fantastical themes; more fastidious as regards slaughterous details and hardboiled idiom; averse to underworld brutalities (no woman could have written *The Maltese Falcon*), and inclined rather toward social and domestic criminality in refined surroundings; less robust in characterization, and usually with less climactic power, but with more consistency in their treatment of love and keener psychological appraisal of their own sex. Mary Roberts Rinehart, Margery Allingham, Patricia Wentworth, Leslie Ford, Margaret Armstrong, Ngaio Marsh are a few of those who represent the specific instillation of feminine appeal into detective and mystery fiction. But it should be noted that a good many writers in this field lead double, sometimes triple, lives, and produce simultaneously under different names different kinds of mystery fiction. Thus, the feminine quality of Leslie Ford's tales is offset by the same author's matter-of-fact masculinity as David Frome, in the Mr. Pinkerton chronicles; and the psychological subtleties of Francis Iles are evolved by the same brain that as Anthony Berkeley unravels more tangible crime problems.

Probably an average of some three hundred detective and mystery novels are published in this country each year. Choosing among them is apt to be a matter of following the lead of a few favorite names, or a venture in random experimentation. But as mediocrity is always more common than excellence, satisfactory selection needs discriminating judgment as well as recognition of different reading tastes. The brief standard review-appraisals usually offer a fair basis for individual judgment, but such judgment will be strengthened and clarified by personal appreciation of specific qualities and values. The most common defects may be indicated as: crudity of workmanship, evident in slipshod English, in vulgarity or shallow monotony of expression; fantastic or brutal sensationalism of plot; obvious manufacture of bewilderment, and forced, elaborated perplexities; preposterous, far-fetched solutions; lack of reality in background and of vitality in characterization. Of values, some indication has already been given. The high entertainment value this fiction possesses for intelligent readers and its value as a mental therapeutic are now generally recognized. It has also specific values of informational background and potential reading relationship. Comparatively few realize the varied and fascinating range of topical interest that is to be found in this kind of reading. Regional and local and specialized backgrounds, basically accurate and brilliantly visualized, abound; there is an immense surface deposit of heterogeneous factual detail that, however superficial, is illuminating and stimulating. Consider the elaborate exposition of the virtually unknown lore of English bell-ringing in Dorothy Sayers's *Nine Tailors,* the topographical exactitude of the Oxford setting in her *Gaudy Night;* Leslie Ford's faithful re-creation of Williamsburg, Virginia, in *The Town Cried Murder,* which might serve as a practical guide to the restored colonial capital; the vivid choreographic detail of the "Petroushka" ballet, in that unassuming mystery tale, *A Bullet in the Ballet;* the Elizabethan and Shakespearean detail in Michael Innes's *Hamlet, Revenge!* Ancient Minoan civilization, anthropological researches in Alaska, mountain-climbing in the English lake district, Inca archaeology, chemistry of perfumes—such topical material appears in recent minor detective novels, and the list might be indefinitely extended. The reading relationships suggested may not be actually established, although the mystery tale staged in the imitation palace of Knossus offered a good short bibliography of Cretan archaeological exploration for readers whose interest in the subject might have been aroused. Nevertheless, this factual informational element represents specific values that unconsciously popularize knowledge and enlarge individual interests. The library of Harvard Law School, it may be added, has one of the largest special collections of this kind of fiction, not only because it is popular as a diversion, but also because of the many factual values that relate to law and criminality.

While many readers buy for themselves in this general field—there are a multitude of experts with fine private collections—probably the majority draw their supply from libraries, commercial or public. Indeed, this type of fiction is a chief bulwark of the small rental library and one of the influences that has scattered through every neighborhood these almost unregarded agencies for reading as a form of recreation. In public libraries, although this demand necessarily receives more limited recognition, there is a fairly constant inflow of the better current detective and mystery fiction. In its provision there should, I think, be wider recognition and more effective use of the topical and regional values that it possesses, more appreciation of literary quality and of personal reading appeal. Libraries should be generous in current supply and should build up a good permanent collection, valuable in preservation of the more important older examples, discriminating and flexible in immediate range.

For any such professional library endeavor, as in any personal exploration of this field of contemporary fiction, there is guidance and stimulation in Howard Haycraft's volume *Murder for Pleasure: the Life and Times of the Detective Story*, published in 1941 by Appleton-Century, in commemoration of the centennial of Poe's "Murders in the Rue Morgue," "the world's first detective story." Indeed, the present brief venture into the lure of crime in fiction finds fitting conclusion by setting up a guidepost to this encyclopedic history and handbook, which records the growth from the seed sown by Poe of the far-spreading twentieth-century forest of crime and mystery fiction.

In his subject Mr. Haycraft is connoisseur, historian, and bibliographer of authority. His book is the first to appear in this country that presents the detective story as a distinct form of literary art; that offers adequate factual and analytical record of its development; and that provides an immense store of interesting and useful information for the edification of addicts, of the mass of general readers, and of beginning writers who seek to try their powers in this field. Wide as is the range of the volume, it is held within closely specialized limitations. Mr. Haycraft's concern is with the "pure" detective story and its writers, not with the broader, far-ramifying fiction of mystery and crime in which technique of detection is subordinate or absent. Within the boundaries set, emphasis is laid upon work that has influenced the development of detective fiction either in method or in popularity. The volume follows chronologically the development of the art, and records its practitioners in their progress through time.

It includes virtually all the writers of detective fiction of whom the present-day reader has heard and many of whom he is ignorant. For the most significant ones there is biographical information and illuminating commentary, and from the mass are elicited the influences, the trends, the changing materials and methods that are still shaping and enlarging this immense body of contemporary literature. This historic-biographic chronicle is rounded out and supplemented. "The Rules of the Game," or the most essential requirements of approved detective fiction, are set forth in comprehensive summary; the chapter "The Murder Market" gives practical commercial counsel to the craftsman entering the field. There is an excellent list of critical and analytical articles on detective fiction; and a readers' recommended list of "detective story cornerstones." And, most welcome boon, there is a long, authoritative "Who's Who in Detection," in which you may trace your favorite sleuth among a total of some 1,200 master detectives, their assistants and familiars. There is a quiz, too, and you may test your wits in answering such questions as What detectives do you associate with the following hobbies: (*a*) roses; (*b*) rare coins; (*c*) vegetable marrows; (*d*) orchids; (*e*) mathematics? What was Professor Moriarty's given name? What was Dr. Watson's given name? What is Mr. Pinkerton's given name? What famous detective had eleven children? Name at least three detectives who are blind. What detectives, if any, have died? To all susceptible to the lure of crime, *Murder for Pleasure* offers justification and satisfaction.

XI. REVIEWING A NOVEL

"She's a very conscientious person," said Miss Lyd-gate, "but she has an unfortunate knack of making any subject sound dull."—DOROTHY SAYERS: *Gaudy Night*

T O KNOW what's in a novel, to appreciate the values it offers, does not mean that it is easy to formulate that knowledge and pass it on to others, in clear, effective, and interesting fashion. This endeavor, however, has become one of the popular activities of the day; it enlists a multitude of exponents—professionals, amateurs, novices, and veterans—and it has given a new connotation to the familiar term "book reviewing." Radio has been the great factor in extending a field of book reviewing that is independent of the medium of print. The spoken review supplements the older, impersonal, relationship of reviewer and reader with the more personal relationship of reviewer and listener. The reviewer on the air brings to his audience commentary on recent books and also acts as "personal conductor" for authors in interviews or discussion of their work. Book review programs are a specialty of many lecturers for clubs and for subscription groups; they are offered by libraries, in radio talks or in free lectures; they are sponsored by bookshops and department stores, educational and commercial organizations; and they are a staple product of the women's clubs, large and small, whose interests are interwoven in American life.

Indeed, club women today form probably the largest body of book reviewers in the country. In women's clubs from Maine to Hawaii, from Florida to Alaska, books find place on programs throughout the club year. Many such programs are presented by professional reviewers, who have developed a skillful technique of entertainment that calls for little individual response from their audiences; and there is a growing inclination to prefer this, if possible, because it imposes no direct personal responsibility, requires no individual mental concentration, and supplies "literary" comment and opinion available as current coin of conversation. But the reviewing that prevails most generally in smaller clubs is done or participated in by club members themselves. It is essentially amateur reviewing: expression of individual taste, individual judgment, by women who read because they enjoy books, who have intelligence and common sense, who sincerely wish to know and appreciate the best books of the day, but who do not have the background of general book acquaintance, the facility in organization and presentation, that are prime requirements of good professional reviewing. Anyone who has a fairly wide acquaintance with the reviewing done by club members for their own programs must have realized how much time and thought are given in this endeavor to convey to others the nature of a book assigned for review. There are many good reviews, conveying character and quality of a book with responsiveness and insight (attributes of good reviewing that should go hand in hand); but there are many more that are defective or weak in structure or in presentation. The reviewer's conscientious effort may be evident, but she is unable to make the content and personality of the book either significant or interesting to her audience.

It is for amateurs and for beginners in the widening field of oral book reviewing that these suggestions are made.[1] The writing of reviews for publication is not dealt with; it has much in common with the spoken book review, but the latter has its own distinctive requirements, which have been less widely formulated. In general the points here considered are applicable to reviews of books in any field, but specifically they apply to novels; for current fiction is the most difficult, the most debatable, and usually the most inadequately handled material on the ordinary book review program. This is partly the effect of that certain condescension toward the novel that prevails in the American educational and intellectual

[1] Fuller consideration of book reviewing, in principle and practice, may be found in Helen E. Haines, *Living with Books*, New York, Columbia University Press, 1935, chaps. vi–viii.

world and is reflected in an apologetic attitude on the part of readers somewhat self-consciously in quest of culture; and it is partly
because discriminating judgment of fiction requires appreciation of
literary art rather than certitude regarding moral standards.

Two principles dominate virtually all book reviewing. One is the
principle set forth by Anatole France, when he defined criticism
as "the adventures of the soul among the masterpieces of literature."
This is essentially the principle of the literary and critical essay, not
of the book review. It interprets in terms of intellectual or emotional
analysis; it may convey a work in part rather than as a whole; and
it follows no conventionalized form of organization or treatment.
The second principle represents an impersonal (or as impersonal as
possible) consideration of an author's work. This is essentially the
principle of the book review, as a logically organized summary and
appraisal of a book as a whole. And in the field of book reviewing
Anatole France has been responsible for sad havoc. The adventures
of a reviewer's soul may be edifying, illuminating, entertaining.
When they record the conclusions of an expert critic, a literary
artist, they invigorate and enrich the study of literature; but in their
more ordinary manifestation they give us, in sum, a review of a
reviewer in his personal relation to a given book rather than a review of the book itself. Impersonal consideration of an author's
work, on the other hand, is founded on the familiar dictum: a review should tell what the author set out to do, what he did, and how
he did it. This remains, I think, the basic principle of good reviewing.

Both principles are represented in many variations, singly or together, in reviews of different degrees of excellence. The soul-
adventuring reviewer is apt to convey enthusiasm with more ardor
than discrimination, to center appreciation—or, conversely, to focus
disapproval—so strongly on some special interpretation of theme
that the proportions of the book as a whole are obscured; while
the reviewer who seeks objectivity may be led into flippant commentary, cursory characterization, that cheapens or ignores the real
values of a book. The best reviewing will draw something from

both principles. It will be based on the dictum already noted; it will be impersonal in the sense that it will avoid egotism, but it will convey the reviewer's own personal response to the book, his perceptiveness of literary art, his intellectual point of view. Each individual book will be approached with an open mind and judged according to its own merits.

This leads to the question, "What is an open mind?" Well, an open mind is not a vacuum; it is not a mortar into which a book's contents are poured and pounded with the pestle of prejudice or of conviction; it is not a funnel through which all that enters passes, leaving no sediment. Rather, it is a strainer, with a flexible, yet strong, mesh of reason and understanding. An open mind should be open both to the past and the present, with a periscopic aperture directed toward the future. There are many reviewers whose appreciation of literature stopped with 1910. There are many more on whose mental horizon no literature more than ten years old has ever loomed. Thoroughgoing traditionalism will deaden any review. So also, entire immediacy will impair judgment, for it has no perspective and no consciousness of what is derivative.

To judge a book according to its merits requires, first of all, a sense of values and a background of acquaintance with literature. It is difficult to have one without the other, for realization of values requires appreciation of literary art, and there must be some acquaintance with any art—even if only "a smattering of ignorance"— before it can be appreciated. In other words, a good book review should have proportion and authority. Proportion means balance in analysis and characterization and also in judgment expressed. The review that is essentially an expression of personal friendship, that hails some novel as a masterpiece because the author is a fellow townsman or a friend or a protégé of the reviewer, is one of the familiar examples of reviewing that lacks a true sense of values. On the other hand, the review that is a vehicle of attack because the book it deals with offends the reviewer in subject or point of view is thrown out of proportion by this undue emphasis. As a rule, violence in reviewing is likely to defeat itself, whether it be violence in panegyric or in condemnation; it raises expectations that are not fulfilled when the book is read, and induces in its hearers a cynical disbelief that anything is really what it is said to be. But this does not mean that enthusiasm should be lacking or that critical judgment should be unexpressed. Prejudices, of course, exist in every one of us. A reviewer without personal likes and dislikes would be spineless and mindless and not worth listening to. There must always be enthusiasm, and enthusiasm for something always means distaste for something else. The reviewer who is entirely noncommittal and aloof has no real fiber of thought or appreciation; but the reviewer who condemns or ridicules a book simply because he doesn't like the author or is opposed to the theme or the treatment is equally at fault. Competent reviewing is what its name implies: a looking over the whole body of a book to convey its nature. The good reviewer does not indulge in unreasoning destruction or infatuated adulation, but analyzes and appraises with the purpose of rendering fair judgment on a piece of literature that, whether he likes it or not, is to be considered for what it is. In any such judgment there is necessarily a critical element—valid indication of merits or demerits, of excellence or crudity in expression, of triviality or significance, of values obvious or implied. A colorless statement of a novel's content is the easiest and most negligible form of reviewing.

It is true that there is often strong temptation to review a book in a wholly satirical or condemnatory vein. Also, such a review may have entertainment value for its audience. To justify it, however, qualities of humor, of deft phrasing, and of essentially sound critical perception are needed that few amateur reviewers possess. Christopher Morley's memorable review of Charles Morgan's *Sparkenbroke* [2] is a masterpiece of brilliant satirical writing turned to parody, but it is also good critical appraisal, without shallowness or show-off. Among expert professional reviewers the "devastating" attack upon a book or writer is still wielded as a critical weapon, though much less frequently nowadays than in the past. Carl Van Doren,

[2] *Saturday Review of Literature*, XII. (No. 25, April 18, 1936), 13-16.

in his *Three Worlds*, remarks that "the only reviews which ever give instant delight are the ferocious or feline ones," and adds: "It is not quite like watching a fight. Rather, it is like watching a public execution, and it seems to fascinate." His inference that there is an element of sadism or latent envy in this attitude seems true enough. There is, at any rate, an instinctive tendency to disparage the novel that everyone is praising; not on a basis of reason or understanding, but in the mood of reaction that exiled Aristides because people were tired of hearing him called the Just. The spoken book-review program that exalts this tendency is as deadening to any true appreciation of literature as is the program that indulges in the opposite extreme, of indiscriminate rhapsody. Indeed, the two infections to which the immature or inexperienced reviewer is particularly susceptible are contemptuosmosis, or infiltration of the flow of enthusiasm by a septic element, and superlativitis, or adjectival inflammation of the nerves of appreciation. Both are pernicious; both need preventive watchfulness.

If proportion is based on fair comparative relations between material and judgment, authority is rooted in background knowledge of literature. It makes possible an almost instinctive comparison of books that have proved their qualities with those newborn and untested and is thus one of the greatest aids to discriminating judgment. Establishing the existence and the differentiation of literary values, it is a means for orientation amid confusion and diversity. Authority builds itself from wide reading, from experience, from study; but, however gained, it is one of the qualifications of the expert reviewer. It is strange how many intelligent people, whose interest in reading is quite genuine and whose confidence in their own judgment is rarely shaken, remain completely insensitive to the quality of a book as literature; for them the subject and the "moral tone" are the only things that count; nor do they seem able to consider a book in relation to its author—to his style, his characteristics, and his other work.

Good reviewing cannot be done by everyone. Ability can be elicited and stimulated, but it cannot be instilled, if specific taste and instinctive fitness are absent. Even when the genuine personal response exists, there are certain requirements essential to discriminating and effective reviewing. One of the first of these is interest on the part of the reviewer; a languid or indifferent approach or a grim determination to carry through a formidable task will stultify the more subtle qualities of any novel. There should be power to concentrate, a responsive mind, sensitivity to literary expression—the richer the background of varied reading, the better—and a natural facility in expression, in the choice of words and phrasing. Spontaneous critical or analytical interest is desirable; so are a sense of beauty, some grains of imagination, a generous measure of enthusiasm, also skepticism to temper fervor. Balanced judgment, the ability to compare and contrast, is necessary. Special interest and individual taste are always to be considered: in the review of a book that has been deeply enjoyed there are likely to be special values of sympathy or interpretation; and, concurrently, no reviewer should review the kind of book that he personally dislikes, unless he can be truly impersonal—honest, but fair. An overpersonal attitude is usually strongly tinged with egocentricity. There are many readers who precipitate themselves upon specific aspects of a novel —phases of character development, equivocal situations, climactic actions—which they seize and hold up as generalizations, true or false, according to whether what the novelist has depicted coincides with their own individual experience. In a way, they are paying unconscious tribute to fiction's power of communicating the actual experience of living; but they are demanding that what is communicated should not be the novelist's interpretation of human existence as he has known it, studied it, and given it form within a certain structure of expression, but a duplication of the reader's own ideas, a reaffirmation of his pre-established codes, that will diffuse a further ambience of self-satisfaction.

The first step in preparation of a review is to read the book. Professional reviewers are able to do this with great rapidity; they skim, yet manage to absorb the substance. The amateur needs and should take more time. How much will depend upon the length and the character of the book. Such a novel as *The Star-Gazer*, Harsanyi's erudite, close-packed study of Galileo's life, is much slower of assimilation than is a novel in quick tempo of everyday experience, like Morley's *Kitty Foyle*. The work of novelists like Thomas Mann, Jules Romains, and Martin du Gard is world literature and will demand and repay all the time, thought, and study that can be given to it; but there are many current novels that in social or critical or literary significance deserve more careful reading than they usually receive. Read the book with interest; if possible, with sympathy. No book can be reviewed fairly if read simply as a task. Read with pencil at hand and make brief notes (if only page references jotted on a bookmark) that will later give clue to specific facts or some sentence significant for quotation or will help to indicate distinctive characteristics. Watch for and note "human interest" material—episodes, delineations, commentary that in homely truth or charm or wit or graphic touch will appeal to an audience and deepen its interest. But don't attempt to formulate a review while reading the book. Read and enjoy (if you can); then analyze and formulate the impression the book has made. The thoughtful reader generally has a changing sequence of impressions. At first there may be a response of enthusiasm, an apparent happy accord between author and reader. Then reservations rise: here is monotony; here a lapse into sentimentalism; the smooth flow becomes dull going, confusing or overweighted; the first impression closes with the opening mood reversed. Or the reversal may be directly opposite: a first impression that opens with enforced patience, continues with latent boredom, is pricked to quickened apprehension, strengthens to rising appreciation, and closes with enthusiasm. Often the impression may be checkered throughout, leaving no definite commitment to praise or blame; the reader is aware of merits and of shortcomings.

While reading, try to correlate and clarify the impressions as they rise and change. Then, afterwards, consider them in retrospect and from their almost certain conflict draw a more unified conclusion, adjusted to the novel's material, theme, purpose, and mode of expression, rather than to the reader's predilections. While avoiding personal prejudice, don't surrender reasoned personal judgment. Opinion should be independent and honestly indicated. Don't praise, if the only reason for doing so is that others do; but try fairly and sympathetically to estimate the book itself, in its own manifestation. And in doing this, avoid moral indignation. There is no veil drawn today over the recognition and discussion of social evils. The mature mind is fully aware that abnormality, sordidness, violence, and degradation exist in human life. Much painful or repellent fiction is as vital and significant an expression of the life of our day as are the social and political currents on which we are borne along; and no sound critical judgment of a novel can be made solely from a moralistic viewpoint.

Briefly, to the question "How should I read a novel?" the answer is: Read it for yourself, according to what are apparently diametrically opposed principles, namely: with freedom, with control; with surrender, with criticism; with sympathy, with judgment. Such a reading involves a threefold perceptive process: comprehension (understanding of the novel's structure and treatment); appreciation (response to its appeal as an evocation of human experience); criticism (analytical consideration of its qualities and defects and of your own individual reactions).

Back of the actual process of reading lie the bases of judgment. There must be some general understanding of the nature and art of fiction as creative literature, some specific recognition of the characteristics and qualities of the novel that is being read. In the analysis of any novel salient points concerning scope, substance, and structure must be considered. Perhaps it is well to note briefly what they are.

Theme, subject, plot.—Theme is commonly defined as the subject of a composition, but it may also be considered as the motif or dominant idea, that is an undercurrent or overtone of both subject and plot. Subject is the specific phase of human experience with which a novel deals. Plot is the skeleton of the story. Thus, according to such an analysis, in *The Grapes of Wrath* theme (implicit in title) is the portent of revolution rising from economic injustice;

subject is the great forced migration from the Southwest to California of farmers ruined by bank foreclosures and soil exhaustion—"tractored off the land"; plot is the experience of the Joad family on their journey from Oklahoma and what happened to them after they reached California. In Aldous Huxley's *After Many a Summer Dies the Swan* theme is the need of escape from materialism into the nonpersonality, timelessness, and peace of oriental philosophy; subject is the vulgarity, animalism, fear of death, and greed that make up modern living, spectacularly exemplified in Southern California; plot is the satiric, fantastic narrative of a millionaire's quest for prolongation of life. While virtually all novels are subject novels, not all convey a theme in this sense of a dominating idea implicit in the whole composition. Continental novelists use this element more generally than do American or English novelists; but almost all novels of distinctive quality have a theme-idea underlying their concrete subject. Plot expresses itself in action: sometimes in a sustained movement toward a dramatic climax; sometimes in more desultory sequence of episode and incident. It directs the reader's interest along the line the novelist has traced for his story pattern, and it gives opportunity to clarify and vitalize character portrayal. It should be a means of progression from a beginning through a middle to an end.

Setting and period.—In historical and regional novels time and place are of special importance; but virtually all novels have some distinctive setting, and in the majority some time relationship is indicated, even if vaguely. Observe the extent of the period covered and the exactitude with which it is denoted. Does it run a long and carefully traced continuous course, as in *The Tree of Liberty* (1754–1806)? Is it revealed in successive chronological vistas, as in the separate panels of Doris Leslie's *Fair Company?* Is it part of a remembered past, as in Llewellyn's *How Green Was My Valley?* Is it a single specific contemporary interval (a year in Josephine Johnson's *Jordanstown*, a day in Kenneth Fearing's *The Hospital*)? Is it obviously but indefinitely in "the past" or "the present," or is it a projection into the future, as in Sherriff's *The Hopkins Manu-*

script? Awareness of the time-span, whatever it may be, gives clearer realization of the novel as a whole and often helps in testing the validity of incidental material. Setting is an important factor, closely related to subject and form and treatment. Consider whether it is made an indispensable and living background, integrated in the nature and development of the novel, as in Rölvaag's *Giants in the Earth* or Rawlings's *The Yearling;* whether it is impersonal, flatly photographic, as with Sinclair Lewis, or a high-colored, stylized backdrop, as with John Dos Passos; whether it is used to enhance social significance, as in Steinbeck's *In Dubious Battle;* whether its influence tinges the medium of expression, as it does in *How Green Was My Valley;* or whether the setting itself is protagonist, and nature becomes a mystic arbiter of human destinies, as in Francis Brett Young's *Undergrowth.* Observe the visualization of place, the apprehension of the effect of environment upon character that is made possible by this element of the novelist's art. Note the descriptive and factual values that authenticity of setting imparts to many undistinguished novels; and note also the pitfall of the so-called "pathetic fallacy," which invests nature with human emotions and turns simple reality into artificial romanticism. This pitfall finds illustration, I think, in *Undergrowth.*

Characterization.—Primarily the novelist is concerned with human beings; his art is determined by his power to impart the illusion of life to the characters whose experiences are set before the reader. Consider the skill, sympathy, and penetration with which the nature of the characters is revealed; whether they are sentient creatures with their own dimensions, their own personalities, or whether they are cut-outs pasted on a flat background, puppets pulled to galvanized movement. Are they types, embodying some trait or quality, symbolic or satiric or allegoric (this is in part true of *Anthony Adverse*); or are they individuals, even though typical individuals, with characteristics and temperaments essentially their own? Have they free will? Is the development of each consistent with the individual personality, or are their actions conditioned by a formalized plot pattern or the exigency of a dramatic climax? Are their natures revealed in their own direct speech and action and immediate thoughts (as in *The Grapes of Wrath*), or through stream-of-consciousness retrospect (as in *Kitty Foyle*), or by dialogue and descriptive commentary (as in *Gone with the Wind*), or by elaborate analysis (as in *The Last Puritan*)? Sound appreciation of a novel's qualities of character delineation requires of a reviewer a sense of values both in human behavior and in literary expression. Too many reviewers accept as "strong" or "convincing" character portrayal the crude and stenciled pattern that sets virtuous characters and villainous ones in black and white contrast (as in Caldwell's *The Dynasty of Death* and sequel); that presents everyone as either worthy or contemptible, and so offers no real character portrayal at all. Others dismiss with resentment or shrinking distaste characters they find unpleasant or reprehensible, without recognizing fundamental truth or inherent vitality in the portrayal.

Structure.—Theme (idea), subject, plot (action), setting, characterization (human nature), are the chief elements that compose the structure of a novel. The structure should have unity. That is, while there may be many different parts and many complex variations in the whole body of material used, that material should be so organized as to establish a unified experience that is realizable in a progressive development from beginning to conclusion. There is unity in this sense (though with much irrelevant surplusage) in the immense varied congeries of *Anthony Adverse*, just as unity is lacking in the development of the much shorter, more limited biographic novel by Kathleen Coyle, *Immortal Ease*. Perfection of unity in organization and artistry may be found in Hergesheimer's *Balisand* or in the many-faceted concentration of Willa Cather's *Lucy Gayheart*, which crystallizes into unified experience the fleeting life-phase of girlhood. In determining whether a novel has unity, consider whether it holds continuity of interest. Can you look back from the closing scene and see a clear and logical connection between the opening and the conclusion? Are the successive incidents, crises, climax, and aftermath in valid relationship with one another, or are they disconnected and irreconcilable? Have all the characters a reason for their existence in the narrative? Do superfluities of episode, exposition, or detail impair unity? Redundancy and prolixity (as in *Anthony Adverse*) are weaknesses common to many of the very long novels to which present-day novelists are addicted.

Form and type.—Consideration of form should be both specific and generic. Observe in what mold the novelist has cast his work, whether it is an autobiography, a memoir, a diary, told in letters, a retrospect, or a mixture of these and other forms with the third-person narrative that is still the most familiar form of fiction, in spite of the many metamorphoses effected by modern technique. *The Late George Apley* was molded in the form of a memoir, so skillful in its sedate satire that many readers believed it was a genuine contribution to biographic literature. Note also the type-group to which a given novel belongs. Anyone who reviews fiction should know what are the characteristics of an expressionistic novel, a stream-of-consciousness novel, a regional, or proletarian, or other novel that bears a distinctive stamp of form or treatment. Types, of course, merge and fluctuate and superimpose upon one another, but generic relationships should be distinguishable.[3]

Treatment.—This is the novelist's technique, the method of construction and style of presentation. Consider whether the narrative is long and loosely woven (the "epic" manner), as in Priestley's *The Good Companions*, or short and closely knit (the "dramatic method"), as in Hughes's *In Hazard*, or whether it combines length with solidity and sustained dramatic integration, as in *South Riding*. Are there many characters, participating in diverse, scattered incidents or adventures, or a small group upon whom action is focused? Does the narrative make use of the movie technique of the flash-back (a sudden doubling back upon itself) to bring out some essential prior scenes or incidents, or the close-up (interpolated vivid emotional detail or interior monologue) to deepen emotional response or convey motive for action? Today many different techniques may be used in a single novel (*In Hazard* is an example of this). The obvious gives way to allusion, to indirection, to latency; the stream

[3] For a general survey of type-groups see Chapter II: "Values and Relationships."

of consciousness percolates the most arid plain of narrative. Try to determine whether treatment is predominantly romantic or realistic, objective or subjective, and observe how its nature is conveyed in verbal expression. Remember that present-day realism makes no concession to fastidious taste; profane, obscene, raw, and brutal language may be a means of evoking the particular kind of experience the novelist seeks to depict. There should be recognition of this by the reader; and also a perceptiveness of the literary art, the essential truth, and the significant purpose that justify the use of sordid or repulsive material.

Significance.—Significance of a novel may lie in its intrinsic nature, in its purpose, in its accessory material. Consider whether it is primarily a novel of character, of setting, of specific subject or purpose; whether it is a study of individual character (as in Pearl Buck's *Other Gods*), or of a segment of human society (as in *South Riding*), or of conflicting ideas (as in Thornton Wilder's *Heaven's My Destination*); whether it expounds a special thesis (as in *Dynasty of Death*), or records aspects of the contemporary world scene (as in *Europe to Let*), or launches a social challenge (as in *Native Son*). Specialized factual exactitude may give significance to novels otherwise of minor import: as *Horse Shoe Bottoms* offers a well-founded two-generation chronicle of mine workers in Illinois and as *Snow-Water* has significance as an authentically based narrative of the beginnings of irrigation in Colorado. Or significance may be conveyed, not factually, but by way of fantasy, symbolism, or allegory, as in many of Robert Nathan's novels, in H. G. Wells's extravaganzas, in Sylvia Townsend Warner's delicate, prismatic tales; by satirical gaiety (*The Ugly Dachshund*); or by spontaneous humor, as in Ross's *The Education of Hyman Kaplan*. Many novels have a significance of idea, of implicit meaning, as well as explicit significance of obvious subject, of plot and character development; often they have also an added factual or informational significance, as in Nevil Shute's *An Old Captivity*, with its careful technical detail of transatlantic aviation. These subsidiary significances should be discerned, and the values they hold indicated.

Besides reading the book itself, it is desirable in preparation for a review to read also any available criticisms or commentary relating to it. Information on the book jacket is often a present help in time of need, giving personal facts that may not be commonly familiar. But avoid the temptation to "lift" the blurb-writer's alluring and skillful sentences and incorporate them into what is presumably an original review. If the author is unfamiliar, material about his previous work and personal background should be sought; for this any public library will supply reference material; or a request to the author's publishers will usually bring prompt and helpful response. Related material of this kind is a great help in making both book and writer take on specific identity for an audience. Indeed, the reviewer should always seek to establish a sense of personal friendship or vital relationship with the writer whose personality is infused into his work; when such a sense of personal relationship is realized, it will often bring that later and continuing companionship which is one of the enduring joys of reading. This sense of personal relationship is born of intellectual or imaginative sympathy; it is not at all dependent upon actual acquaintance with an author as an individual. A review that centers upon a reviewer's brief contact or casual acquaintance with the author under discussion is too often a rather tiresome excursion into egocentricity—a setting forth of personal trivia, a preening of plumage because the reviewer once went up a canyon with John Burroughs or spent an afternoon with Gertrude Atherton.

Consider now the formulation of a review. Here, too, proficiency cannot be acquired without study, experiment, and practice. Current review periodicals should be read and their reviews studied for organization and technique, but the review that is to be spoken must have its own different individuality. Good reviewing in periodicals and newspapers is more formalized, more detailed in critical analysis, and more elaborate and "literary" in expression than the spoken review should ever attempt to be. For the latter, simplicity, clarity, and the establishment of a magnetic current between speaker and listeners are first requisites. There must be co-ordination and progression in the presentation of the book. The review should have a skeleton, a basic plan; it should be pleasing and flexible in expression; it should arrest and hold the listeners' interest. Whatever order of progression is chosen should be consistently followed, neither jumbled nor disconnected, but—like effective plot development—an ordered movement from a beginning through a middle to an end. There is no fixed pattern. A review may open with information about the author and pass on to the book; it may open with consideration of the book and close with information about the author. Transitions should be clear and sustained, not confused and fragmentary; and the interest aroused at the beginning should be clinched in closing. The special test of the reviewer's skill lies in an effective beginning and an effective ending. A good spoken review should open with an arresting statement, perhaps linking the book to some immediate topic of interest, perhaps crystallizing its theme, or visualizing its setting, or evoking the author's personality and purpose. It should close with a definite finale, that may be a summation of qualities, or a reaffirmation of judgment, or a climactic scene, or a selection that illuminates or interprets the nature of the book; but whatever it is, it should leave the listeners with unquenched interest and a deepened sense of book values.

A review often gains in accent and variety from provocative selections from the book. It may present some vivid scene that indicates emotional or dramatic qualities, or it may include extracts that reveal striking character portrayal, that show play of humor or charm of expression. It will almost always have to emphasize certain aspects of the book and condense or telescope others, rather than attempt completeness of exposition; yet it should manage to convey adequate realization of the novel as a whole. Make clear the meaning of an obscure title that in itself subtly transmits the author's theme—*Eyeless in Gaza; The Eye of the Fish.* Never "tell the story" in a long and involved narrative, larded with proper names and wound about with monotonous connectives. Plot should be treated as the outgrowth of the subject, the manifestation of the theme. Specify its chief elements and suggest its course of action as vividly as possible, but never suck out the whole content or reveal the full climax, leaving the reader only an empty shell, for the purpose of a review is not to satiate, but to stimulate, to invite others to participation in a rewarding or provocative experience. Try to transmit a sense of the book's own personality and thus to convey its strength and weakness, but avoid prolixity and entanglement in detail.

Clear, simple, and graphic expression is of great importance. A varied vocabulary and interest in word use are needed to escape the bondage of the clichés, those worn-out superlatives that are common denominators of a book's popularity. Here a good thesaurus (say, Roget or March) offers a lifeline. Avoid elaborate phrasing and the use of the more recondite terms of literary criticism. A review sprinkled with words such as "adumbration," "perdurable," "pastiche," "mimesis" and phrases such as "the criteria of social norms," "affirmations of surrealisme" may be deeply impressive as evidence of a reviewer's profundity, but it is likely to cast a blight upon his audience. Humor is a sharpener of perceptions, a tonic to assimilation. It conveys criticism cogently, yet with amenity; its effect upon an audience is both stimulating and mellowing. But it should be discerning humor, intelligently directed, not a wisecracking flippancy that finds derision easier than understanding.

A review should always be adapted to its audience. Sometimes, when the personnel of the audience proves to be quite different from what had been expected, this may mean a lightning-change readjustment of the reviewer's material. Ordinarily, it involves a variation from an intended approach, a modification of tone, deft omissions, and a different placing of emphasis, according to the reviewer's awareness of audience response. A review repeated before different groups must undergo many such minor transformations.

A good review may lose many of its values, a poor review may gain values it lacks, by the way in which it is presented. Mannerisms should be avoided. Overdramatization is a serious weakness; so is a relentless, overconscientious monotony of detail. Indefiniteness, vague generalizations, belong in the calendar of sin, as does evangelical fervor in eliciting and proclaiming an author's presumable "message." Informality and directness have the strongest audience appeal, and most professional reviewers have trained themselves to speak apparently spontaneously and without notes. The satisfactory spoken book review, however, must be based upon carefully prepared notes. A script is necessary in all radio reviewing, and this requirement has set standards of condensation and precision that other audiences have come to expect. Among amateur reviewers best results are obtained from skillful and unobtrusive use of notes that will convey the impression of informal speaking based on brief memoranda, not of "reading a paper." Yet the notes should, in fact, be the speaker's text, carefully organized, precise in phrasing: a base from which quicker, more immediate, comment may rise without danger of losing its bearings. They should be inconspicuous (half-size letter sheets are satisfactory), clearly legible, carefully folioed, held informally and casually consulted. If each sheet, after the eye has covered its content, is slipped behind the remaining sheets, not deposited upon a desk, the effect produced will be of speaking, not of reading; but speaking with a compactness, clear sequence, and effective expression that extemporaneous reviewing seldom possesses.

In presenting a review, keep to the time limit set, whatever it may be. A fifteen-minute review should last fifteen minutes. Estimate about 175 words a minute, as a fairly rapid rate of speaking, and shape the review to fit the time allotted. Almost any novel can be adequately and effectively reviewed in fifteen minutes; for a review of half an hour or longer it is desirable to link together several books that offer interesting reading relationships. Many novels, of course, justify more extended review time, but a good book review is not a critical lecture and should not expound a book so exhaustively that no incentive remains to read it for oneself.

Follow Benjamin Jowett's advice to his students regarding their theses: "Cut off the porch." In other words, omit introductory remarks and preliminaries; step at once into your subject. Never explain that you have very little to say; and don't say that you don't know why you were asked to speak—your audience is likely to agree with you.

Make clear when you are quoting from the book under review. This can be done by a simple phrase, such as "as the author says," or something similar; but an audience should never be left in doubt as to whether they are listening to the words of the reviewer or those of the author.

Always remember that the most eloquent review must be heard to be appreciated. Inaudibility is a total loss to reviewer and to audience. Therefore, a woman reviewer should not heighten (and thin) her voice, but should deepen and strengthen it; and she should constantly be aware of the (imaginary) presence of a deaf old lady in a back seat, whose interest must not be allowed to flag. Don't speak too fast, give your words time to enter your hearers' minds; don't speak too slowly, your hearers will get tired waiting. But the larger your audience, the slower your speech should be. Don't be expressionless; speak naturally, but with inflections. Don't drop your voice at the end of a sentence. Consider accent and pronunciation: they reveal family history, social and educational background, and personality.

These suggestions have ranged from theory to practice, from the obvious to the implicit. For the experienced reviewer they cover familiar ground; but the continuing influx of newcomers into this field of book influence should justify a formulation of purpose and procedure. The spoken book review is the most recent medium for bringing current literature into more immediate relation with life, for enabling its values of information and enlightenment to be more widely realized and used. In *The Provincial Lady in America*, it may be remembered, the Lady remarked that in her lecture tour through the United States she found that conversation chiefly consisted in the question, "Have you read *Anthony Adverse?*" and an answer, Yes, or No; and then the question, "Did you like it?" and an answer, Yes, or No; and that was all. It is in some such fashion that the rich and various art of contemporary fiction is ordinarily linked to everyday life. From the direct personal appeal of the spoken book review, as it multiplies and flourishes through women's clubs and community groups, through every kind of public and private organization, there should develop a more stimulating and fruitful relationship. These reviews provoke discussion, they increase materials of conversation, they incite to personal acquaintance with books reviewed or referred to. They are a form of entertainment, but entertainment that stimulates intelligence and enlarges mental horizons. Their full values are not yet developed, for oral book reviewing is still in an early stage of confused and heterogeneous growth. It needs to establish standards and to improve technique. There should be greater discrimination and broader range in selection of books for review, more balanced appraisal of values, fewer follow-my-leader opinions, less commercial exploitation, and a fuller realization that the literature of today is the expression and interpretation of the life of today.

INDEX

COLUMBIA UNIVERSITY STUDIES IN LIBRARY SERVICE